BUILDINGS AND LANDMARKS OF 20TH- AND 21ST-CENTURY AMERICA

BUILDINGS AND LANDMARKS OF 20TH- AND 21ST-CENTURY AMERICA

AMERICAN SOCIETY REVEALED

Elizabeth B. Greene with Edward Salo

An Imprint of ABC-CLIO, LLC
Santa Barbara, California • Denver, Colorado

Copyright © 2018 by ABC-CLIO, LLC

All rights reserved. No part of this publication may be reproduced, stored in a retrieval system, or transmitted, in any form or by any means, electronic, mechanical, photocopying, recording, or otherwise, except for the inclusion of brief quotations in a review, without prior permission in writing from the publisher.

Library of Congress Cataloging-in-Publication Data

Names: Greene, Elizabeth B., author.
Title: Buildings and landmarks of 20th- and 21st-century
   America : American society revealed / Elizabeth B. Greene with
   Edward Salo.
Description: Santa Barbara, California : Greenwood, 2018. | Includes
   bibliographical references and index.
Identifiers: LCCN 2018009512 (print) | LCCN 2018026180 (ebook) |
   ISBN 9781440839931 (ebook) | ISBN 9781440839924 (alk. paper)
Subjects: LCSH: Architecture—United States—History—20th century. |
   Architecture—United States—History—21st century. | Historic
   buildings—United States. | Architecture and society—United
   States—History—20th century. | Architecture and society—United
   States—History—21st century.
Classification: LCC NA712 (ebook) | LCC NA712 .G74 2018 (print) |
   DDC 720.973/0904—dc23
LC record available at https://lccn.loc.gov/2018009512

ISBN: 978-1-4408-3992-4 (print)
       978-1-4408-3993-1 (ebook)

22 21 20 19 18   1 2 3 4 5

This book is also available as an eBook.

Greenwood
An Imprint of ABC-CLIO, LLC

ABC-CLIO, LLC
130 Cremona Drive, P.O. Box 1911
Santa Barbara, California 93116–1911
www.abc-clio.com

This book is printed on acid-free paper ∞
Manufactured in the United States of America

CONTENTS

Preface vii
Acknowledgments ix
Introduction xi
How to Evaluate Buildings and Structures xvii
Chronology xxiii

CIVIC ARCHITECTURE

Pennsylvania Station   3
Los Angeles Memorial Coliseum   9
Attica Correctional Facility   17
Hoover Dam   25
Golden Gate Bridge   31
Interstate Highway System   39
Portland Public Service Building   47
Central Library   55

COMMERCIAL ARCHITECTURE

Asch Building (Now Known as Brown Building)   63
Luna Park   73
Equitable Building   81
Ford River Rouge Complex   89
Grauman's Chinese Theatre   97
Woolworth's Store   105
Empire State Building   111
Flamingo Hotel   119
Northgate Shopping Center   127
Sun Record Studio   133
Lever House   141
McDonald's   149
Fontainebleau Hotel   157
Seagram Building   165
TWA Flight Center   173
Watergate Complex   181
Sears Tower (Currently Known as the Willis Tower)   187
World Trade Center Twin Towers   193
Walt Disney Concert Hall   201
One World Trade Center   207

DOMESTIC ARCHITECTURE

First Houses   215
Fallingwater   223
Cabrini-Green Homes   229
Levittown   235
Seaside   243

MILITARY ARCHITECTURE

Japanese American Relocation Camp   251
The Pentagon   259

MEMORIAL ARCHITECTURE

Lincoln Memorial   267
Vietnam Veterans Memorial   277

Biographical Appendix 281
Glossary of Terms 289
Bibliography 295
Index 311

PREFACE

This volume, *Buildings and Landmarks of 20th- and 21st-Century America: American Society Revealed*, examines 37 separate buildings and landmarks in the United States. These structures span the entire century and the entire breadth of the nation. At the birth of the 20th century, the United States was still a young nation that had not yet achieved its status as a world power. With the relentless supply of new immigrants from Europe flooding into the cities in the early 20th century, manufacturing flourished and factories like the Triangle Waist Company exploited swarms of young immigrant women and girls in unsafe conditions. The Progressive Movement forced the public to face up to the human cost of a completely deregulated society. With additional regulation came an escalation in the power of the federal government as the country grew more urban and industrialized. This power increased even more with the onset of the Great Depression in the 1930s. The nation was no longer a decentralized agglomeration of mostly rural states, but an industrial juggernaut with a powerful federal government, with the muscle to create great feats of engineering for the public good, like the Hoover Dam and the Interstate Highway System. The increasing affluence of the American public led to an accrual of leisure time that resulted in the advent of the consumer economy. Shopping, attending organized sporting events, eating out, going to the movies, and traveling on vacation were pursuits that became increasingly popular and available to the American family as the 20th century forged ahead. The technology revolution that started at the end of the 19th century transformed the nation again at the end of the 20th century with the invention of computers, the Internet, and cell phones. The post–World War II boom resulted in the growth of the suburbs as the automobile's impact on American society increased.

Throughout the book, buildings and landmarks are analyzed to reveal their influence on many aspects of 20th- and 21st-century society, including the growing importance of the consumer economy, the increasing power of government and the military, the civil rights movement, and the impact of suburbanization. The book is organized in chronological order within five categories: Civic Architecture, Commercial Architecture, Domestic Architecture, Military Architecture, and Memorial Architecture. The Civic Architecture category comprises buildings and landmarks that promote civic life, and they include government buildings, engineering projects, bridges, libraries, educational institutions, sports stadiums, and prisons. The Commercial Architecture category comprises buildings and landmarks that are built for a commercial interest such as department stores, hotels, office buildings, factories, and entertainment venues. The Domestic Architecture category comprises all types of dwellings, whether single-family or multiple dwellings. The Military category deals with landmarks that are built by or for the U.S. military. The Memorial Architecture category comprises important 20th- and 21st-century monuments and memorials.

ACKNOWLEDGMENTS

I would like to thank my editor Michael Millman for giving me the opportunity to complete this project. After publishing *Buildings and Landmarks of 19th-Century America* with Michael's help in 2017, I was more than excited to be able to switch my focus to this more recent time period. Once again, I have to thank my ever-supportive husband George, who is learning almost as much I am with these fascinating projects. He lends me his wise comments as well as his patience after my many hours holed up in my office. I again have to thank my son Chris, who is the real writer in the family, for his support, and brother Chris for his interest, enthusiasm, advice, and historical knowledge, which he is always happy to impart.

—Elizabeth B. Greene

INTRODUCTION

Frederick Jackson Turner signaled the closing of the American frontier in his speech at the Chicago World's Fair in 1893. The 20th century was about to begin and the frontier would no longer serve as the relief valve for a restless nation. What would the new century bring? Would the traits that Turner illuminated—individualism, egalitarianism, inventiveness, and a streak of violence—continue to breathe life into the American society? With the closing of the frontier, would this brash young country continue to exhibit its capacity for innovation and wealth creation? Would the fever to spread democracy and remake the frontier create an imperialist power or would the United States opt to maintain its borders? The dawn of the 20th century was a period of transformation for the country. Changes that began occurring at the beginning of the century would have broad impact for decades to come. But, despite some fits and starts, the nation was soon to morph into the hegemon that it would become by the mid-20th century. For, as Henry Luce, the publisher of *Life Magazine*, would posit in an essay written in 1941, the 20th century was the "American Century."

ADVENT OF THE CONSUMER ECONOMY

The 20th century began with a number of new inventions that had the power to transform the daily lives of Americans. The mass production of consumer-based durable goods made a variety of products available for families to purchase inexpensively. With electrical and telephone wiring now connecting many homes, electrical labor-saving devices like irons, vacuum cleaners, refrigerators, and other appliances allowed women more leisure time. Telephones revolutionized communications. The enhancement of leisure time allowed such early amusement parks as Luna Park in Coney Island to become the favorite destination for millions of New Yorkers. Americans began flocking to the motion picture shows in the 1920s and '30s. Grauman's Chinese Theatre in Los Angeles, California, is an example of the ornate movie houses of the day. Invented in the late 19th century, the automobile did not reach the homes of most Americans until Henry Ford perfected the assembly line at the massive River Rouge plant in Michigan. The ubiquity of the motorcar was one of the most dominant influences in American society in the 20th century. The car transformed where Americans lived, how they ate, how they vacationed, and how they shopped. Northgate Shopping Center in Seattle, Washington, an early shopping mall, was an innovation that was a paean to the ballooning suburbs, the omnipresent automobile, and the domination of consumer culture. McDonald's was also a creature of car-based culture; it started as solely a drive-in restaurant in California in the 1950s. Besides the car, the passenger airplane transformed American life after World War II. For the first time, Americans could travel long distances in a very short time. In the 1950s and '60s, "space age" design flourished. The iconic, soaring design of the TWA Terminal in New York designed by Finnish American architect Eero Saarinen reflected an optimistic interpretation of a booming American economy. With airplane travel, new resort cities like Las Vegas and Miami prospered, with modern hotels like the Fontainebleau and the Flamingo making a splash. Americans developed their love of sports in the 20th century. The Los Angeles Coliseum is one of America's oldest sports stadiums, completed in 1923. In 2028, it will host its third Olympic Games. It is also serving as host to the National Football League's Los Angeles Rams for the second time in history until a new stadium in Inglewood is completed in 2020. Another 20th-century innovation was a new type of popular music. As the postwar baby boom generation began to mature, they sought a new musical genre, and rock and roll was invented in a tiny storefront in Memphis called Sun Records. The consumer economy in the United States continued to evolve as the 20th century progressed.

EXPANSION OF GOVERNMENT POWER DOMESTICALLY AND INTERNATIONALLY

The laissez-faire capitalism that dominated the economy during the 19th century faced a challenge from the Progressive Movement in the early 20th century. Big corporations were allowed to conduct business with virtually no regulation in the early years of American corporate power. But life in the unregulated state created all sorts of problems. In the first decades of the 20th century, muckraking investigative journalists as well as other progressive reformers fought for regulations in manufacturing, child labor, and prisons. The horrific fire at the Triangle shirtwaist factory in New York resulted in regulations that improved working conditions for workers in the garment industry. The first zoning regulations and height restrictions for skyscrapers were written after the massive Equitable Life Assurance Building was erected in 1915, effectively blocking the sunlight on Lower Broadway. The demolition of the beloved Pennsylvania Station resulted in another new set of regulations in the 1960s as people rued its loss. Landmarking laws were soon passed in New York, and for the first time, the dynamic city was forced to take historic significance into account when considering a new construction project.

The United States emerged as a world power in the 20th century, eventually becoming the sole world power after the fall of Communism in 1989. It took decades for the nation to fully accept its role as a world power. There has been a constant strain of isolationism in the United States that ebbs and flows depending on the era. When *Life Magazine* publisher Henry Luce dubbed the 20th century "the American century" in 1941, the essay was actually a cri de coeur for the United States to enter World War II and accept its international responsibilities. But at the time, many in the United States were unconvinced that the country should be forced to fight the Nazis in what was deemed to be a European conflict. "America Firsters" were a powerful lobby in the United States. However, after World War II, the power of the United States and its role in international relations were acknowledged in the fight to contain further incursion of the Communist ideology worldwide. A number of landmarks display the recognition of the United States as a player on the world's stage. One of the world's largest office buildings, the Pentagon, was built in 1943 by President Franklin Roosevelt to house military staff at its location in Arlington, Virginia. When the USSR sent its first rocket into space in 1957, the United States was caught flat-footed and hustled to catch up. The American space program, called NASA, was launched in 1958 by President Dwight Eisenhower. The United States became involved in the conflict in Indochina in the 1950s in order to quell the spread of Communism. In the 1960s, the United States increased its involvement in Vietnam. The United States did not withdraw until 1975, ultimately sending 2.7 million American GIs to fight in Vietnam. A total of 58,318 names of the service members who died on the Vietnam War are listed on the magnificent Vietnam Veterans Memorial Wall, in Washington, D.C. This unusual memorial was designed by a 21-year-old Yale design student named Maya Lin and completed in 1982.

SOCIAL ISSUES, SUBURBANIZATION, AND CIVIL RIGHTS

Civil rights emerged as one of the major movements in the United States in the 20th century. Discriminatory Jim Crow laws persisted in the South in the first half of the century. Women continued their decades-long struggle for the right to vote, finally achieving it with the passage of the 19th Amendment in 1920, although hope for the passage of the Equal Rights Amendment has not yet been fulfilled. Although civil rights was already an ascendant issue by the 1940s, the civil rights of Japanese Americans were flouted during World War II as thousands of families of Japanese origin from the West Coast were sent to internment camps against their will. In 1960, as people of color began to assert their civil rights, a group of courageous African American college students from Greensboro, North Carolina, ignited a protest movement to integrate Woolworth's lunch counters in the South. The Lincoln Memorial has served as a destination for a number of civil rights protests in the 20th century, including Martin Luther King's 1963 March on Washington for Jobs and Freedom, where an estimated 250,000 people saw King deliver his legendary "I Have a Dream" speech. The civil rights movement affected minority groups as well as other underrepresented cohorts like the incarcerated. The 20th-century war on crime resulted in a record number of prisoners in the nation's prisons. The abysmal conditions in many prisons were highlighted during the tragic uprising in the New York State's Attica prison in 1971, which resulted in 43 deaths of inmates and hostages.

The movement of the American population from the cities to the outlying suburbs, a demographic shift referred to as suburbanization, has had enormous impact on the nation in the years following World War II. Many factors contributed to the growth of the suburbs, including federal housing policies enacted after the war. Innovative construction techniques, imitating Ford's assembly line method, allowed for cheap and rapid construction of scores of identical houses on former potato fields in New York's Long Island. This successful development, Levittown, was the first of several towns named after the developer Arthur Levitt. President Eisenhower's promotion of a federally financed interstate highway system allowed for the gigantic public works project to be accomplished after 1956. The highways and other roads built in the new suburban developments were crucial in two new commercial enterprises—fast food and shopping malls. McDonald's in California was the first successful fast-food franchise. Northgate Shopping Center in Seattle, Washington, was the first modern shopping mall in the country. In opposition to the proliferation of suburban sprawl, a group of architects who call themselves the "New Urbanists" wrote a manifesto that demanded a return to smaller, walkable communities. Their prototype community was a town in Florida called Seaside, built in 1981.

Another issue that confronted the United States in the 20th and 21st centuries was the curse of income inequality. This has evolved into a crisis but became evident with the economic expansion that took place after World War II. Much of the population benefited from the subsidies provided by the federal government after the war, with housing policy and educational aid. However, not everyone was allowed to enjoy these benefits, as much of the language in these laws included racially discriminatory exclusions. As more poor people migrated to cities for work and more middle-class people fled the cities to the suburbs, many cities devolved into ghettos that housed predominantly indigent minorities. Some effort to improve housing conditions did take place in downtown urban areas. There were a few successful ones, and many that were far from successful. An early effort to provide public housing in New York City, the groundbreaking project called First Houses, was built in 1935. It was a low-rise project that related to the street and is still in use today. On the other end of the scale, large high-rise projects on so-called superblocks were in vogue in the 1950s and '60s. This type of low-income project rarely succeeded in providing safe, comfortable housing for the poor. One of the most infamous projects was the Cabrini-Green development in Chicago. It was one of a number of large housing projects built in the 1950s and '60s that were ultimately demolished. The answer to the housing crisis and to income inequality in general has not yet been provided.

TECHNOLOGY AND MODERNIST DESIGN

Modernist design in the 20th century was a radical departure from 19th-century historicism. Stripped of ornament, this spare style originated in Europe and spread to the United States in the mid-20th century. Early modern buildings include the Empire State Building in New York, which displays Art Deco ornament as well as Modernist austerity. A group of European architects and designers came to the United States as refugees after World War II. Architects like Ludwig Mies van der Rohe influenced American firms like Skidmore, Owings and Merrill (SOM), who became the leaders in Modernist design in the United States. Mies and SOM were responsible for two of the International Style icons in New York: the Seagram Building and Lever House. A later skyscraper from the Skidmore, Owings and Merrill firm was the Willis Tower (formerly, Sears Tower) in Chicago, which was the tallest building in the world for over 20 years. Another Modernist skyscraper was the World Trade Center twin towers, designed by Minoru Yamasaki in 1971. The complex was derided at first by critics and the public alike, although the two towers eventually were accepted and even admired by the time they were tragically destroyed by a terrorist attack in 2001. Their replacement, originally called the Freedom Tower, but now known simply as One World Trade Center, is another design by the venerable Skidmore, Owings and Merrill. The primary architect on the project was David Childs, who was forced by politics, security, and the budget concerns of the real estate developer, to make considerable alterations to the original design. Although it is a wildly popular tourist destination, it too has been panned by the critics. Architects like Michael Graves in the late 20th century utilized a style called Post-Modernism that eschewed the severity of the Modernist aesthetic, utilizing oversized classical elements. Graves's Portland Public Service Building has been criticized for its cartoonish, colorful classical motifs, but it is considered a breakthrough from the unadorned functionalism of the Modernist creed. Other architects went on personal paths, rejecting the Modernist orthodoxy. Frank Lloyd Wright, America's most creative and personal genius, designed his masterpiece, the country house for Edgar Kaufmann, Fallingwater, in Mill Run, Pennsylvania, in 1939. Other architects have contributed to the anti-Modernist movement. A version of Post-Modernism that is dubbed Deconstructivism can be seen in Frank Gehry's 2003 Walt Disney Concert Hall in Los Angeles, a flashy, expressionistic tour de force. Another inventive architect who has influenced design in the late 20th century is the Dutch-born architect Rem Koolhaas, who designed the award-winning Seattle Central Library in 2004.

The revolution of new technologies has influenced American culture in the 20th and 21st centuries. During the early part of the 20th century, technological advancement allowed for development of a number of massive engineering projects. In 1933, the iconic Golden Gate Bridge was completed. To connect the city of San Francisco to Sausalito over the dangerous waters of the Golden Gate was a magnificent engineering feat, performed without the aid of today's computers. Similarly, the construction of the massive Hoover Dam on the Colorado River in 1936 provided needed flood control, irrigation water, and hydroelectric power to the burgeoning western states. Another premier engineering project in the late 20th century was the nationwide interstate highway system. The advent of computer-aided design (CAD) in architecture and engineering has had an enormous impact on design in the late 20th century. Buildings such as Gehry's Walt Disney Concert Hall and the gigantic One World Trade Center in New York would have been extremely difficult if not impossible to design without the aid of modern CAD systems.

In the 20th and 21st centuries, the United States evolved from an upstart nation to an industrial juggernaut and a world power. The evolving consumer culture affected all aspects of American society. With more and more suburbs being developed farther from the cities, walkable neighborhoods became harder and harder to find. Both suburbs and waistlines expanded throughout the country as cities and sidewalks shrank. By the end of the 20th century, the rich were getting richer and the poor and middle class were stagnating. The battle for civil rights grew as more disaffected minorities demanded an equal share, with varying results. Technology had widespread influence as computers insinuated themselves into all aspects of daily life. This technological revolution affected engineering and architectural design as well. With the 21st century already well into its second decade, the United States was facing another transformational era. What would the end of the 21st century bring? If not another "American century," then what would it be?

HOW TO EVALUATE BUILDINGS AND STRUCTURES

In my previous book that examined buildings and landmarks of 19th-century America, I discussed the variety of building types and the available clues that help decipher their architectural styles. I mentioned my walks with my husband through New York City and other locales, examining buildings and structures and guessing their age, time period, and style. The same clues can be used in the buildings and landmarks in this book, although the styles may have changed. The skills can be learned to identify and to "decode" the clues that exist in a building and that give some basic knowledge of its history, style, and significance. This is how one can learn how to evaluate, or "read," buildings. The skill of reading buildings entails a number of factors that illuminate what the building can tell us just by our examination of it. By honing this skill, the casual viewer can look at buildings, monuments, and landscapes and be able to answer the questions that will be reviewed here. Once the viewer has deciphered the major clues inherent in the building, he or she can easily do further research into the building by looking it up. After seeing a building and taking stock of its identifying properties, one can research on the Internet in order to confirm and expand on one's theories regarding its style. In this chapter, we will identify the elements that allow a person to discover the important characteristics to look for in reading a building or landmark.

What does it mean to "read" a building? In this volume, there are a variety of buildings, historic sites, and historic landscapes dating from the beginning of the 20th century until the present day in the United States. The various landmarks display an assortment of styles, forms, materials, and locations across the country. The only factors connecting them to each other are their time period (20th and 21st centuries), locations (United States), and the fact that they are deemed significant in some way. Their significance comes from either their stylistic importance or historical importance, or both. But the skill of learning how to understand what the buildings can teach you, or "reading" the building, applies to all the landmarks discussed in this volume. When you read about the properties listed in this volume, you should ask these questions:

- What type of building or structure is it, and what specific purposes did the building or structure have?
- What is the architectural style?
- When was the building or structure constructed, and what were the circumstances?
- What materials were used to construct this building or structure?
- Why was the building or structure built, and what was the need it addressed?

Learning how to read a building will give you many of the clues that are necessary to answer these questions. There are certain ways to decode a building by examining it. It can give you clues on the use of the building, its age, its style, and its significance. It can even give you some clues as to the historical context that will explain the environment that precipitated the construction of the building.

Answering the first question should be the simplest: "What type of building or structure is it, and what specific purpose did the building or structure have?" In this volume, there are many types of buildings, structures, and engineering projects. Some buildings have been familiar historically, for instance, houses and churches. But in the 20th and 21st centuries, there were a number of new types of structures. These included fast-food restaurants, shopping malls, airline terminals, recording studios, movie theaters, amusement parks, and sports stadiums. Although skyscrapers were a new type of building in the late 19th century, the 20th-century skyscrapers reached a totally new scale with new set of design implications. Although there were certainly paved roads in the United States in the 19th century, the scale and impact of the interstate highway system was unprecedented. The sheer magnitude and ambitiousness of the Hoover Dam and the Golden Gate Bridge projects relied on technology and engineering expertise that was not available previously. With these innovative projects, architects had to ponder how to accommodate the needs of these structures while using the architectural vocabulary that was available at the time. Mies van der Rohe influenced a generation of 20th-century office buildings with his pared-down simplicity of the International Style, utilizing modern materials and eschewing 19th-century ornament. New forms like the airline terminal gave architects an opportunity to explore novel, space age designs, as seen in Eero Saarinen's TWA Terminal in New York. Railroad terminals like Pennsylvania Station were still designed in the Beaux Arts style of the late 19th century that utilized great expanses of glass to let the light stream in and were modern interpretations to great classical precedents. Monuments like the Lincoln Memorial were still being designed in the classical style, whereas the later Vietnam Veterans Memorial interpreted the memory of the dead in a completely new way. Industrial production in the United States reached a whole new level with the invention of the assembly line by Henry Ford in his massive River Rouge plant. Automobiles were a new product in the early 20th century, and their influence would be felt for the rest of the century and beyond. The efficient manufacturing techniques utilized by Henry Ford revolutionized the industrial process and provided more inexpensive products for an ever-more eager consuming public. The assembly line techniques were later applied to the post–World War II building boom, allowing for the rapid growth of the suburbs in new towns like Levittown in Long Island, New York. The small suburban houses provided a new type of simplified colonial style that typified postwar suburban residential design.

The second question to ask is: "What is the architectural style?" Architectural history boasts a plethora of styles, but knowing a shorthand of certain examples of architectural vocabulary will afford the viewer some likely answers. Does the building have classical or medieval influence? Many buildings in the 19th century displayed either classical elements from the Greek or Renaissance styles or medieval elements from the Romanesque or Gothic styles. Some 19th-century buildings also utilized elements from other exotic historical styles, like Byzantine or Moorish. With the introduction of the 20th century, styles changed significantly as the Modernist era was launched and architects sought a new vocabulary that was not based on historical styles. Louis Sullivan's famous creed "form follows function" was magnified in the 20th century with the advent of the Modernist style. This style was created in Europe at the turn of the 20th century, and was a revolutionary style that utilized a machine aesthetic to pare down the building to its essential elements. American office building design surrendered to the version of Modernism called the International Style in the 1950s and '60s as modern skyscrapers with unadorned glass curtain walls were erected nationwide. In the 1920s, a more decorative style called Art Deco applied geometric ornament and used modern materials like plastics and chrome. Although Greek influence could still be seen in some institutional buildings, classical style went out of fashion until the onset of the Postmodernist style in the late 20th century. In a reaction to the ubiquity of the unornamented International Style, the Postmodernists used vivid colors and playfully applied oversized classical elements. The simple suburban house that can be found in every postwar suburban neighborhood, however, still utilized many historical elements from earlier styles, especially Colonial Revival.

A vital skill in guessing the style is defining the shape, or massing, of the building. Is it rectangular in shape? How tall is it, does it have extensions, and what is the roofline like? Does it appear squat or attenuated? Where is the door and where are the windows in relationship to the door? The massing of a building will often give away the style or even the age of a building. Knowledge of these basic elements will afford the viewer a window on identifying these styles.

With the ability to guess the style often comes the answer to the third question: "When was the building or structure constructed, and what were the circumstances?" Certain styles had certain time periods in American architectural design. The Greek Revival style was popular at the middle of the 19th century, Neo-Classical style at the beginning. One can figure out the date of certain buildings by relating them to technological advances: skyscrapers did not appear until the end of the 19th century as they were dependent on steel framing and the use of the elevator. Airline terminals were a new type of building and often utilized modern styles. Structures like the TWA Terminal were built to house airline passengers, indicating the date had to be post World War II. Even engineering feats like the Hoover Dam or the Golden Gate Bridge were modern marvels, and display Art Deco ornament that reveal the time frame of their construction. The tenements of New York had to be built during the surge in immigration that began in the mid 19th century. Later attempts to house the poor, like Cabrini-Green in Chicago, displayed evidence of the influence of the International Style with the construction of the high-rise public housing on "superblocks" during the years following World War II. Hotels built in the postwar decades like the Fontainebleau in Miami Beach or the Flamingo in Las Vegas also displayed playful interpretations of modern styles, often referred to as mid-century modern. Guessing the date of a building, structure, or landmark requires combining a number of factors in your head, but it is one of the most intriguing pursuits in the skill of reading a building.

Having a basic knowledge of construction materials will be useful in answering the fourth question: "What materials were used to construct this building or structure?" Look at the foundation. Is it concrete, block, or rubble stone? Are the walls made of masonry—brick or stone? Are the walls clad in siding? What is the roof made of? Many buildings in the 19th century were constructed of wood or masonry, whereas common construction materials in the 20th century were concrete and steel. Many houses have wood clapboard or shingle, or brick, although some modern houses use material like glass and steel. Most commercial structures were constructed of masonry in the 19th century, especially as the country urbanized and the threat of fire was constant. By the 20th century, steel framing allowed for large windows and masonry cladding that was not part of the building's structural framework. International Style office buildings often used curtain wall construction, with massive walls of glass supported by steel framing.

Probably the most fascinating question to ask is this one: "Why was the building or structure built, and what was the need it addressed?" This question has a multitude of answers. Domestic architecture was built to house humans, but the variation is wide. The First Houses in New York City and Cabrini-Green in Chicago were built to house indigent families. Fallingwater in Pennsylvania was built to provide a wealthy Pittsburgh family a vacation home. Levittown in Long Island was built to house hundreds of desperate young families who were looking to settle down after World War II. Seaside in Florida was built to also house families, but without the dreariness, sameness, and conformity of the typical car-based suburban development. Alternatively, Attica Prison in New York State was built to house a growing downstate prison population. And the Japanese American Relocation Camp in Rohwer, Arkansas, was rapidly constructed in order to house a population of Japanese American internees during World War II. The institutional and commercial structures in this book were built for a number of reasons as well. With the technology revolution in the 20th century, engineers made extraordinary advances with the Hoover Dam, Golden Gate Bridge, and the extraordinary River Rouge Ford plant in Michigan. The rise of the corporation with its requisite professional and clerical staff required that downtown office buildings expand in size as the skyscraper grew ever taller. The consumer culture that evolved in the 20th century produced a number of unique building types, including the music studio, movie palace, shopping mall, sports stadium, and amusement park. The emergence of the United States as a world power led to new types of structures in the 20th century like the Pentagon and other military installations that faced up to the new nuclear threat. The Pentagon as well as the new One World Trade Center was fortified to include extra security measures in order to forestall another terrorist attack. The buildings and landmarks of the 20th and 21st centuries demonstrate a huge variety of raisons d'être. Learning to evaluate the variety of buildings and landmarks from the 20th and 21st centuries will prove to be a fascinating exercise.

BIBLIOGRAPHY

Cragoe, Carol Davidson. 2008. *How to Read Buildings: A Crash Course in Architectural Styles.* New York: Rizzoli International Publications Inc.

Jones, Will. 2012. *How to Read New York: A Crash Course on Big Apple Architecture.* New York: Rizzoli International Publications Inc.

McAlester, Virginia Savage. 2015. *A Field Guide to American Houses.* New York: Alfred A. Knopf.

Poppeliers, John C. 1983. *What Style Is It?* Washington, DC: Preservation Press.

Upton, Dell. 1998. *Architecture in the United States.* Oxford: Oxford University Press.

CHRONOLOGY

1901	Asch Building opens in New York home to the Triangle Waist Company factory.
1903	Wright Brothers make the first controlled, sustained flight at Kitty Hawk, North Carolina.
1903	Luna Park amusement park opens in Coney Island in Brooklyn.
1906	San Francisco earthquake leaves 500 dead or missing.
1910	Pennsylvania Station is built by the Pennsylvania Railroad, bringing rail travel to Manhattan for the first time.
1911	Triangle shirtwaist factory fire kills 150 young women and girls.
1915	The Great Migration begins, resulting in the relocation of 6 million African Americans from the rural South to the industrial North and Midwest.
1915	Equitable Life Insurance Company Building opens, sparking protests that result in the creation of zoning laws in New York City that require buildings to have setbacks that allow more light to reach the street.
1917	United States enters World War I.
1917	Henry Ford's River Rouge Complex project is begun.
1918	Worldwide influenza epidemic kills half a million Americans.
1919	Prohibition begins as 18th Amendment to the Constitution is passed banning sale of liquor.
1920	Women given right to vote with passage of 19th Amendment to the Constitution.
1922	Lincoln Memorial is dedicated.

1925	The Ku Klux Klan marches on Washington, receiving a "warm reception."
1927	Charles Lindbergh makes the first solo nonstop transatlantic flight.
1927	Grauman's Chinese Theatre in Hollywood, California, opens.
1929	Stock market crash precipitates the Great Depression.
1931	Empire State Building in New York City opens and becomes the tallest building in the world.
1931	Attica State Prison opens, the most expensive prison of its day.
1932	Los Angeles Memorial Coliseum hosts Olympic Games.
1935	Social Security Act is passed.
1935	First Houses, the nation's first public housing project, is opened.
1936	Hoover Dam is completed at a cost of $49 million.
1937	Golden Gate Bridge in San Francisco is opened, the longest suspension bridge in the world until 1964.
1939	Fallingwater, Frank Lloyd Wright's masterpiece in rural Pennsylvania, is completed.
1941	United States enters World War II after being attacked by Japan at Pearl Harbor.
1941	The first buildings are built at Cabrini-Green, an infamous public housing project in Chicago that was largely demolished by 2011.
1942	Japanese immigrants and Japanese Americans are interned in relocation camps for the duration of World War II.
1943	The Pentagon, one of the world's largest office buildings, is dedicated.
1945	World War II ends after Germany surrenders and United States drops the first atomic bombs on Hiroshima and Nagasaki in Japan.
1946	Flamingo Hotel in Las Vegas is opened, developed by notorious mobster Bugsy Siegel.
1947	Construction is begun on the new suburb named Levittown in Long Island.
1950	Northgate Shopping Center, one of the first suburban shopping malls, opens in Seattle, Washington.

1950	Sun Record Studio opens in Memphis, where many early rock and roll artists were discovered.
1952	Lever House in New York is completed. It is the second building in New York City with a glass curtain wall.
1953	The first McDonald's franchise opens in Phoenix, Arizona, followed by one in Downey, California.
1954	*Brown v. Board of Education* Supreme Court decision declares that racial segregation is unconstitutional.
1954	Fontainebleau Hotel is opened in Miami Beach, designed by Morris Lapidus.
1956	Interstate Highway System is authorized with passage of the Federal Aid Highway Act of 1956.
1958	Seagram Building in New York, designed by Mies van der Rohe, and considered a masterpiece of the International Style of architecture, is completed.
1960	The birth control pill is approved by the Food and Drug Administration.
1960	Four students sit at the segregated Woolworth's lunch counter in Greensboro, North Carolina, in a nonviolent protest that influenced the civil rights movement.
1962	John Glenn is the first American to orbit the earth.
1962	TWA Flight Center in New York is dedicated, designed by Eero Saarinen.
1963	Pennsylvania Station in New York is demolished, which sparks a protest that leads to the creation of the Landmarks Preservation Commission in New York.
1963	Martin Luther King Jr. delivers his "I Have a Dream" speech at the March for Jobs and Freedom in front of the Lincoln Memorial.
1963	President John F. Kennedy is assassinated in Dallas, Texas. Lyndon Johnson is sworn in as president.
1964	The first building of the Watergate Complex in Washington, D.C., is completed. The office building/luxury apartment complex is the location of the break-in that brought down the Nixon presidency in 1974.
1965	Gateway Arch in St. Louis, the world's tallest arch, is completed.
1966	Vehicle Assembly Building at Kennedy Space Center is completed.

1968	Martin Luther King Jr. is assassinated in Memphis, setting off riots nationwide.
1968	Robert F. Kennedy is assassinated in Los Angeles while he was campaigning for president.
1971	Riot in Attica State Prison results in 43 deaths.
1973	Abortion is legalized after Supreme Court's decision on *Roe v. Wade*.
1973	The World Trade Center Complex is opened and is mocked by architectural critics who detested the design.
1973	Sears Tower in Chicago, the tallest skyscraper in the world for the next 25 years, is opened.
1974	President Richard Nixon resigns after Watergate scandal; Gerald Ford sworn in as president.
1981	Seaside, Florida, is opened, a new town built based on the precepts of "New Urbanism."
1982	Vietnam Veterans Memorial is completed, designed by Yale design student Maya Lin.
2001	The World Trade Center Complex is destroyed in the worst terrorist attack in American history.
2003	Walt Disney Concert Hall in Los Angeles opens, designed by Frank Gehry.
2004	Central Library in Seattle opens, designed by Rem Koolhaas.
2014	One World Trade Center, also known as the Freedom Tower, is completed.

Civic Architecture

Pennsylvania Station

Los Angeles Memorial Coliseum

Attica Correctional Facility

Hoover Dam

Golden Gate Bridge

Interstate Highway System

Portland Public Service Building

Central Library

Pennsylvania Station

New York, New York
1910

BACKGROUND

By the turn of the 20th century, there were webs of railroad tracks in virtually every pocket of this vast country. The railroad industry had transformed transportation, agriculture, and manufacturing as passengers were now able to travel more quickly and comfortably, while goods could be transported both speedily and efficiently throughout the nation. But nevertheless, in 1900, Alexander Cassatt, the powerful president of the largest corporation in the world at that time, the Pennsylvania Railroad, was not able to travel by train to New York City in order to board the ocean liner on his yearly trip to Europe. Cassatt was a cultured and wealthy man, the brother of America's famous Impressionist painter Mary Cassatt. On his annual trip to see his sister in Paris, Cassatt was once again dismayed that he was forced to board a crowded ferry to Manhattan at the Jersey City terminal after debarking from his train from Philadelphia. He had considered building a rail bridge to Manhattan, but the estimated $100 million price tag was too high. Tunnels were a possibility, but the existing train technology used steam, which led to possible asphyxiation inside the tunnel as well as blocking the vision of the train conductor, which caused deadly accidents. On one of his trips to Paris, Cassatt made a visit to the newly built Gare d'Orsay, an innovative railroad station that used electrification to bring the trains into the center of the city through tunnels. Electrified trains had only been used for trolleys and other light rail systems, but the technology was advancing enough to utilize electricity to haul heavy locomotives. Cassatt thought he might have a solution to his problem.

Cassatt was determined to build a railroad terminal in Manhattan and chose a down-at-the-heels district called the Tenderloin on the west side of midtown for the building. He hired an architectural firm in 1902 that was the premier firm at the time that specialized in civic projects using the Beaux-Arts style. McKim, Mead and White had designed buildings at the 1893 Chicago Columbian Exposition as well as the Boston Public Library and Columbia University. Charles Follen McKim, who was the primary designer for the Pennsylvania Station project, had studied at the Ecole des Beaux-Arts in Paris and was steeped in the vocabulary of classical (Greek and Roman) architecture. Cassatt, a man who also appreciated the monumentality of classical design, looked forward to working with McKim on his massive project. But first he had to find an engineer who could provide a solution to his quandary: How to build safe tunnels under the Hudson River? Cassatt's plans were even more grandiose—he wanted to build tunnels under the East River on the east side of Manhattan and a bridge to the Bronx so that the Pennsylvania Railroad could extend its reach to Long Island and New England from the terminus in Manhattan. Cassatt tapped engineer Samuel Rea from his own company as well as tunnel engineering expert Charles Jacobs. The entire tunneling project encompassed 16 miles of tunnels, of which 7 were under water. This massive engineering project was considered to be one of the greatest of its time. However, the project did not involve any public funding; it was totally financed by the Pennsylvania Railroad, which owned every inch of the tunnels and the terminal. In order to obtain the necessary land for the tracks and the terminal, men were sent out into the Tenderloin district with pockets full of cash that they would offer to the owners of the buildings in the selected area. This was done surreptitiously so that the owners would not recognize the rising value of their property. The proposed use of the land was kept secret until the entire 7.5 acres of land were acquired. The Pennsylvania Station took four years to build. It was completed in 1910.

CHARACTERISTICS AND FUNCTIONALITY

Pennsylvania Station was considered one of the great works designed by Beaux-Arts architects of the early 20th century. The classical design by Charles Follen McKim was based on the ancient precedents. The exterior of the building, covering four city blocks, had a colonnade on all four sides, with heavy Tuscan Doric columns, in pink Milford granite from Massachusetts. The entrances were guarded by six gigantic eagles. The periphery of the building was not tall, but in the center of the building, two portions of the interior of the building rose high above the periphery with huge windows. These were the famous, grand public spaces within the station. The towering 300-foot-long waiting room was 150 feet tall, with high half-moon-shaped lunette windows that let in light as well as ventilation. The vaulted ceiling was coffered and the vaults were supported by Corinthian columns, and the walls were covered in travertine marble imported from Italy. This waiting room was designed by McKim to be a replica of the tepidarium, or warm bathroom, of the Roman Baths of Caracalla, only 25 percent larger. The waiting room had a grandeur and dignity that impressed all its visitors. The concourse, or train shed, had a totally different atmosphere. It was also light-filled, but here, the decorative steel supports were covered in a soaring vaulted glass roof. Instead of classical solemnity, this giant space had an airy quality that used modern materials. Even though the solidity of the granite and marble make it look like a masonry structure, the framing was all steel. The main rooms of the station were one story below grade. Ramps were built along Seventh Avenue, which brought taxis and carriages inside. The president of the Pennsylvania Railroad, Alexander Cassatt, wanted to add a hotel to the design, but McKim refused to include it.

KEY STATISTICS

The Pennsylvania Station was located on four blocks in midtown Manhattan, between West 31st and West 33rd Streets and between Seventh and Ninth Avenues, said to be the largest block of commercial property in Manhattan. It was the largest railroad station of its day, and it cost $114 million to complete. The station hosted 100,000 visitors on its first day of operation, and by 1929, it had a daily passenger count of over 200,000. At the height of its usage during World War II, Penn Station had over 100 million passengers annually. The construction of Penn Station required 27,000 tons of steel and half a million cubic feet of granite, as well as 17 million bricks.

CULTURAL SIGNIFICANCE

Pennsylvania Station had enormous significance when it was opened in 1910 to admiring hordes. It provided a grand gateway to the city from throughout the country. It was a monumental public space. One unique factor in the building of Penn Station was that it was a purely private venture. Cassatt wanted to provide a majestic entrance into the world's center of commerce, and this station represented the power and wealth of the city of New York, yet no taxpayer money was involved. This private infrastructure investment was a gift to the city of New York, admired and utilized by millions of people. The gift was not solely the station itself, because the tunnels that cross the Hudson and the East Rivers were part of the project and are still being used. One of the unintended consequences of this investment was the growing use of the suburban transit lines into New Jersey and Long Island. However, the ultimate tragic loss of the grand station can also be blamed on the fact that it was a private investment. After World War II, the use of railroads declined significantly as the economy boomed and Americans began using their cars to travel on the new Interstate Highway system or to fly on one of the many new airplanes from the burgeoning airline industry. By the early 1960s, the station had been insensitively renovated in order to make it look more "modern," which only made it look more tired, as did the caked-on dirt on the exterior. The owner, the Pennsylvania Railroad, knew it had a goldmine in the large, midtown property it owned. It wanted to modernize the station, as well as take advantage of the valuable property asset that it owned. It announced the demolition of the station to make way for a new Madison Square Garden above a new underground station. There were protests by groups of activists; however, it was to no avail. Pennsylvania Station was demolished in 1963. Many members of the public as well as the architectural establishment were devastated. The *New York Times*' former architectural critic Ada Louise Huxtable wrote a column decrying the decision to demolish Pennsylvania Station, which has become a mantra of the preservation movement: "Any city gets what it admires, will pay for, and ultimately deserves. Even when we had Penn Station, we couldn't afford to keep it clean. We want and deserve tin-can architecture in a tin-horn culture. And we will probably be judged not by the monuments we build but by those we have destroyed" (Huxtable 1963). There was no law in place that could protect a privately owned building, even one that was as beloved as Penn Station. The profession of historic preservation did not yet exist, and neither did laws that designated buildings as landmarks that could not be destroyed. The crucial cultural significance of this great monumental building turned out to be its very loss. Because of the grief felt by so many after the demolition of Penn Station, legislation was promptly passed in New York City that established the New York City Landmarks Preservation Commission in 1965. This law actually has the power to penalize property owners who destroy buildings that are designated as landmarks. The other great railroad station in New York City, Grand Central Terminal, was soon landmarked to prevent it from meeting the same fate. Soon, other cities would pass similar legislation, and in 1966, Congress passed the National Historic Preservation Act.

FURTHER INFORMATION: IMPORTANT PRINT, ELECTRONIC, AND MEDIA RESOURCES

American Rails. "Pennsylvania Station, An Architectural Wonder." http://www.american-rails.com/pennsylvania-station.html. Accessed July 10, 2017.

Gelernter, Mark. 1999. *A History of American Architecture: Buildings in Their Cultural and Technological Context*. Hanover and London: University Press of New England.

Huxtable, Ada Louise. October 30, 1963. "Farewell to Penn Station." *The New York Times*. https://nycarchitectureandurbanism.files.wordpress.com/2015/03/huxtable-farewell-to-penn-station-1963.pdf. Accessed July 10, 2017.

Plotsky, Eric J. 1999. "The Fall and Rise of Pennsylvania Station: Changing Attitudes toward Historic Preservation in New York City." Master's in City Planning Thesis, Massachusetts Institute of Technology.

Roth, Leland M., and Amanda C. Roth Clark. 2016. *American Architecture: A History*. Boulder, CO: Westview Press.

Wiseman, Carter. 2000. *Twentieth-Century American Architecture: The Buildings and Their Makers*. New York and London: W. W. Norton.

Penn Station and the Tenderloin District

During the second half of the 19th century, New York City was growing into a great metropolis. However, there was an immense amount of poverty in certain neighborhoods like the Lower East Side. The district on the west side of midtown, called the Tenderloin, was another neighborhood beset by poverty. However, it also had the dubious distinction of being the "red light district" of the city. Crime was endemic, and one of the major businesses in the area was prostitution. A section of this neighborhood was occupied by a large population of African Americans, and the Tenderloin became one of two major black enclaves in Manhattan. The southwestern section of the Tenderloin that encompassed Seventh Avenue between the West 20s to the West 40s was referred to as "African Broadway." When plans were made to build the tunnels, tracks, and terminal that would become Pennsylvania Station, Alexander Cassatt of the Pennsylvania Railroad sent out third-party salesmen to purchase the properties in the district at bargain-basement prices. The neighborhood was subsequently destroyed and the residents were displaced. Many moved uptown to a neighborhood that had a growing black population: Harlem. The construction of Pennsylvania Station, with the adjacent U.S. Post Office, Macy's department store, and the Pennsylvania Hotel, in the early years of the 20th century was a major contributing factor in the growth of Harlem as a primarily African American district.

Los Angeles Memorial Coliseum

Los Angeles, California
1923

BACKGROUND

Although it is now the second largest city in the United States, Los Angeles, California, is, in fact, a young city. It was founded in 1781, but it was a tiny village, with a population of only 315 by 1800. Originally named El Pueblo de Nuestra Senora la Reina de Los Angeles de Porcincula, which means Our Lady the Queen of the Angels of Porcincula, it was owned by Spain until Mexico won its independence in 1821, when it became part of Mexico. In 1847, the U.S. military captured it in one of the skirmishes of the Mexican–American War, which ended in 1848 when Mexico ceded California to the United States in the Treaty of Guadalupe Hidalgo. The growth of the city of Los Angeles continued at a slow pace during the first half of the 19th century, with the population reaching a little over 5,000 by 1870. Although the state was booming as a result of the California Gold Rush of 1849, San Francisco benefited from the bulk of the population growth. Los Angeles, which was not included in the path of the transcontinental railroad until 1885, was primarily an agricultural center and was known as the "Queen of the Cow Counties" for its role in providing beef, vegetables, and fruits to the prosperous northern cities of California. When the Santa Fe railroad finally connected Los Angeles to the Midwest, a fare war ensued between Santa Fe and Union Pacific, which installed the railroad line connecting Los Angeles to San Francisco, and the cost of a train fare from St. Louis to Los Angeles fell to just $1. This enticed more Americans to undergo the trip west, and the population of Los Angeles finally grew substantially. Southern California was gaining a reputation as a healthy destination, for its abundant sunshine and dry weather. With the expansion of the population came a real estate boom, which became a bubble, as prices for land soared. The bubble burst in 1887 and many investors lost all their money. But when oil was discovered in Los Angeles in 1892, the population increased more, reaching 100,000 by the year 1900. In the first decades of the 20th century, Japanese and Mexican immigrants flooded into Los Angeles, as well as African Americans. The city was growing exponentially. Its desperate need for drinking water to nourish its growing population led to a movement in the early years of the 20th century to build an aqueduct that would bring water into the city. In 1905, the voters of Los Angeles approved a bond issue to build an aqueduct from the Owens River, 250 miles northeast of the city. The aqueduct was completed in 1913. The city continued to grow and had a population of half a million by 1920, and 1.2 million by 1930. The city of Hollywood became part of Los Angeles in 1910, and by the 1920s was the center for burgeoning new film industry. The 1920s was a boom time for Los Angeles.

With its exponential growth, but scant history, Los Angeles was anxious to prove itself as a player on the American cultural block. There were few cultural resources in the young city. The tax base was increasing, so community leaders began to agitate for investment in educational, recreational, and cultural infrastructure. One of the early improvements in the city was the transformation of Exposition Park, located on the south side of the city abutting the campus of the University of Southern California (USC). Once named Agricultural Park due to its use as grounds for agricultural fairs, the Exposition Park had belonged to the state but had been taken over by private investors who turned it into a center for gambling and other shady pursuits. It boasted a racetrack, brothels, and multiple saloons. In 1899, a prominent judge and local politician named William Bowen began a crusade to clean up the park. In 1908, the California Supreme Court ruled that the land was state property, thereby allowing it to be developed as a public cultural and recreational center. Bowen took on this assignment as a mission, and became known as the "Father of Exposition Park." The first cultural institution constructed in the park was the Los Angeles Natural History Museum, completed in 1913. Bowen continued to advocate for the development of the large park and suggested assigning part of the park for recreational use, even going so far as to suggest building a stadium. He had influence at USC, as an adjunct law professor, and convinced the board of trustees to promise to utilize a new stadium for all the USC home football games. This assurance by the private university to commit to the park became a major incentive for the state to pursue the venture. A nonprofit group of community leaders was formed in 1919 by Mayor Meredith P. Snyder. This group included William May Garland, a real estate developer; Harry Chandler, the publisher of the *Los Angeles Times* newspaper; and Frank P. Flint, former U.S. senator. They announced later that year that a new stadium was a prerequisite to give the city an appropriate venue for all types of sporting events and other events. With the end of World War I fresh in their minds, they decided to dedicate the new stadium as a memorial to the soldiers who died in the war. It was to be named the Los Angeles Memorial Coliseum. Their proposed location was Exposition Park.

The nonprofit organization, now named the Community Development Association (CDA), pledged to build a coliseum in the spirit of ancient Rome, and put "in reach of the public the class of amusements which are ordinarily too costly to be seen by the average amusement patron." The CDA convinced the most prominent local architectural firm, Parkinson & Parkinson, to donate its time and expertise to design a world-class stadium. John Parkinson and his son Donald devoted time and energy to the project. They even traveled to Europe to glean inspiration from designs of other large stadiums. The CDA then unveiled its secret wish: to be awarded the rights to hold the 1924 Olympic Games. William Garland trekked to Europe in 1920 to promote the city to the Olympic Committee in a bid for the 1924 Games. The bid failed, but the notion was already planted in the minds of the Los Angeles community leaders. They wanted to see this great coliseum built and they wanted to host an Olympic Games.

The concept of the Olympic Games was resurrected in 1896 when the first modern Olympic Games were held in Athens, Greece. The event had grown in prestige and in participation by the 1920s. After Los Angeles was denied in its bid for the Games in 1920, the city continued to move ahead with its plans to build the coliseum in the hopes that it would be considered for a subsequent Olympics. On August 22, 1921, the Municipal Arts Commission approved the plans for the coliseum, and ground was broken on December 21, 1921. The construction was executed through a public–private partnership, which included the city and county, the architects, the banks who provided the loans, and the contractors who worked on the construction. Funding was provided through an $800,000 loan made out to the CDA; no public funding was included. A long-term lease was signed for the area of the former racetrack in the new Exposition Park. Construction began on the stadium soon after the groundbreaking took place in December. The stadium was completed on time, in May 1923, with the first football game between USC and Pomona College taking place on October 6, 1923. Recognizing the city's commitment to constructing a world-class stadium in 1923, the International Olympic Committee approved the request for Los Angeles to host an Olympic Games. The Xth Olympiad would now take place in Los Angeles in 1932.

CHARACTERISTICS AND FUNCTIONALITY

The Los Angeles Memorial Coliseum was designed by a father–son team of architects, Parkinson & Parkinson. The elder Parkinson, John, was an immigrant from England who was not formally trained as an architect although he had some training as a technical draftsman. He left England in 1885 at the age of 21 and initially settled in northern California, working in construction. Moving to Seattle, Washington, Parkinson opened his first architectural office. Parkinson relocated to Los Angeles in 1894 and formed a partnership with G. Edwin Bergstrom. Los Angeles was booming at that time, and Parkinson received many commissions. Parkinson's buildings were influenced by the Beaux-Arts style, which was very popular at that time, especially for large public buildings. The firm was responsible for many of the major buildings in the downtown area of Los Angeles. John Parkinson was also very influential in the early city planning policies of the city of Los Angeles. He was a proponent of the "City Beautiful" movement. This movement emerged as an outgrowth of Beaux-Arts planning, which was showcased at the 1893 Chicago World's Columbian Exposition. The celebrated exposition, also known as the "White City," was designed by Daniel Burnham. The embryonic city of Los Angeles was just starting to consider design and planning for its upcoming development. John Parkinson exerted a major influence on the further development of the city as a member of the Municipal Art Commission. He was also instrumental in establishing the city's planning commission in 1920. He advocated for laying out the city with broad avenues, using symmetry and harmony as promoted by the City Beautiful movement. His most significant contribution to the appearance of the city was the passage of the ordinance that limited the height of all buildings in the city, a law that remained in effect from 1905 until 1957. This restriction was intended to allow for maximum sunlight and fewer shadows on the streets. In addition, there was the perennial concern for earthquakes. The effect of this height limit law, combined with the broad avenues, was the iconic appearance of the city with its low scale. However, after the law was changed and with more modern anti-earthquake construction techniques, many skyscrapers have been built in the city that have altered that scale in the downtown central core.

In 1921, John Parkinson teamed up with his son Donald to form the firm Parkinson & Parkinson. The elder Parkinson had already been commissioned to begin design on the proposed coliseum. He was so excited about the plan that he offered his services at no fee. The site of the new stadium was at the east end of the former racetrack, in an area where the city had been removing sand and gravel for years. This gravel pit was already below grade and served as the starting point for the excavation of the foundation for the stadium. The field level of the stadium is 32 feet below grade, with the first and second tiers of seating set into the excavated embankment. The structure is made of cast-in-place reinforced concrete and is in the shape of an elliptical bowl. The architectural style of the coliseum is a simplified version of the popular "Moderne" style of the 1920s and 1930s. The ornament on the structure has Egyptian and Spanish elements. The stadium was designed to seat 75,000 guests. However, in 1930–31, in preparation for the Olympics, seats were added onto a third tier, resulting in a new total capacity of over 101,000. The most celebrated feature of the coliseum is the peristyle. This grand facade at the east end of the elliptical stadium features a central giant propylaeum, or triumphal arch, surrounded by seven smaller arches on either side. On top of the triumphal arch is a tall, narrow concrete torch, which was added in 1932 for the Xth Olympiad. At the top of the concrete torch is a bronze cap. The torch was lit while the Olympic Games were under way. The Memorial Coliseum did not receive significant renovations until after World War II, when various repairs were made, and a two-story office structure and a press box, tower, and elevator were added. Several modernized scoreboards were also added.

KEY STATISTICS

The Los Angeles Memorial Coliseum is located on 3911 South Figueroa Street in Exposition Park in Los Angeles on a 17-acre property. It was completed in 1923, with a capacity for 75,000. With its expansion for the 1932 Olympics, an additional tier was added that brought to capacity up to 101,574. The structure is 1,038 feet long and 738 feet wide at the widest point of the ellipse. The height of the structure totals 106 feet from the field level to the top rim. The field itself is 684 feet by 345 feet. There are three banks of seats, two with 25 tiers of seating and one with 29, with a total of 79 tiers of seats. The "Court of Honor" located in the peristyle contains over 50 commemorative plaques of "outstanding persons or events that have made a significant contribution to the Coliseum or Sports Arena through positive athletic participation, or a positive contribution to the historical significance of the Coliseum or the Sports Arena." The construction of the stadium, when it was initially completed in 1923, cost $954,000.

CULTURAL SIGNIFICANCE

Nearing 100 years old, the Los Angeles Memorial Coliseum has had a long and illustrious life span, providing a venue for many types of sporting events as well as countless other types of events. The 1932 Olympic Games were originally faced with some serious headwinds coming into the event. The devastating effects of the Great Depression were being felt worldwide, and a number of participating nations threatened not to come due to the expenses involved. The United States, too, was suffering from the consequences of the global downturn, with the homeless and the unemployed setting up shantytowns called "Hoovervilles" in downtown Los Angeles. In addition, Europe was concerned about the rise of Adolf Hitler, and Japan was already showing aggression to neighboring regions. However, in the end, it worked out. A novel concept instituted by the planners of the 1932 Olympics convinced the foreign nations to decide ultimately to attend. For the first time, an Olympic Village was constructed that would house all the male athletes in a communal setting. (The female athletes were also housed, though in a luxury downtown hotel.) For the first time, athletes from around the world were able to live comfortably and inexpensively and to instill friendly relationships with athletes from around the world. This idea was retained and expanded on ever since. The initial fears of the Olympic planners for the 1932 Games were proven wrong, and the Games were a rousing success, with American athletes receiving the most medals with a total of 103. The opening ceremonies were attended by 101,022 fans, an astounding number even by today's standards. The coliseum was used again successfully in the 1984 Olympics in Los Angeles. The stadium was used for the Super Bowl twice. It hosted the 1959 World Series. It has served both professional baseball and football teams and was the temporary home of the Los Angeles Dodgers and the Los Angeles Raiders. Many other historic events took place in this venue. These include the acceptance speech made by John F. Kennedy after he was nominated at the Democratic National Convention in 1960. Franklin Roosevelt held a campaign event there. It was also the venue for Billy Graham's Crusade for Christ, in 1963, when it hosted record number of patrons, totaling 134,254. The vision of the early Los Angeles boosters like William Bowen, William Garland, the Parkinsons, and others has proven to be prescient. The USC football team still plays in the stadium. Two Olympiads took place there, in 1932 and again in 1984. In fact, it was announced in September 2017 that Los Angeles was chosen to host the Games once more in 2028. The opening ceremonies will take place in the century-old Los Angeles Memorial Coliseum.

FURTHER INFORMATION: IMPORTANT PRINT, ELECTRONIC, AND MEDIA RESOURCES

Charleton, James H. 1984. "Los Angeles Memorial Coliseum." National Park Service. https://npgallery.nps.gov/pdfhost/docs/NHLS/Text/84003866.pdf. Accessed October 14, 2017.

"Coliseum History—LA Coliseum." http://www.lacoliseum.com/index.php/coliseum-history/. Accessed October 11, 2017.

Lambert, Tim. "A History of Los Angeles." http://www.localhistories.org/losangeles.html. Accessed October 12, 2017.

"Los Angeles Memorial Coliseum—Los Angeles." Los Angeles Conservancy. https://www.laconservancy.org/issues/los-angeles-memorial-coliseum. Accessed. October 11, 2017.

Meares, Hadley. July 21, 2016. "The People's Playground." Curbed LA. https://la.curbed.com/2016/7/21/12215982/los-angeles-olympics-coliseum-history. Accessed October 11, 2017.

Los Angeles? Where's That?

The city of Los Angeles was not the world-class city in the 1920s that it is today. In fact, the name was barely recognized outside of California. When William May Garland first went to Europe to put in the bid for the 1924 Olympics to be hosted by the city of Los Angeles, one of the International Olympic Committee members told him, "Billy, I voted for Los Angeles because I like you personally. But where is Los Angeles? Is it anywhere near Hollywood?"

Source: Meares, Hadley. "The People's Playground." Curbed LA. https://la.curbed.com/2016/7/21/12215982/los-angeles-olympics-coliseum-history. p. 3.

Attica Correctional Facility

Attica, New York
1931

BACKGROUND

The study of the punishment of crime and of prison management is called penology. In the United States during the colonial period, prisons did not exist. Punishment was meted out in various ways. Serious crimes were punished by public execution, and less serious crimes were also punished publicly, by whipping or maiming the offender or placing him or her in a pillory for a prescribed amount of time. The Age of Enlightenment in the late 18th century ushered in a different theory of punishment. The idea of public shaming was rejected and replaced by the concept of long-term confinement, which was considered more humane. The states of New York and Pennsylvania were on the cutting edge of penology in the early 19th century. Pennsylvania, influenced by Quaker religious beliefs, invented a system of punishment that was meant to require the convict to do penance. The offender was placed in a new type of state-run facility that was called a penitentiary, where the prisoner would be encouraged to repent. Prisoners were provided with a cell and a private exercise yard. There they would be confined totally alone, away from the pernicious influences that had led them astray. Provided with a Bible to study and a small craft project, the prisoner would have time to contemplate and restore his or her faith. A parallel system was developed in New York at about the same time. This method was developed at Auburn Prison, which was opened in 1819 and was called the Auburn system or the congregate system. Unlike the pious Quakers, New Yorkers were less religious and more motivated by business concerns. Like the Pennsylvania Quakers, the builders of the Auburn Prison believed in keeping prisoners away from unhealthy influences. However, they saw that the Pennsylvania method was expensive and did not provide any return on the investment in the prisoners. They designed a prison with smaller individual cells and brought the prisoners out every day for work, building factories with the labor force of involuntary workers. "Industry, obedience and silence" was the motto at the Auburn Prison. Although the prisoners ate and worked as a group, they had to remain totally silent. In addition, Auburn developed a system of marching in lockstep, where each prisoner had to grab the shoulder of the one in front and look down in shame as they shuffled along. The famous black-and-white striped prison uniform is also a creation of the Auburn Prison. The two systems of incarceration, both New York's and Pennsylvania's, fascinated Europeans, who were also looking for a penal system that could replace public punishments. Alexis de Tocqueville, who came to the United States and studied the American culture in the 1831, was actually sent here by order of the French government to study the American prison systems. Other European nations also sent emissaries to observe the American methods of incarceration. The Europeans preferred the Pennsylvania system, but the Auburn system proliferated in the United States well into the 20th century.

When the Attica State Prison was opened in 1931, New York State was in desperate need for a large, new prison. The existing prisons were very overcrowded. Two prison riots had taken place in 1929 in New York's Auburn and Clinton prisons, and the state officials were worried. The last prison built in the state was Great Meadow prison, completed in 1911. The other large prison complexes, Auburn, Sing Sing, and Clinton, were built between 1819 and 1844. As these prisons were built before the invention of electricity and indoor plumbing, inmates in these ancient prisons were still given a bucket of fresh water and a bucket for waste every day in their cells. The new prison at Attica was designed with modern amenities. It had electricity, running water, mess halls, kitchens, and recreational facilities. It was the most expensive prison ever built at the time. Besides its amenities, it had multiple safety features that made the prison purportedly riot-proof. The brand new design of the Attica State Prison was hailed as a secure and modern facility to house the most dangerous of the state's prisoners. The location, 35 miles east of Buffalo, in northwestern New York State, was selected because of its proximity to the railroad line and the availability of fresh water. The tiny village of Attica, however, was 350 miles away from the huge city of New York, home to most of the prison's inmates.

When Attica was opened in 1931 during the Great Depression, it was populated by a variety of murderers, rapists, and bank robbers. However, Attica's prison population changed after World War II as the Great Migration brought many African Americans to northern cities seeking better opportunities. Likewise, Puerto Ricans also sought work and opportunity in cities like New York in the decades after the war. By the late 1960s and 1970s, two-thirds of the inmates at state prisons like Attica were minorities. The laws had changed as the "war on drugs" was beginning to bring in young offenders who were drug sellers or users. Because of severe overcrowding in the New York City jails, a new law was passed in 1970 that allowed New York City prisoners who were sentenced to over 90 days to be transferred up to "the Big House" at Attica. This comingling of New York

City street toughs with the long-term prison population created a more turbulent atmosphere. In addition, the culture war of the late 1960s and early 1970s was exploding throughout the country. Protests against the Vietnam War were continuing, political groups were becoming more radicalized, and antagonism between protesters and the police was intensifying. The radicalization of young African Americans manifested itself in groups like the Black Panther Party. This party, as well as the conversion of many prisoners to Islam, had a major influence on the minority prison population. Attica, sitting in the rural farmland of northwestern New York, was run by a force of almost exclusively white corrections officers, who had scant understanding of the life of a New York City street kid. The cultural divide was vast. The Muslims sensed the sting of religious discrimination. A prison leader named George Jackson, who had recruited many African American inmates nationwide to the Black Panther Party, was murdered in San Quentin Penitentiary in California on August 21, 1971, which distressed many of the Attica inmates. Tension was building in the cell blocks.

On September 8, 1971, a scuffle broke out between two inmates in the yard. The prisoners protested the punishment of the men, and the following day, a full-blown riot broke out throughout the prison. Inmates took 40 hostages and killed one of the guards. This outburst did not come as a surprise to many observers. A group of prisoners had been peacefully protesting throughout the hot summer. They had written to the Commissioner of Correctional Services Russell Oswald, a man who professed to be committed to prison reform. On the list of the prisoners' demands were simple requests like more toilet paper (a prisoner was given only one roll per month) and more frequent showers (once a week even during the torrid heat in the non-air-conditioned cells). Oswald had come to the prison to discuss the demands but was called away before anything was accomplished. The prisoners felt betrayed. The anger exploded on September 9 as the inmates took over the prison and took hostages, in a standoff that lasted four days. One corrections officer was killed in the riot. Negotiations went on between Commissioner Oswald and the inmate leaders. Black Muslims protected the hostages. Oswald was ready to accede to the demands, with the exception of their demand for complete amnesty for the prison takeover. He feared that it would lead to copycat riots in prisons across the country. After four days of unsuccessful negotiations, Oswald recommended to New York State governor Nelson Rockefeller to take the prison by force. Rockefeller agreed. A helicopter hovered over the prison and proceeded to drop tear gas, as the gas-mask-clad State Troopers stormed the prison. It only took six minutes for the prison to be retaken by the State Troopers, who fired off 4,500 rounds of ammunition. Ten hostages and 29 prisoners were killed. The initial reports falsely stated that the prisoners had slit the throats of the hostages. In fact, the State Troopers were responsible for all the deaths. The hostages were killed by friendly fire. The siege was over, with a final total of 43 dead and scores more injured.

CHARACTERISTICS AND FUNCTIONALITY

Attica State Prison was designed as a riot-proof and escape-proof facility. The architect of Attica was William J. Beardsley, a prominent architect based in Poughkeepsie, New York. Over his career, Beardsley had designed a number of institutional facilities, including hospitals and courthouses. Attica is the only prison he designed that was actually built, although he won a competition for his design to replace the old prison at Sing Sing, which was never carried out. Beardsley's plan was replete with features that were designed to prevent escape or riots. The facility was encircled by a 30-foot-high concrete wall, which extended 12 feet into the ground. The wall had 14 gun towers spaced along the top. The design of these towers alluded to French medieval castle walls, with crenellations, corbels, and long, narrow openings called embrasures. On top of the gun tower was a smaller octagonal tower with a tall pointed roof and a small lantern on the top. This small tower had round-topped windows on each of the eight faces. The wall and the towers appeared monumental, but the French medieval allusions gave the exterior of the facility an incongruous Disneyland feel. The complex had 18 buildings, which included administration buildings, the hospital, mess halls, kitchen, laundry, metal trades shops, the powerhouse, and maintenance building. But the heart of the prison was the four original cell blocks, A, B, C, and D. A fifth cell block, Cell Block E, was completed in 1966. The four original cell blocks formed a square that enclosed an open area, creating an interior courtyard. Extending out from the middle of the cell blocks were corridors, called "tunnels," that divided the large square into four smaller squares. These tunnels met in the middle of the courtyard at a central location dubbed "Times Square." The entry into each tunnel and into Times Square was a manned and locked gate. Another innovation at Attica was the Van Dorn Automatic Locking System, which allowed the corrections officers to open or lock any cell or gate from a centralized location. The cell blocks contained three floors of cells, and each cell block held 500 inmates. In addition to the walls and the gates, another security feature designed into the plan was tear gas bombs built into the walls in high-traffic areas like the mess hall and the auditorium, which corrections officers could release at the first sign of disturbance. The tear gas bombs have been used on a number of occasions.

KEY STATISTICS

Attica State Prison, now officially called Attica Correctional Facility, is located at 639 Exchange Street Road in Attica, New York. The complex comprises 55 acres. When it was built in 1931, it cost the state $9 million.

The massive wall enclosing the facility cost a whopping $1.275 million to complete. The original plan called for a capacity of 2,000 inmates. There are presently over 2,200 inmates.

CULTURAL SIGNIFICANCE

The infamous deadly prison riot provoked outrage as the facts of the siege on the prison were discovered. Not only did the State Troopers kill the hostages with their indiscriminate fire, but they also tortured the inmates and left the injured to die. The state proceeded to cover up as much evidence as it could. Governor Rockefeller falsely reported to President Nixon that the dead hostages were dead before the siege. The cover-up continued as the evidence in the yard was destroyed by a bulldozer. The public was horrified by the news coming out of Attica. A statewide commission was set up to investigate the incident. Lawsuits were filed by both the inmates and the guards' families, which continued for years. In 2000, the inmates won a $12 million lawsuit, although the state never apologized. In 2005, a settlement was reached with the surviving hostages, widows, and children of those who were killed. A Pulitzer Prize–winning new book by Heather Ann Thompson that was released in 2016, *Blood in the Water: The Attica Uprising of 1971 and Its Legacy*, reveals that the state is still trying to hide crucial evidence of the riot and its aftermath, although Thompson has done the most thorough investigation so far.

The outcome of the riot and the unnecessary deaths were due to a number of concomitant factors. First, the change in the racial makeup of the prison, as well as the radicalization of the civil rights movement and the polarization of the country politically, contributed to the explosive situation. Richard Nixon was elected in 1968 on a platform of law and order. He reached out to what he called the "silent majority" and utilized the so-called Southern strategy, using racial code words to appeal to the covert racism of many Southern Democrats in order to win the election. The Republican Party had started its inexorable tilt to the right. Nelson Rockefeller, the governor of New York State, had ambitions to run for president. Unfortunately, he had a record of liberal policies that did not play well in the conservative southern and western states. Rockefeller did not want to be known as "soft on crime" as crime was rising in the cities. If he had allowed the prisoners at Attica to win their demands, especially the demand for amnesty, Rockefeller feared that the prisons nationwide would erupt. There was no way that the prisoners could win. The case for prison reform, once a real hope, seemed doomed. In the 46 years since the riot at Attica took place, the incarceration rate in the United States has mushroomed. Nelson Rockefeller signed a litany of laws against the use and sale of illegal drugs, now called the "Rockefeller drug laws," that were draconian in nature. Some states are attempting to reduce their prison populations by repealing mandatory sentencing laws and "three strikes you're out" legislation. But the so-called prison-industrial complex creates crucially needed jobs in rural areas. The end of the problems with penology, prison management and prison reform, is nowhere in sight.

FURTHER INFORMATION: IMPORTANT PRINT, ELECTRONIC, AND MEDIA RESOURCES

"Attica Prison Riot." American Experience. PBS.org. October 15, 2000. http://www.pbs.org/video/2112801229/. Accessed July 31, 2017.

The Official Report of the New York State Special Commission on Attica. 1972. New York: Bantam Books. Digitized by New York State Library, 222 Madison Avenue, Albany, NY 12230. 2011. http://www.nysl.nysed.gov/mssc/attica/atticareport.pdf. Accessed July 31, 2017.

Slade, Kathleen E. 2012. "Attica State Correctional Facility: The Causes of the Riot of 1971." *The Exposition* 1(1), Article 3. http://digitalcommons.buffalostate.edu/cgi/viewcontent.cgi?article=1000&context=exposition. Accessed July 1, 2017.

Thompson, Heather Ann. 2016. *Blood in the Water: The Attica Uprising of 1971 and Its Legacy*. New York: Pantheon Books.

Attica Prison

A number of notorious prisoners have been incarcerated at Attica prison over the years, including the following:

David Berkowitz is a serial killer known as the "Son of Sam." He was convicted of shooting and killing eight people during a spree that terrorized New York City during the summer of 1976. He has been incarcerated since his arrest and is serving six consecutive life sentences.

Mark David Chapman is imprisoned for the murder of rock legend John Lennon outside of his home at the Dakota Apartments in New York City, on December 8, 1980. Chapman has been denied parole nine times.

Colin Ferguson, a Jamaican American, was convicted of killing six people and wounding 19 more on a Long Island Railroad train on December 7, 1993. He is serving a 315-year-and-8-month sentence, which means that he will not be eligible for parole until 2309. In response to the shooting, Carolyn McCarthy, whose husband was killed on the train and son was seriously wounded, ran for Congress on a gun control platform. She served as a representative of her Long Island District from 1997 to 2015.

Joseph "Mad Dog" Sullivan, a New York mobster of Irish descent, was the only person to have escaped the Attica prison.

Willie Sutton was a successful bank robber whose career spanned a 40-year period that started in the 1920s. Known as "Slick Willie" or "Willie the Actor," the charming Sutton is said to have come up with the so-called Sutton's law although the story is most likely apocryphal. Asked why he robbed banks, he supposedly answered "because that's where the money is." Sutton's law, which has been used in medical education as well as in economics, states that the most obvious answer or diagnosis should be investigated first, as it is likely to be the right one. In economics, it is known as "the Willie Sutton Rule."

Hoover Dam

*Clark County, Nevada, and
Mohave County, Arizona
1936*

BACKGROUND

The cities of southern California were growing at a rapid pace in the early years of the 20th century. But they had one crucial shortcoming: lack of water. Both drinking water and water for irrigation were necessary elements in the continued success of the western cities and growing agricultural region. Constructed in the 1930s to provide water and power to the western United States, the Hoover Dam (originally known as the Boulder Dam) represents a period of American history where the government constructed large dams for water reclamation and for power generation. This occurred in the South by the Tennessee Valley Authority and in the West and Northwest by the Bureau of Reclamation, and by the U.S. Army Corps of Engineers all across the nation. These dams facilitated the development of large cities like Los Angeles and other areas that needed the water and electricity provided by the dams. However, they also destroyed natural habitats and people's homes in the name of progress.

The government had been trying to control the Colorado River since the late 1800s. However, flooding still occurred in the 1900s. After a horrific flood that caused millions of dollars of damage, in 1909 Congress authorized a new levee project for the Colorado River. However, by the 1920s, the engineers were recommending the construction of a dam near Boulder Canyon as a means to provide flood control, improved navigation, drinking water, and electrical energy generation for the region. In 1929, Congress approved the new dam; however, there was still opposition from engineers who did not believe the dam would work, holding back the powerful waters of the river.

Despite the skepticism, in 1931 the federal government awarded the construction contract to Six Companies, Inc., of San Francisco, and it quickly started work on planning and preparing the site. Construction began in 1933 and was finished in 1935, two years before the estimated completion date. The fact that the nation was in the middle of Great Depression allowed the company to never fear about not having enough labor, which assisted in the speed in completing the dam. President Franklin Roosevelt dedicated the dam on September 30, 1935. Sadly, during construction, 112 men lost their lives at the dam site, with many entombed in the walls of the dam.

CHARACTERISTICS AND FUNCTIONALITY

Construction of the dam began in June 1933; however, planning had begun in 1931. Hoover Dam is a concrete arch-gravity storage dam, which uses both gravity and horizontal action to hold back the water. The dam is located on the Colorado River in the Black Canyon, and sits between Clark County, Nevada, and Mohave County, Arizona. Although it only dams up one river, the drainage area is over 167,800 square miles, which includes parts of the states of Wyoming, Utah, Colorado, Nevada, Arizona, and New Mexico. The size of the Hoover Dam is incredible and hard to contemplate. The dam measures 1,244 feet long at the crest and is 726.4 feet above the ground. The walls of the dam are 660 feet thick at the base and taper to 45 feet at the top of the dam. The top of the dam is so large that U.S. Highway 93 runs across its top. Also, towers and ornaments on the parapet rise 40 feet above the crest. During the construction of the Hoover Dam, four 50-foot-diameter diversion tunnels were built on each side of the river to drain the dam site for construction. The upper portions of the tunnels were later plugged and have been used for spillways.

A significant engineering innovation that facilitated the dam's construction was the addition of water pipes through the concrete blocks that pumped ice-cold water through the concrete, allowing it to cool at a rapid pace. Normally, concrete requires "setting up," which would have taken more than a century at the Hoover Dam, considering the massive amounts of concrete that were required. The cooling of the dam's concrete blocks was accomplished within two years. The architectural style of the ornament at the Hoover Dam is Art Deco. The ornament can be found on the elevator shaft houses at the summit of the dam and two similar houses that contain public restrooms. The ornament on the parapets of the intake towers is also in the Art Deco style. The towers include sculpted bas-reliefs depicting symbolic representations of power, water storage, and other related subjects. The construction of the Hoover Dam resulted in the creation of Lake Mead, a reservoir that serves the states of Nevada and Arizona. It is the largest reservoir in the United States, at 112 miles long, with 247 square miles of surface area. The level of the water has been depleted, however, in the last 30 years due to drought and increased water demand.

KEY STATISTICS

The Hoover Dam is about 28 miles southeast of Las Vegas, Nevada, and approximately 7 miles east of Boulder City, Nevada. Even though it was a massive project, the dam was completed two years ahead of schedule.

The size of the dam is breathtaking. Over 3.25 million cubic yards of concrete were used in the dam itself, with an additional million cubic yards in the power plant and appurtenant works. The Hoover Dam weighs more than 6,600,000 tons, and more than 5,500,000 cubic yards of material were excavated.

CULTURAL SIGNIFICANCE

The highest dam in the world at the time it was completed, the engineering feat that is the Hoover Dam can be compared to the construction of the Panama Canal in the first decade of the 20th century. The Hoover Dam was one of the earliest of the Bureau of Reclamation's massive multiple-purpose dams, which was designed to provide electric power, flood control, and irrigation waters. The Bureau of Reclamation had already constructed the Cheesman Dam in Denver and the Theodore Roosevelt Dam. However, the Hoover Dam towers over those examples because of its size, the amount of power it produced, and the way it opened parts of California and Arizona for settlement and agriculture. In fact, Los Angeles and Las Vegas would not have developed into the megacities that they are today without the power and water from Hoover Dam.

After its construction, the Hoover Dam had a huge effect on the region. Electrical energy generated at the largest plant in the world was transmitted to southern California, southern Nevada, and parts of Arizona, allowing for the rapid development of towns and suburbs in regions that did not have proper power sources. The dam also provided irrigation water for over 2,270,000 acres. One of the effects of the irrigation is allowing for year-around planting of vegetables in California that are shipped across the nation. The dam was added to the *National Register* in 1981, and was declared a National Historic Landmark in 1985.

FURTHER INFORMATION: IMPORTANT PRINT, ELECTRONIC, AND MEDIA RESOURCES

Ellis, Luke, Bruce M. Nash, and Max Raphael. 2005. *Hoover Dam.* [New York]: A & E Home Video.

Hiltzik, Michael A. 2010. *Colossus: Hoover Dam and the Making of the American Century.* New York: Free Press.

National Park Service. September 7, 1979. "Hoover Dam." *National Register of Historic Places Inventory-Nomination Form.* https://npgallery.nps.gov/pdfhost/docs/NHLS/Text/81000382.pdf. Accessed December 18, 2017.

Stevens, Joseph E. 1988. *Hoover Dam: An American Adventure.* Norman: University of Oklahoma Press.

Western Construction News. 1931. "Hoover Dam Specifications." *Western Construction News* 6 (1) 2–11.

Hoover Dam

The naming of the Hoover Dam resulted in a political fight among the Roosevelt administration and the Republicans. When the dam was first authorized, it was not officially named, and was referred to as a dam at Boulder Canyon. In 1930, the secretary of the interior named the dam after current president Herbert Hoover, who was a famous and well-respected engineer. After Hoover's defeat in 1932, the new Roosevelt administration declared the dam was to be named Boulder Dam. However, it soon became clear that Congress had referred to the dam as Hoover Dam in at least five pieces of legislation, and therefore, it was considered the official name of the dam.

Although the Roosevelt administration referred to the dam as Boulder Dam, the public continued using the Hoover Dam name, and Congress finally officially named it as Hoover Dam in 1947.

Brandon Holmes/Dreamstime.com

Golden Gate Bridge

San Francisco, California
1937

BACKGROUND

The iconic city of San Francisco is known for its equally iconic bridge, the Golden Gate Bridge. Finished in 1937, the Golden Gate Bridge was a triumph of engineering and chutzpah, and was a signature achievement. The city of San Francisco was the largest metropolis in California until being superseded by Los Angeles in the 20th century. San Francisco was founded in 1776 by Juan Bautiza de Anza who established a mission and presidio, or fort, there. The mission, called San Francisco de Asis, was one of the early missions in California founded by Spain. In 1821, Mexico won its independence from Spain, and San Francisco as well the rest of California became part of Mexico. At that time, San Francisco was still a small western outpost named Yerba Buena. In 1847, the Americans renamed it San Francisco. In 1848, the United States officially took over Upper California to end the Mexican War in the Treaty of Guadalupe Hidalgo. The small outpost of San Francisco was soon to be transformed. On January 24, 1848, gold was discovered at Sutter's Mill, near Coloma, northeast of San Francisco. All of a sudden, the region was teeming with expectant prospectors in their eager quest to find gold. The small town of San Francisco ballooned into a dynamic metropolis. In fact, the population swelled from 1,000 to 25,000 in the first two years of the Gold Rush. The city continued to expand as the 19th century came to an end, with 342,000 residents in 1900 and a ranking as ninth largest city in the nation. The growth of San Francisco was temporarily halted by the devastating 1906 earthquake and subsequent fire that destroyed 80 percent of the city. Undaunted, the city went ahead and rebuilt. To celebrate the renaissance of San Francisco after the earthquake, as well as the opening of the Panama Canal, the Panama-Pacific International Exposition took place in San Francisco in 1915. The city was buoyed by youthful enthusiasm. However, the geographical location of San Francisco was beginning to hamper its growth. Surrounded by water on three sides, San Francisco is located on a narrow peninsula with San Francisco Bay to the east and the Pacific Ocean to the west. To the north are Marin County and the small city of Sausalito. But separating Marin County from San Francisco is the treacherous constricted one mile wide strait that was dubbed the Chrysopolae or "Golden Gate" by Captain John Fremont, who surveyed the region for the U.S. Army in 1846. The slender waterway reminded him of the so-called Chrysoceras or "Golden Horn" harbor in Byzantium, modern-day Istanbul, in Turkey. The Golden Gate channel separated the promontory that contained the entire city of San Francisco from the northern western coast up to Oregon. The only way to get to Marin County and the rest of the west coast was by ferry. Regular ferry service began in the 1840s when the Gold Rush added thousands to the local population. The Southern Pacific Railroad eventually took over the ferry service from San Francisco to Sausalito. By the early 1900s, the ferries plying the Golden Gate were proliferating, but eventually the number of ferries crowding the narrow strait was becoming unsustainable. Marin County was the playground for the metropolis, mainly a rural region that was a destination for San Franciscans to enjoy a day out. However, the area was not convenient as a commuter suburb, and real estate development was not taking place in Marin County, which inhibited economic growth there. The dearth of accessible land in San Francisco began to hinder further population expansion. With the introduction of the automobile, planners began to consider alternate options for the region. As early as 1872, suggestions to build a bridge to Sausalito were made but there was little follow-up. However, after the Panama-Pacific world's fair was over in 1916, San Franciscans were excited about the growth implications that a bridge across the Golden Gate would provide. A journalist for the *San Francisco Bulletin*, James Wilkins, proposed a radical idea to build a bridge over the Golden Gate. The city engineer, Michael O'Shaughnessy, was inspired by the proposal but feared that such a project would cost upward of $100 million, an unacceptable price tag. O'Shaughnessy requested that a well-known bridge designer Joseph B. Strauss apply his skills to the task, in order to lower the cost. Strauss had enjoyed a modicum of success as a designer of bascule bridges. The name "bascule" comes from French for balance scale, and is the technical term for drawbridge. Strauss had studied engineering at the University of Cincinnati. He opened up his own engineering firm in Chicago and proceeded to develop a new type of bascule bridge that was built in a number of cities around the country; approximately 400 of his bascule bridges were already built. Michael O'Shaughnessy in San Francisco was impressed with Strauss's bridge design skills. However, in the end, it was not the design skills that ultimately got the bridge built. It was the visionary zeal and marketing skills of Joseph Strauss himself.

Strauss arrived at City Hall in San Francisco with a set of plans in his hands in 1921. He had labored over the design dilemma. His solution was a combination cantilever and suspension bridge. As a specialist in bascule bridges, Strauss had provided many successful spans over rivers in inland cities. This massive project was something completely new to Strauss. The mile-long strait posed a unique challenge: the waters of the Golden Gate had strong currents, and the winds were fierce. The depth of the channel was 335 feet in the center. Engineers had protested for years that a bridge could not be built in such adverse conditions. There was the ubiquitous San Francisco fog. And of course, the threat of another earthquake from the San Andreas Fault that was located only 12 miles away was omnipresent. The bridge had to be strong enough to withstand these conditions over time as well as being able to span the broad width of the Golden Gate Strait. In addition, the miserable conditions present at the site made it extremely difficult to build the bridge using construction techniques available at the time. It was truly a risky venture. Strauss was a man who was not afraid of risk. He was a consummate promoter and had complete confidence in his abilities. However, when he presented his set of plans to the city officials, they were not impressed. This design had two cantilevers extending out into the water, with a short suspension bridge in the center. The cantilevers were supported by multiple steel girders that gave the bridge a cage-like appearance. One of the critics called it "an upside down rat trap." No one liked it. But the city elders were enthusiastic about the idea of having a bridge. Unfortunately, despite the low-ball estimate of $27 million given by Strauss to the city, no funding was forthcoming from the federal or state government. Eventually, the state of California passed enabling legislation, which was called the Golden Gate Bridge and Highway District Act in 1923, which gave rights to the surrounding counties to organize, borrow money, issue bonds, construct a bridge, and collect tolls. Another delay occurred when the War Department objected to the project, contending that the bridge would hinder navigation. In 1924, it finally issued a provisional permit to move ahead with the design. The Golden Gate Bridge and Highway District, which included the counties of San Francisco, Marin, Sonoma, and Del Norte, and parts of Napa and Mendocino, was formed in 1928. The stock market crash of October 1929 created another hurdle in building the bridge. Although the district counties voted to issue $35 million in bonds, no one would purchase them. Joseph Strauss was completely invested in this project. He was desperate to have the bridge built, so he visited A. P. Giannini, the founder of San Francisco's powerful Bank of America, and pleaded his case. Although facing tough times himself, Giannini agreed that the city needed the bridge and promised to purchase all the bonds. The project was ready to proceed. Construction commenced on January 5, 1933, and on February 26, 1933, a groundbreaking was held at the nearby Crissy Field.

CHARACTERISTICS AND FUNCTIONALITY

While the project made its way through numerous hurdles to its funding, the engineers were busy designing the bridge. Strauss, the master of the drawbridge, was not the ultimate designer of the Golden Gate Bridge, although he appointed himself as chief engineer. He punted the engineering design to a member of his firm, a former professor at the University of Illinois named Charles Ellis. Another prominent bridge engineer named Leon D. Moisseiff worked with Ellis. However, Ellis was ultimately responsible for all the calculations that were required to design this revolutionary structure. Using only his slide rule, adding machine, and multiple algebraic formulas, Ellis was able to predict how the various stresses would act on the cables of the suspension bridge. The bridge had to be strong yet flexible, for it had to be able to sway in the fierce winds of San Francisco Bay. Strauss also hired an architect to work with the team, a local architect named Irving Morrow, who was not a well-known figure at the time. Morrow had the ability to get along with the mercurial Strauss, and was responsible for the unique Art Deco elements of the bridge's design. Charles Ellis, however, despite all his work on the engineering for the bridge's design, was fired by Strauss in 1931. It is believed that Strauss was intimidated by the intellectual Ellis, and resented the attention he received in meetings with the administrators. Although his name was not mentioned on the plaque that was installed on the bridge at its opening, Charles Ellis has now been credited with being responsible for the major engineering work on the Golden Gate Bridge.

When the bridge construction began, the economy was in the depths of the Great Depression. Desperate men who were out of work flooded the city from distant locations looking for jobs as iron workers as the project ramped up. The John A. Roebling's Sons Company, the firm formed by the family that designed and built the Brooklyn Bridge, provided the cable for the Golden Gate Bridge. As the construction on the bridge proceeded, chief engineer Strauss became more and more obsessed with safety. The work was extremely dangerous. Strauss feared that he would be criticized for promoting this radical plan if some of his workers fell to their deaths into the roiling waters below. He purchased and installed an innovative and costly safety net, which hung under the length and breadth of the bridge while it was under construction. This net saved many lives. Only 11 men died during the construction, with 10 of them perishing in an accident that happened when the bridge was almost complete. A platform gave way and fell into the net and the net collapsed, and the workers fell 220 feet into the water.

The architect Irving Morrow was responsible for the Art Deco and Moderne features on the bridge. The towers display Art Deco elements in the horizontal struts, which are distinctive in their design. Towers on other bridges at the time were designed with X-shaped cross bracing. The towers on the Golden Gate Bridge become slightly narrower in elegant steps as they rise. The struts also boast steel faceplates that have decorative faceting in the Art Deco style. Under the struts are decorative stepped corner brackets. The lights and rails on the bridge, as well as the toll booth, are examples of the Moderne style. Lacking ornamentation, these features are graceful and streamlined in appearance. The most consequential decision that Morrow made in his design was the selection of "International Orange" as the color for the bridge. The color is one of the bridge's most iconic features.

KEY STATISTICS

The Golden Gate Bridge was opened on May 27, 1937, with a grand celebration. It spans the Golden Gate Strait and connects San Francisco to Sausalito in Marin County. It is a suspension bridge and was the longest in the world until the completion of the Verrazano Narrows Bridge in New York, which was completed in 1964. It is 8,981 feet long and the central span is 4,200 feet. The towers reach 746 feet high. The two suspension cables each contain approximately 27,572 wires that were compacted into 122 strands. A total of 80,000 miles of wire were spun to create the cables. To build the structure of the bridge, 1.2 million rivets were required. The cost of the project was $35 million.

CULTURAL SIGNIFICANCE

When the Golden Gate Bridge was opened to vehicles in 1937, it was hailed as one of the wonders of the world. President Franklin Roosevelt pressed a telegraph key in Washington, D.C., to announce to the world that it had opened. A cacophony of car horns, sirens, and cannons went off to celebrate the event. Aircraft carriers and a fleet of battleships were assembled in the San Francisco Bay and 500 war planes whizzed overhead. This was an enormous accomplishment. This "bridge that can't be built" was completed on time and under budget. It once again represented the ingenuity of the American people as the United States, even in the depths of the Depression, demonstrated its expanding influence as a new world power. The irrepressible Joseph Strauss, obsessed with the project for years, suffered exhaustion after the bridge was opened and died within a year. However, his vision and his creation still live on as one of America's most beloved and beautiful 20th-century feats of engineering.

FURTHER INFORMATION: IMPORTANT PRINT, ELECTRONIC, AND MEDIA RESOURCES

San Francisco Planning Commission. Resolution 14754. December 17, 1998. The Golden Gate Bridge. Draft Landmarks Board Case Report.

Shiff, Blair. May 27, 2017. "The History of the Golden Gate Bridge as It Turns 80." ABC News. http://abcnews.go.com/Lifestyle/history-san-franciscos-landmark-golden-gate-bridge-turns/story?id=47657315. Accessed October 31, 2017.

Sigmund, Pete. June 2, 2006. "The Golden Gate: 'The Bridge That Couldn't Be Built.'" Construction Equipment Guide.com. https://www.constructionequipmentguide.com/redirect/7045?story=7045&headline=The%20Golden%20Gate:%20%EBThe%20Bridge%20That%20Couldn%EDt%20Be%20Built%ED. Accessed October 19, 2017.

United States Department of Transportation, Federal Highway Administration. "Two Bay Area Bridges—The Golden Gate and San Francisco-Oakland Bay Bridge." https://www.fhwa.dot.gov/infrastructure/2bridges.cfm. Accessed October 31, 2017.

The Golden Gate Bridge as a Magnet for Suicides

For years, the Golden Gate Bridge had the ignominious record as having the highest number of suicides. The current record is now held by the Nanjing Yangtze River Bridge in China, with the Golden Gate following close behind. Since its completion in 1937, more than 1,600 people have died by jumping off the bridge into the frigid waters of the San Francisco Bay. The bridge is a magnet for people who want to kill themselves, and unfortunately, the height of the bridge makes it a very efficient method. The deck of the bridge sits 245 feet above the bay. The would-be suicides fall at a rate of 75 miles per hour, and 95 percent die upon impact as they hit the water. Most of the 5 percent who are still alive will perish from drowning, hypothermia, or internal injuries. There have been some lucky jumpers who have survived, however. Many of the survivors say that while flying through the air, they suddenly rue their decision to jump. But it is too late for most of them.

For years, there has been local opposition to adding netting that could prevent suicides. Many people claimed that adding unsightly netting would detract from the exquisite splendor of the bridge as seen from the city of San Francisco. However, due to the unending scourge of successful suicides, a movement has been growing to add suicide prevention barriers to the bridge, similar to those installed at the Empire State Building, the Eiffel Tower, and other locations for attempted suicides. For years, there have been signs posted on the bridge claiming that "The Consequences of Jumping from This Bridge Are Fatal and Tragic" but their effectiveness seems negligible. Beginning in April 2017, a four-year project has been initiated to build suicide prevention nets. These stainless steel nets will sit 20 feet below the bridge's pedestrian walkway and will span 1.7 miles on each side of the bridge. The netting will extend out 20 feet from the edge of the walkway over the water. The funding for this $200 million project will come from federal, state, and local sources.

Interstate Highway System

Nationwide
1956

BACKGROUND

When Henry Ford began producing affordable automobiles for the American middle class in 1908, families eagerly snatched them up. Drivers of these shiny new Model-T vehicles that were produced on the innovative Ford assembly line were then forced to contend with the atrocious conditions on the nation's roads. The lands that comprised the United States were vast. Frederick Jackson Turner had recently proclaimed that the American frontier was closed. The assertion of manifest destiny had extended the American border from the Atlantic Ocean to the Pacific Ocean. The massive American continent was crisscrossed with a web of railroads. But the state of American roads was abysmal. An influential group of bicyclists had been lobbying for improved roads since the 1890s when the safety bicycle was invented and bicycle touring became a fad. This group, calling itself the League of American Wheelmen, initiated a nationwide movement, the Good Roads Movement. This group advocated for paved roads. However, its success was minimal: the government estimated that only 12 percent of American roads were paved by the first years of the 20th century. Those roads were generally located in the cities, where municipalities collected the requisite taxes to upgrade the roads. The roads that connected the cities to the suburbs and beyond were most often dirt or gravel, which became mud or dust depending on the weather, and giant potholes were endemic. The Good Roads advocates had some influence with national policy. President Woodrow Wilson signed the Federal Aid Road Highway Act in 1916. This act created the Bureau of Public Roads. As roadbuilding was traditionally the responsibility of states and localities, the condition of the roads was totally dependent on the taxes collected and the priorities of the communities themselves, which led to an unpredictable trip in the family's new Model-T. The creation of the Bureau of Public Roads was intended to aid local governments in upgrading their roads by providing 50 percent of the funding. However, the offer was slow to catch on. World War I further slowed the progress. In 1919, Dwight D. Eisenhower, a young officer in the U.S. Army, participated in a planned trial run to assess the conditions of America's roads. This army convoy, called the Cross-Country Motor Transport Corps, traveled on the newly built Lincoln Highway, the first transcontinental highway. It was barely paved, and the trip took the truck convoy 62 days to complete the trip from Washington, D.C., to San Francisco, with an average speed of 5 miles per hour. The convoy suffered from multiple flats and breakdowns due to the potholes and muddy ditches, and trucks fell through bridges with inadequate supports. The trip proved once and for all that the country's roads were incapable of supporting the popular motor car, not to mention heavy trucks and military vehicles. Eisenhower was convinced that the nation needed an upgraded road system. But it would take decades before he was able to successfully provide it as president of the United States.

During the booming years of the 1920s, some highways were built. These were mostly in the wealthier states like New York, Massachusetts, and Pennsylvania. The states in the South and the West did not have adequate funding to build roads, and dirt roads were still ubiquitous. A new piece of legislation called the Federal Aid Highway Act of 1921 was passed, which also promised 50 percent funding to states for road construction. Federal officials were beginning to understand the importance of a national highway system. A map was drawn by General John J. Pershing in 1922, which was dubbed the Pershing Map. This map showed locations for a nationwide system of roads that could accommodate military vehicles for national defense. The Great Depression slowed the progress of roadbuilding throughout the country, but President Franklin D. Roosevelt understood the value of the national road system, if only as a job-creating enterprise. He lobbied for highway construction, and eventually succeeded in providing funding through the Works Progress Administration for the Pennsylvania Turnpike, the country's first limited-access highway, completed in 1940. Popular support for a nationwide highway system was limited, although an exhibit at the 1939 New York World's Fair helped to change that. General Motors (GM), which had become the most powerful car manufacturer in the country, built a pavilion at the fair that was called "Futurama." This exhibit displayed GM's interpretation of a view of the United States in 1960 that showed a vastly transformed nation. Throngs of visitors rode past the gigantic model designed by Norman Bel Geddes, a celebrated theatrical and industrial designer. The visitors saw elevated superhighways soaring through cities of the future, with cars traveling at 100 mph. Futuristic architecture in the cities contrasted with model farms, all connected by the ubiquitous highways, on which 50,000 miniature cars automatically moved smoothly. No traffic jams, pollution, or accidents. This was a view of the future of American automobile culture, perfected. Five million visitors waited on lines for hours just to see this future. They were impressed.

The progress of the effort to build a nationwide highway system was facilitated by a consortium of interest groups that could benefit by such a system. This group, informally called the "Road Gang," formed a secretive but influential lobbying syndicate that was determined to ensure the completion of a nationwide system of high-speed roads using federal funds. The Road Gang included car and truck manufacturers and dealers, automobile clubs, oil companies, truckers, and officials of the state highway departments. Not only did they promote road construction, but also they dreaded any competition from existing mass transit in the cities. Trolleys took riders away from buses and cars. In the 1940s, a group of the large car and truck companies proceeded to buy out trolley companies in cities and replace them with buses. These nefarious deeds eventually killed the trolley systems in virtually all American cities. However, most local residents were not pleased with the corrupt privately owned trolley companies or their service. So there was no outcry from local citizenry. By the end of World War II, the United States was moving away from a wartime economy. Dwight D. Eisenhower was now president. He remembered the interminable transcontinental trip he made as part of the army convoy. He also recalled the wide, fast highways, called the Autobahn, that he had admired in Germany. Eisenhower was determined to build a highway system that would connect all parts of the nation. He appointed a commission to study the feasibility of the project. Knowing that many voters were not convinced that a national gasoline tax should be used to build a massive highway system, he shrewdly packed the commission with men who had links to the car and truck manufacturers, engineers, and members of the Teamsters Union that represented truck drivers. The ruse worked. In 1956, Eisenhower signed the Interstate Highway Act, which is now called the "Dwight D. Eisenhower National System of Interstate and Defense Highways." The Cold War had begun and Americans were afraid of nuclear war. The Interstate system was sold as a method of easy evacuation from population centers in the event of a nuclear attack; hence the moniker "defense highways." This explanation also made the gas tax charged for this enormous project more palatable to the voters.

CHARACTERISTICS AND FUNCTIONALITY

The Interstate Highway System was initially planned to create 41,000 miles of highway. A budget of $27 billion was assigned for the task. What made this project exceptional was that, for the first time, the federal government was offering to pay for 90 percent of the cost of the highways, by charging a three cent tax on a gallon of gas. The taxes that were collected were parked in the Highway Trust Fund, and the money was not allowed to be utilized for any other purpose. There were a number of standards that the federal government set. These new highways were unique in that they were limited-access highways, with a limited number of entrances and exits. They were a minimum of four lanes in width. There were no cross streets and no traffic lights. Any road that crossed the highway had to be shunted either above or under the highway in order not to impede traffic flow. And the traffic did flow at high speeds. Uniform design specifications were used nationwide. Sign design was standardized as well. There was a system of numbering set up by the federal government. East–west major highways used even numbers; north–south highways used odd numbers. The new interstates were different from the existing parkways that were built in the 1920s. While the parkways were designed for slower speeds and to take advantage of the beautiful scenery, the interstates were not. There were many tighter curves on the parkways that were eschewed on the interstates for safety reasons. Higher speeds meant the highways needed longer curves, and some interstates had no curves at all. The ride on the interstate was more uniform and less pleasing to the eye, but safer and much faster.

KEY STATISTICS

The Dwight D. Eisenhower National System of Interstate and Defense Highways is located throughout the continental United States as well as Alaska, Hawaii, and Puerto Rico. It was originally budgeted to cost $27 billion over 12 years of construction. The final cost, however, was $114 billion and the project took 35 years to complete. The total number of miles proposed for the highway system was 41,000. However, with additional highways added to the map, the present total is 46,876 miles. Each individual state is responsible for maintaining its portion of the highway in the state, and enforcing traffic laws. The states are also responsible for setting speed limits. (In the 1970s, the federal government wanted encourage drivers to save gas due to the gas crisis and passed a law that cut all federal funding to any state that did not change its speed limit to 55 mph. Needless to say, all the states did it, although technically the states were still responsible for setting their own speed limits.) The numbering of the interstates is related to the numbering of the U.S. highways, which existed before the interstates were built. The interstate numbers reflect a mirror image of the U.S. highways, in order to prevent confusion. A driver will never be confused by seeing signs for Interstate 80 near a U.S. Highway 80. Therefore, there is no Interstate 50, which would run through the same state as U.S. Highway 50. The longest interstate highway is I-90, which links Seattle, Washington, with Boston, Massachusetts, clocking in at 3,020 miles long. The longest north–south interstate is I-95, which links Houlton, Maine, with Miami, Florida. The state of Texas has the most interstate miles, totaling 3,233. The state of New York has the most interstate routes at 29.

CULTURAL SIGNIFICANCE

There are two sides to the debate about the significance and results of the building of the Interstate Highway System. The federal government has trumpeted the benefits of the system since its founding in 1956. There is no question that this project, one of the largest public works projects ever completed, has been a boon to the American economy in the last half-century. A safe, reliable, and fast transportation system is essential to the economic development of a nation. The vastness of the country combined with the dreadful conditions of the roads was a serious drag on the economy before the interstate system was built. The fact that the federal government paid 90 percent of the costs was a gift to the poorer states in the South that could not afford the huge investment that the highways required. Every $1 spent on the interstate system resulted in $6 worth of economic growth. Commerce benefited as trucks were able to haul goods farther and faster at a reduced cost. Families benefited and were able to enjoy longer vacation trips in their beloved automobiles. Parts of the country that were underpopulated grew.

But the results have been mixed and the outcomes have been infinitely more complicated. Although there was economic growth in some areas, there was decline in others. The winners were rural areas and suburbs. The losers were the cities. Cities lost out in several ways. First, one of the objectives of the system was to bring people into the cities from the suburbs and remove city slums through a process known as urban renewal. By replacing a poor neighborhood with a gigantic elevated highway, the city would be cleared of a portion of its unwanted slums, according to city planners in the 1960s. The unintended consequence was that the highway slashed through existing vibrant neighborhoods, effectively killing them. This was done in cities throughout the country. In addition, the interstates that brought people in from the suburbs also carried them out to the suburbs, and the scourge of white flight was exacerbated. This was aided by the discriminatory policies of the Federal Housing Administration that barred African Americans and other minorities from purchasing homes in the burgeoning suburbs. Of course, the addition of easy access to the city by car meant that the existing public transit was used most often by the poor who had been left behind in the urban core. This left the mass transit system dying on the vine in many cities. The fact that the Highway Trust Fund could only be used for highway construction and never diverted to public transportation aggravated the situation. In addition to the large cities, smaller cities and towns were hurt by the interstate highway system. In general, the highways were designed by the engineers for their safety and speed. Eminent domain was used to purchase the land for the highways, and in cities as well as in rural areas, the cheapest land was preferred. Downtown main streets were skirted to avoid traffic lights and slower speeds. This hurt small towns as people scurried to the new malls on the new highways and left the downtowns essentially forgotten. The interstates also devastated the passenger train industry, as people preferred the freedom of their car to the tyranny of the train schedule.

Although the Interstate Highway System continued its inexorable path to complete 46,000 miles of road, it did not proceed without protest. During the 1960s and 1970s, civic groups in a number of cities fought the construction of the highways and sometimes won. The law that disallowed using the Highway Trust Fund for public transit was amended in 1973 to allow the diversion of targeted funds to mass transit. The Interstate Highway System has been derided as a gift to real estate developers and big businesses to the detriment of the poor who were frequently left with a destroyed neighborhood and nonexistent public transportation. Although the system helped the economy in general, it hurt a number of its constituents. The federal government paid for much of the suburbanization of the country through its subsidy of highways. It did not, however, subsidize the passenger train industry to the same extent. Neither did it build replacement housing for the people who were dislocated by the highways built in the cities. Although it was a magnificent public works achievement, the Interstate Highway System turned out to be both a blessing and a curse.

FURTHER INFORMATION: IMPORTANT PRINT, ELECTRONIC, AND MEDIA RESOURCES

Divided Highways: The Interstates and the Transformation of American Life. September 27, 1997. Directed by Lawrence Hott and Tom Lewis. https://www.youtube.com/watch?v=PLr-8QPbiAY. Accessed November 29, 2017.

"The Dwight D. Eisenhower System of Interstate and Defense Highways Part VII—Miscellaneous Interstate Facts." U.S. Department of Transportation, Federal Highway Administration. https://www.fhwa.dot.gov/highwayhistory/data/page07.cfm. Accessed November 29, 2017.

Fox, Justin. January 26, 2004. "The Great Paving." *Fortune* 149 (2): 86–90. http://archive.fortune.com/magazines/fortune/fortune_archive/2004/01/26/358835/index.htm. Accessed November 29, 2017.

Hayden, Dolores. 2003. *Building Suburbia: Green Fields and Urban Growth, 1820–2000*. New York: Vintage Books.

Hilke, Jens. "History and Cultural Impact of the Interstate Highway System." University of Vermont. http://www.uvm.edu/landscape/learn/impact_of_interstate_system.html. Accessed November 13, 2017.

Jackson, Kenneth T. 1985. *Crabgrass Frontier*. New York, Oxford: Oxford University Press.

Rose, Mark H., and Raymond A. Mohl. 2012. *Interstate: Highway Politics and Policy since 1939*. Knoxville: University of Tennessee Press.

Stromberg, Joseph. May 11, 2016. "Highways Gutted American Cities. So Why Did They Build Them?" *Vox*. https://www.vox.com/2015/5/14/

8605917/highways-interstate-cities-history. Accessed November 13, 2017.

Weingroff, Richard F. Summer 1996. "Federal-Aid Highway Act of 1956: Creating the Interstate System." U.S. Department of Transportation, Federal Highway Administration. Vol. 60. No. 1. https://www.fhwa.dot.gov/publications/publicroads/96summer/p96su10.cfm. Accessed November 13, 2017.

Did You Know?

- The longest interstate route is I-90, stretching from Boston to Seattle. It is 3,020 miles long. I-80 is the second longest. It connects New Jersey with San Francisco.
- The shortest interstate route is in Maryland, I-97. It connects Annapolis with Baltimore.
- New York State has 29 interstate routes, the most of any state.
- Texas has the most interstate mileage at 3,232 miles.
- I-95, which connects Maine with Florida, passes through the most number of states, 16. I-95 also was the most expensive interstate highway to build, as it goes through some of the most congested areas in the country.
- I-405 in Southern California is the most heavily traveled interstate.
- Four state capitals do not have an interstate that goes through them: Juneau, Alaska; Dover, Delaware; Jefferson City, Missouri; and Pierre, South Dakota.
- Highways running north–south are odd numbered, whereas highways running east–west are even numbered. The lowest numbers are in the west and in the south.
- If the first digit of a three-digit interstate route number is odd, it is a spur into a city. If it is even, it goes through or around a city.
- Three-digit interstate highway numbers represent beltways or loops, attached to a primary interstate highway (represented by the last two numbers of the beltway's number). Washington D.C.'s beltway, known as the Capital Beltway, is numbered 495, because its parent highway is I-95.

Portland Public Service Building

Portland, Oregon
1982

BACKGROUND

When Michael Graves, a country boy from a middle-class family in Indianapolis, attended the University of Cincinnati, he knew he loved to draw. He considered studying studio art, but his mother encouraged him to select a profession with better financial prospects, so he entered the school of architecture. It was the late 1950s, and American architectural schools were in the thrall of International Style modernism. The leader of the International Style in the United States was the German architect Ludwig Mies van der Rohe, who had emigrated from Germany in 1937. Graves's professors were students of Mies and proponents of his style. After Graves graduated with his bachelor of science in architecture, he opted to study at Harvard where he received his master's in architecture in 1959. The students were taught Modernist creed in design, but no architectural history. Graves was frustrated by his lack of knowledge about the historical context of traditional architectural design. He is quoted as saying that the teaching was not just "anti-historical" but "ahistorical," showing no concern for history or tradition. He applied for, and won, the prestigious Rome Prize or Prix de Rome. With this scholarship, Graves was able to study for another two years at the American Academy in Rome. For the first time, he learned about the history and iconography of classical architecture. He soaked up the Roman, Renaissance, and Baroque designs that were all around him, and he was smitten. The two years he spent in Italy had an enormous impact on his life's work.

When he returned, he was hired by Princeton University to teach architecture. He opened an office in the city of Princeton, New Jersey. His first commissions were for large houses, and his work showed an influence of Le Corbusier. Corbusier, a Swiss transplant to the United States, was known for his spare, white houses perched on top of slender pilotis (piers) and his expressionistic use of concrete, as well as his theories about urban planning. Corbusier's principles had a profound influence on the design of public housing projects in the United States post World War II. There was a group of five young architects who were producing work in the Corbusier tradition, using austere, geometric constructions in their designs for the homes of wealthy clients. These homes were unfailingly white in color. These five young architects, Graves among them, were dubbed "the New York Five," and also "the Whites." In 1973, another group of five New York architects, calling itself "the Grays," responded in a series of essays to the Modernist designs of "the Whites" with a different approach. The "Grays" called for designs that expressed a sense of place. Modernist architecture, following the lead of Mies van der Rohe and Le Corbusier, did not relate to the local traditions. Their buildings, as examples of the "International Style" could be anywhere, displayed an anonymous unadorned simplicity. In contrast, the "Grays," who aligned themselves with the firm of Venturi and Brown, a married team of architects from Philadelphia, were early pioneers advocating for the emerging style of Post-Modernism. Graves took note of the precepts being proposed by Venturi and the Grays and proceeded to develop his mature style, veering away from the stark, white shapes he used in his early work.

Graves, an inveterate artist and painter as well as Princeton professor, spent the first years of his career drawing beautifully delicate drawings for proposals that were never built and writing about architectural theory. His writings described his designs as symbolic, anthropomorphic, and mythic. His drawings had elements taken from Greek, Roman, and Egyptian precedents. His graceful drawings, which became popular as "paper architecture," have been described by Carter Wiseman as "warm, unthreatening, innocent." He adds that, "They were, to a large degree, buildings as children might like to make them if they had the drawing skills" (Wiseman 2000, 261). Graves used classical vocabulary in a novel way, often exaggerating the size of the elements or rearranging them in an innovative, abstracted way. He also utilized much more color than his Modernist colleagues and predecessors, eschewing the all-white, all-the-time of his earlier work.

CHARACTERISTICS AND FUNCTIONALITY

Michael Graves received his first public commission in 1980 when he won a competition for a new public services office building in Portland, Oregon. In 1979, the city of Portland advertised for a design competition for a new building in the downtown. Because the building was built with public funds, a very small budget was allotted for the project. The renowned architect Philip Johnson was asked to be the chair of the selection committee. Three finalists were chosen, and one of them was Michael Graves. The proposal submitted by Graves caused a stir. The beautiful presentation drawings displayed a large cubic box of a building, covered with colorful applied decoration. Some critics, led by Philip Johnson, defended the unusual design. It was called "colorful, active and engaging" by one critic in the journal *Architectural Record* (National Park Service 2011). But many architectural critics panned the building's design, calling it "an oversized beribboned Christmas package," and "like a woman past her prime who puts on too much makeup" (ibid.). However, the dearth of funding was on Graves's side. The City Council, seeing that all the entries were over budget, requested the three finalists to submit a second proposal, using cost-saving measures to lower the cost of the project. Graves was the most successful in value engineering his design, removing several amenities, changing some of the applied decoration, and promising "no change orders." By reducing the cost of the project, Graves was hired as the architect for the project in 1980.

The Portland Building, as it became known, is a 15-story block of a building, appearing like a gigantic square box. The four facades have colorful decorations, consisting of highly abstracted interpretations of classical elements. The composition of the building is a conceptual rendering of the classical column, with a base, shaft, and capital. Graves described it anthropomorphically, as a base, body, and head. He also related it to nature, with a green base representing grass and a blue top representing the sky. The base is covered in a blue-green ceramic tile, and encircles the entire building, rising several stories. On the facade where the main entrance is located, above the entrance, sits a mammoth sculpture conceptualized by Graves and executed by the sculptor Raymond Kaskey, who was also selected in the competition. The sculpture is covered in hammered copper over a steel frame. The sculpture is a representation of "Lady Commerce," which is an element of the Portland City seal. The woman is clothed in classical garb and is reaching down from the podium with one hand, while holding a trident in her other hand. Kaskey was celebrated for the statue and won numerous awards for it. It is unusual in that it is an example of representational art, at a time that abstract art was the norm. Above the base of the building, each facade has a section that is the body or shaft of the virtual column, with earth-tone-colored terracotta pilasters rising seven stories. The east and west facades have two of these pilasters; the north and south facades have four. At the top of the two pilasters on the east and west facades are oversized projecting capitals of the same color. Surrounding these pilasters are areas of blue reflective glass. Above the capitals is a gigantic truncated "V" design, representing a classical element called the keystone. The keystone traditionally sits at the top of an arch, where the opposite sides meet, but here there is no arch. The abstract keystone element consists of alternating tile that matches the pilasters, and dark bands of windows. It is one of the elements that Graves liked to use in his designs. On the north and south facades, the pilasters are topped with graceful pale blue ornamental swags. On all the remaining wall surfaces on the four facades, square windows punctuate the beige wall cladding, giving the building an added polka-dot appearance. The 14th floor is slightly set back and is blue.

KEY STATISTICS

The Portland Building is located at 1120 SW Fifth Avenue in Portland, Oregon. It is in the civic center of the city, where most of the government buildings can be found. The property sits between the Portland City Hall and the Multnomah County Courthouse, both century-old structures. Across the street on one side of the building is the Chapman Square Park, with Lownsdale Square Park and Federal Park nearby. The building takes up a full 200-foot square city block. It has 362,422 square feet on the interior, and contains 15 floors. The height of the building is 200 feet. The frame and the walls were constructed of reinforced concrete. The floors are reinforced concrete waffle slabs. The exterior is clad in stucco, with areas that are covered in decorative tile. The composition of the decoration of the four sides of the building is virtually identical on the west (the main entrance) and east facades, and the north and south facades. The main facade, however, has the sculpture of Portlandia. The four facades each have a symmetrical design, as if there is an imaginary line down the center of the facade, and the design is a mirror image on each side. The regularly spaced windows are all 4-foot squares.

CULTURAL SIGNIFICANCE

The exterior of the Portland Building, with it cartoonish, oversized classical elements, has been controversial from its inception. Some loved it; many despised it. It was criticized for bringing the overly intellectualized, eastern elite academic abstractions to a small western city in a condescending way. Graves's analysis of the building, as a base, body, and head, did not seem too obvious to all the general public. Graves wanted to build a structure that would be "double-coded," that is, have symbolism that appealed to the common man as well as to the architectural theorist. In some ways it succeeded, and the city of Portland was inundated with news reports nationally because of its new controversial building. However, the city workers destined to be assigned to the building were not happy. The small windows and small offices inside made the interior dark and gloomy. The exterior did not hold up well in the wet Oregon weather. In fact, the building was considered for demolition in 2014, although a budget for extensive renovation has been approved and is moving ahead. The Portland Building is significant because it introduced the architectural style of Post-Modernism. The architect Philip Johnson, one of the America's leading Modernist architects, also designed Postmodernist buildings in his later years, including the AT&T Building, now the Sony Building, in New York City. This building, also using oversized classical elements, has a colossal crown that resembles a Chippendale highboy cabinet and a giant rounded arch entrance. With this building, and with Graves's subsequent project, the Humana Building in Louisville, Kentucky, Post-Modernism was accepted as a legitimate alternative to the unadorned, spare functionalism of the Modernist orthodoxy. As the architecture critic Paul Goldberger stated in describing the Portland Building in 1982, "it is the most important public building to open thus far in this decade. It is a monument of Post-Modernism, a determined rejection of the cool, unadorned forms of orthodox modern architecture" (Goldberger 1982). Post-Modernism broke the grip of the Modernists on architectural design.

FURTHER INFORMATION: IMPORTANT PRINT, ELECTRONIC, AND MEDIA RESOURCES

Brake, Alan G. "Postmodern Architecture: The Portland Municipal Services Building, Oregon, by Michael Graves." September 12, 2015. *Dezeen*. https://www.dezeen.com/2015/09/12/postmodernism-architecture-portland-municipal-services-building-michael-graves/. Accessed March 10, 2017.

Goldberger, Paul. "Architecture of a Different Color." October 10, 1982. *New York Times*. http://www.nytimes.com/1982/10/10/magazine/architecture-of-a-different-color.html?pagewanted=all. Accessed March 12, 2017.

National Park Service. "Portland Public Service Building." October 25, 2011. *National Register of Historic Places Registration Form*. https://www.portlandoregon.gov/omf/article/509212. Accessed March 12, 2017.

Wiseman, Carter. 2000. *Twentieth-Century American Architecture: The Buildings and Their Makers*. New York and London: W. W. Norton.

WTTW. "Ten Buildings That Changed America. #8—Portland Municipal Services Building." http://interactive.wttw.com/tenbuildings/portland-municipal-services-building. Accessed March 12, 2017.

Michael Graves: Architect, Consumer Product Designer, and Proponent of Accessible Design

Although he made his name as an architect in the Post-Modernist style, Graves was also popularly known for his consumer product designs that were sold at Target, and later at J. C. Penney. His design for a teakettle that had a whistle shaped like a red bird, sold by Alessi, is one of his most famous. He is credited with producing designs for 2,000 consumer products.

Michael Graves suffered a spinal cord infection in 2003 that paralyzed him from the waist down. Although wheelchair-bound, he continued to work until his death in 2015 at the age of 80. Graves spent the last years of his life designing objects and architecture that were accessible to people with disabilities. In 2011, Graves lent his design skills to the Wounded Warrior Home Project in Fort Belvoir in Virginia, for which he designed two homes that would be accessible for wounded veterans coming home from the wars in Iraq and Afghanistan. These vets had a variety of injuries, including lost limbs, traumatic brain injuries, hearing loss, vision loss, and posttraumatic stress disorder. The 3,000-square-foot homes are all on one floor and contain design features like adjustable kitchen counters, automatic doors, curbless showers, video monitoring systems, and contrasting floor colors for improved visibility.

Central Library

Seattle, Washington
2004

BACKGROUND

The city of Seattle, Washington, is known for its hip vibe and its myriad of mighty international corporations that include Microsoft, Amazon, and Starbucks. Seattle relishes its "cool" factor, which makes it a popular tourist destination despite its reputation for dreary, rainy weather. But it has not always been such a corporate giant and tourist attraction. Over the century and a half that Seattle has been a city, it has suffered a series of booms and busts. The timber and coal industries, as well as an expanding port, made Seattle successful in the 1880s but it was the discovery of gold in the Klondike in 1897 that really gave the city its first boom cycle. The city grew and became the center for shipbuilding during World War I. After suffering through the Great Depression, the city again recovered as the new airplane industry, led by the Boeing Company, brought wealth to Seattle once again. The ups and downs of the volatile airline industry led to several more booms and busts for the city. However, by the time that Microsoft began its inexorable growth in the 1970s, the city of Seattle was diversifying its industrial base. It is now home to eight of the Fortune 500 companies, which are the largest corporations in the United States, which include retail giants like Costco and Nordstrom, the lumber company Weyerhaeuser, Starbucks, and tech companies like Microsoft and Amazon.

The city of Seattle had a public library as early as 1890. It was run by the city government. It burned down in 1901, and the city made an official appeal to the philanthropist Andrew Carnegie to help with funding for a new library building. Carnegie was the millionaire industrialist who was known for having made the historic decision to give away all his money before his death. He set out on a program to build free libraries in cities throughout the country. Carnegie complied with Seattle's request for funding and donated $200,000 to the city to build a new library. The city contributed the building site and the maintenance costs. The new Carnegie library was to be situated on a property on a city block located between Fourth and Fifth Avenues in downtown Seattle. In 1906, a stately new library was completed, in the

Beaux Arts style that was popular at the time. Although the city had a population of almost 150,000, the library only accommodated 500 people, and soon it ran out of space. By the 1930s, a report stated that the library was so overcrowded that visitors would have to stand along the sides of the reading room, waiting for chairs to become available. With the Beaux Arts structure demolished, a new library building was built in 1960 at the same location. This building was another example of a popular architectural style of the period. A total reversal from the classical solemnity of the Carnegie building, the new library espoused the International Style, a Modernist style based on the work of Mies van der Rohe. This Seattle Central Library had clean, simple lines that eschewed ornament. But, with the boom times hitting the city of Seattle once again, the new building again outgrew its space. In 1998, Seattle voters approved a bond measure called "Libraries for All" that would fund a new central library on the existing site, as well as increase the number and capacity of its branch libraries. The city selected the architect Rem Koolhaas, a Dutch native who was known for his architectural theory as well as his avant-garde designs. Seattle, with its expanding tech industry, saw itself on the cutting edge. With this grand investment in a public building, the city would put itself on the architectural map.

Rem Koolhaas, principal in the firm Office of Metropolitan Architecture (OMA), was born in 1944 in the Dutch city of Rotterdam. Koolhaas began his career as a writer, first as a journalist and then as a screenwriter. Deciding to revise his career plans, he went to London to attend the Architecture Association School in 1968. He received a fellowship to study in the United States in 1972. After spending several years in New York as a visiting Fellow at the Institute for Architecture and Urban Studies, he made his name in architectural circles in 1978 when he wrote a book called *Delirious New York*. This treatise on urban design examines the relationship between architecture and culture in the context of the history of the buildings and institutions in New York. He saw the deteriorating city of the 1970s and made a plea for the advantages of an urban lifestyle. Critics loved the book, but Koolhaas had yet to have any of his architectural designs actually built. In 2000, Koolhaas won the prestigious Pritzker Architecture prize. Koolhaas eventually received commissions to design several buildings in Europe, and opened an office in Rotterdam. His American commissions include the McCormick Campus Center at the Illinois Institute of Technology, two stores for Prada, and Milstein Hall at the Cornell College of Architecture, Art, and Planning. He has also designed buildings in Europe and Asia.

Rem Koolhaas's firm OMA was not on the list of preferred architects when the project to design the Seattle Central Library was announced. However, Koolhaas's partner, Joshua Ramus, was a Seattle native even though he was working in the firm's headquarters in Rotterdam. Ramus's mother gave him a call in 1999. Apparently there was this wonderful publicly financed project for a new central library in his hometown. The catch was that the deadline for applying to be considered was the next day. Ramus hopped on a transatlantic flight, arrived in Seattle, and was interviewed for the project. The firm got the commission. The Seattle Central Library opened in 2004.

CHARACTERISTICS AND FUNCTIONALITY

The novel design of the Seattle Central Library came out of months of discussions and analysis with the stakeholders. The major influence was Deborah Jacobs, the city's chief librarian. She, with some of the board members and staff members, visited libraries throughout the country and consulted with the local tech companies to assess the required design elements of the public library of the future. The changing landscape of the print business, the use of digital technologies, and the future outlook for books was debated. The decision was that the library of the future had to contain spaces that were extremely flexible, without the rigid confines of rooms and floors of a traditional library space. No one knew the actual future of the library and the technological changes that would occur, so their best guess was to make the spaces as adaptable as possible, allowing for expansions or contractions of collections as the needs arose. This innovative concept would lead to a library like none other.

The library is designed to be five staggered boxes, or platforms for the fixed uses, like the parking garage, the entrance, the children's library, administrative offices, and meeting rooms. The largest fixed block is the four-story book stack. In between the fixed platforms are the flexible spaces that can be altered according to future needs. The innovation of the four-story book stack, coiling around the seventh to tenth floors, is "probably the most unique element" of the building, according to architect Joshua Ramus. Remembering his miserable experiences in library buildings in his past, which he called a "trail of tears," Ramus recalled using the Dewey Decimal system searching in vain for the desired books in room after room. His design of a "book spiral" is a continuous gradual ramp system, twisting around the center of the building from the Dewey Decimal 000 at the bottom until 999 at the top. The books in the stacks are therefore available to view, encouraging browsing. The other spaces in the library were named by the architects with signature inventiveness: the Living Room, the Mixing Chamber, and the Reading Room. The atrium-style Living Room is located on the third floor. It is an open space with plenty of seats for the community to sit and read. The Reading Room, on the tenth floor, is another area for reading, but in a quieter venue. The so-called Mixing Chamber, located on the fifth floor, is a souped-up version of the traditional reference desk, where librarians can help the public in finding books or doing research on computers. All these spaces are wrapped in a skin, a type of exoskeleton, which consists of glass with a diamond-shaped grid of structural steel. The glass has a mesh interlayer that allows in light but controls the glare and heat. The pattern of the steel is part of the earthquake-resistant seismic engineering. Light floods into the soaring spaces through the glass. The Reading Room on the tenth floor has views of the surrounding Seattle skyscrapers with glimpses of Elliott Bay beyond. The Living Room is a grand, inviting space. The entire interior boasts quirky, colorful elements. The escalators and elevators are painted in bright chartreuse. Supergraphics are used for signage, identifying areas within the space.

KEY STATISTICS

The Seattle Central Library is located on the city block bounded by Fourth and Fifth Avenues, Madison and Spring Streets. The property is raked, so the entrance on Fourth Avenue is one story higher than the entrance on Fifth Avenue. The new building opened on May 23, 2004. It has a total of 11 stories, and 362,987 square feet, with capacity for 750,000 books. The project cost $165 million to build. For its construction, 18,400 cubic yards of concrete in the building and 4,644 total tons of steel were used. There are 9,994 total pieces of exterior glass. The structure is 196 feet high.

CULTURAL SIGNIFICANCE

The Seattle Central Library received rave reviews from most architectural critics when it opened. Paul Goldberger of the *New Yorker* compared it to the 1911 Carrere and Hastings New York Public Library on Fifth Avenue in its celebration of a public space in the center of the city. He asserted that the Koolhaas building not only reinvented the idea of the public library, but also reaffirmed the importance of building one. Some critics have revisited the library in recent years since its opening and made some negative comments about it and how the condition of the interior has survived its heavy use. The quirky and almost too cute elements may not wear well with time. It has attracted thousands of tourists over the years who are wowed by the dazzling exterior and interiors. However, some visitors have found the open reading rooms too noisy and cavernous for the contemplation and thought required in a library. The library has also been criticized for not being as inviting or as community oriented as it claims to be, with the public spaces not really connected to the street. Yet it is still one of the beloved of the buildings constructed so far in this century, and represents a public investment that Seattle residents are proud to claim as theirs.

The Seattle Central Library is culturally significant because it represents a serious investment in a facility that is for public use. Such investments are getting ever more uncommon with the tight budgets and tax-cutting tendencies of today's governments. Large investments in public facilities are getting less and less popular. However, in the city of Seattle, a progressive bastion with a variety of cash-rich tech companies, investments like the Seattle Central Library are still possible. The $196.4 million "Libraries for All" bond measure was overwhelmingly approved by the citizens of Seattle in 1998, to double the square footage of existing libraries and to build a new central library. It was a proclamation made by the citizens of the city that public investment that would benefit people of all classes and incomes was something they wanted to pursue. Rem Koolhaas, the architect of the library, explained it this way: "It's a very specific culture here. There is a very highly developed common sensibility and a highly developed sense of solidarity between the rich and the poor. I think it's the only part of America where the rich are angst-ridden and want to do good. It is also a culture where many people have been involved in the digital world. What connects everyone is a dedication to reason and to reasoning, and I think that enabled us to do the project and explained the way it turned out" (Koolhaas, http://lynnbecker.com/repeat/seattle/seattlepl.htm).

FURTHER INFORMATION: IMPORTANT PRINT, ELECTRONIC, AND MEDIA RESOURCES

Becker, Lynn. "Sleekness in Seattle: Rem Koolhaas, Joshua Ramus, OMA and the Seattle Public Library." *Repeat.* http://lynnbecker.com/repeat/seattle/seattlepl.htm. Accessed May 25, 2017.

Cheek, Lawrence. March 26, 2007. "On Architecture: How the New Central Library Really Stacks Up." *Seattle PI.* http://www.seattlepi.com/ae/article/On-Architecture-How-the-new-Central-Library-1232303.php. Accessed May 25, 2017.

Fried, Benjamin. July 1, 2004. "Mixing with the Kool Crowd." Project for Public Spaces. https://www.pps.org/reference/mixing-with-the-kool-crowd/. Accessed May 25, 2017.

Goldberger, Paul. May 24, 2004. "High-Tech Bibliophilia." *New Yorker.* http://www.newyorker.com/magazine/2004/05/24/high-tech-bibliophilia. Accessed May 25, 2017.

"History of the Central Library." The Seattle Public Library. http://www.spl.org/locations/central-library/cen-about-the-central-library/cen-history. Accessed May 25, 2017.

Muschamp, Herbert. May 16, 2004. "Architecture: The Library That Puts on Fishnets and Hits the Disco." *New York Times.* http://www.nytimes.com/2004/05/16/arts/architecture-the-library-that-puts-on-fishnets-and-hits-the-disco.html?_r=0. Accessed May 25, 2017.

Ouroussoff, Nicolai. September 2012. "Why Is Rem Koolhaas the World's Most Controversial Architect?" *Smithsonian Magazine.* http://www.

smithsonianmag.com/arts-culture/why-is-rem-koolhaas-the-worlds-most-controversial-architect-18254921/. Accessed May 25, 2017.

Rem Koolhaas. 2000 Laureate Biography. *The Pritzker Architecture Prize.* http://www.pritzkerprize.com/2000/bio. Accessed May 29, 2017.

The Pritzker Architecture Prize

Rem Koolhaas, the architect who designed the Seattle Central Library, was awarded the Pritzker Architecture Prize in 2000. The Pritzker Architecture Prize is the most prestigious prize in the field of architecture, often compared to the Nobel Prize. It is awarded annually to an architect or architects whose body of work has displayed talent, vision, and commitment that has made significant contributions to humanity and the built environment. The recipient of the prize is awarded $100,000, a citation certificate, and a bronze medallion. The prize was founded in 1979 by the Pritzker family. The Pritzkers, owners of the Hyatt Hotel chain, are based in Chicago and are one of the wealthiest families in the United States.

Commercial Architecture

Asch Building (Now Known as Brown Building)

Luna Park

Equitable Building

Ford River Rouge Complex

Grauman's Chinese Theatre

Woolworth's Store

Empire State Building

Flamingo Hotel

Northgate Shopping Center

Sun Record Studio

Lever House

McDonald's

Fontainebleau Hotel

Seagram Building

TWA Flight Center

Watergate Complex

Sears Tower (Currently Known as the Willis Tower)

World Trade Center Twin Towers

Walt Disney Concert Hall

One World Trade Center

Hulton Archive/Mario Tama/Getty Images

Asch Building (Now Known as Brown Building)

New York, New York
1901

BACKGROUND

At the turn of the 20th century, New York City had grown into the center of the garment industry. New York was not only the business center but also the fashion center during the Gilded Age. It was close to the mills in New England where fabrics were produced; it was also the center of international trade, and the home of fashion designers and their showrooms. And it had a large and eager workforce in the swarms of immigrants landing daily on the shores of the city. After the invention of the mechanical sewing machine, the ready-to-wear garment industry blossomed, growing from 39,000 in 1889 to 165,000 in 1919. For the first time, most clothing in the United States was purchased from retailers and department stores, and not sewn by hand at home. The garment industry flourished in New York among the immigrants living in crowded tenements on the Lower East Side. Members of the family would toil in their tiny tenement parlors, sewing parts of clothing provided by the manufacturer, and paid by the piece. This type of clothing manufacture was called the "home shop." There were two other types of shops in the New York garment industry at the time. The "inside shop" was the factory for the manufacturer itself. In the "outside shop," the manufacturer paid a third party, a subcontractor, to manufacture the clothing. The home shop was dominant in the 19th century before technology allowed for the construction of the modern factory building. The outside shop gained in popularity at the beginning of the 20th century. It took the responsibility of managing the workforce away from the clothing manufacturer. But, in a totally unregulated industry, managers of these outside shops were able to pay very little and pocket huge profits by exploiting their poor, young, and mostly female workforce.

Many of the young girls in the garment industry made the shirtwaist, a popular tailored blouse. In the late 19th century, women's fashion was influenced by the omnipresent "Gibson Girl." The Gibson Girl, a creation of the illustrator Charles Dana Gibson, depicted a modern American girl who was beautiful, healthy, athletic, and stylish. She was often depicted wearing a shirtwaist, which was a high-necked cotton blouse that was fashionable at the time. This fashion emerged as many women entered the workforce, working in offices for the first time. Women began to wear separate shirts and skirts, emulating men's wear. This shirtwaist fad was ubiquitous for middle- and upper-class American women. However, as they are wont to do, fashions began to change in the first decade of the 20th century. As the craze wound down, and dresses came back into fashion, scores of shirtwaist manufacturers were forced into a fiercely competitive market for their goods. One of the largest outside shops for shirtwaist manufacturing was the Triangle Waist Company, established in 1900 by a pair of Russian Jewish immigrants named Max Blanck and Isaac Harris. These two were so successful in the field that they were known as the "shirtwaist kings." Blanck and Harris were archetypes of the American dream, impoverished tailors who had emigrated from Russia and started a business that would eventually make them rich. But they made their wealth on the backs of newer impoverished immigrants flooding the streets of New York. Their several businesses, the largest of which was the Triangle Waist Company, were known as the most cutthroat in this competitive market. In fact, the pair was accused of being the worst employers in the industry. The workweek was longer than many of the other firms, often as long as 14 hours per day, and they paid lower wages to their workers. They required the mostly Jewish and Italian immigrant workers to deduct thread and needles from their average $2 per day salary. They denied the workers the right to unionize as the movement toward unionization was growing. Worst of all, they locked the workers into the building, purportedly to prevent theft.

The industry was changing as the Progressive Era encouraged more workers' rights and safety standards. But it was not changing fast enough. Wildcat strikes began to take place in various factories. Local 25 of the International Ladies' Garment Workers' Union encouraged factory workers to strike for the right to collectively bargain for higher wages and better working conditions. Soon after a successful strike that led to unionization of another shirtwaist factory and a 20 percent wage increase, in September 1909, a group of workers at the Triangle Waist Company met and planned a walkout. After hearing of the plan, Blanck and Harris promptly fired 150 workers whom they suspected of being involved in the scheme. When they advertised for new employees the next day, Local 25 declared a lockout and called for a strike at the Triangle factory. This strike was debated at a meeting at Cooper Union in Manhattan on November 22, 1909, which was attended by the leaders of the labor movement, including American Federation of Labor president Samuel Gompers. An impassioned speech from a young striker named Clara Lemlich resulted in a motion for a general strike that passed unanimously. The next day, thousands of garment workers walked off the job. The massive strike attracted between 20,000 and 30,000 workers from New York, Philadelphia, and Baltimore. The response to the strikers was violent: prostitutes and thugs were hired to beat up the strikers. City police, in the pocket of the factory owners, also attacked and arrested the strikers, who were 80 percent women. The tone changed only later when the Women's Trade Union League, a group of wealthy women who supported women's rights and included Anne Morgan, the daughter of financier J. P. Morgan, began to march with the strikers and helped protect them from the thugs. Popular opinion began to change as the strike and its prominent patrons were covered by the local press. This strike, which lasted 13 weeks, was significant in that it was organized almost entirely by women. The strike was successful in lifting wages for the garment workers, reducing the workweek to 52 hours, and allowing the union to bargain for a contract in many factories. Blanck and Harris's factories, however, refused to allow the union to come in, or to upgrade safety standards like unlocking doors or improving fire escapes. The only concession they allowed was the raise in pay. The workers at Triangle came back to work in February 1910 without winning all that they had fought for, which would unfortunately end in tragedy.

A year later, March 25, 1911, it was near closing time on a late Saturday afternoon at 4:45 P.M. when a fire broke out on the 8th floor of the Triangle factory in the Asch Building. The factory was located on the top three floors of the building, the 8th, 9th, and 10th floors. The crowded open loft space of the building was lined with rows of sewing machines packed together and dripping oil. Near the cutting tables, there were piles of fabric on the floor and wicker baskets filled with fabric. There were also tissue paper patterns above the tables, suspended from a clothesline. It is believed that a discarded cigarette was the cause of the start of the fire, which ignited the flammable fabric, the tissue paper, and the clothes line that hung across the room. The oil on the floors under the sewing machines aided the spread of the fire. The only fire protection available in the room was buckets of water, which the workers tossed onto the fire, to no avail. A manager tried to access the fire hose in the stairwell, but it had deteriorated and the valve had rusted, so it was unusable. The telephone operator, realizing that the situation was dire, called up to the executives on the 10th floor to warn them of the fire. However, she forgot to call up to the 9th floor. That mistake would be the most tragic. Although the workers on the 8th floor were able to get out of the building, and the executives and workers on the 10th floor were able to escape onto the roof and to another building, the workers on the 9th floor were not. By the time the fire had reached their floor, they were getting ready to leave for the day. When the fire suddenly appeared through the windows, the workers tried desperately to escape. The door to the exit on one side of the building was locked. They hurried to the other side of the building through the clutter of machines and chairs, where a barrel of oil exploded, blocking the exit there as well. The workers who knew about the rickety fire escape that led to the tiny courtyard attempted to unlock the shutters that hid it. Although some made it to the fire escape, the weight of the workers and the heat from the fire made the metal fire escape crumple and collapse. The firemen who eventually arrived had ladders that only reached to the 6th floor, useless to the panicked people on the 9th floor. One tiny passenger elevator was able to rescue a number of workers, and the elevator operator risked his life as he kept returning to the floor. However, as the situation deteriorated even more, workers started jumping down the elevator shaft, and the elevator eventually was not able to ascend. As some frantic workers saw their only hope was to jump out the window, firemen's nets were useless as they broke apart after the nine-story drop. After the firemen got the conflagration under control, which took 25 minutes, the catastrophe was complete. A total of 146 workers, 123 women and 23 men, were killed in the Triangle fire. It was the worst industrial disaster in the history of New York City, and one of the worst in the nation's history.

CHARACTERISTICS AND FUNCTIONALITY

The Asch Building was built in 1901 as a loft structure, specifically designed as a modern factory building. Developers from the garment industry were eager to locate in the area, and these new loft structures were large, with wide open floors and amenities such as elevators, electric lights, telephone service, and plumbing. The structures were also considered fireproof, because of their steel structures and masonry cladding, a bonus feature that significantly reduced their insurance rates. The building was developed by Joseph J. Asch, a furrier who was looking to capitalize on the development of the neighborhood, and Ole Olsen, a builder and developer. Asch was attempting to assemble a large building site, not an easy prospect in New York where the building lots were sold in 25-foot widths. He purchased several townhouses, including the one that was the birthplace of American author Henry James, in 1843. He was stymied in his plan when another developer purchased the corner lot at Washington Place, who then sold it to Ole Olsen. The lot was eventually assembled in 1900 when Asch and Olsen came to an agreement, with Asch taking ownership of the four lots. The architect John Woolley was hired to draw up the building plans.

The Asch Building has 10 stories, and is an iron-and-steel structure with terra-cotta fireproofing. The law allowed for wood floors and window frames because the building was less than 150 feet tall. Although fire sprinklers were available at the time, they were not required by the building code. There were only two fire stairs in the plans for the building. This design brought up objections from the building department, but the architect convinced the plan examiners that a third fire stair was not necessary because of the availability of the fire escape. The building is in the

Neo-Renaissance style, with classical elements. It was divided into three sections visually. There are two entrances, one on Greene Street and one on Washington Place. The Asch Building has a two-story stone base with brick and terra-cotta cladding on the upper floors. The first two stories were used for retail space and the upper eight floors were factory lofts. The retail floors had wide window openings, separated by stone pilasters with recessed granite bands and decorative terra-cotta capitals at the top of the second story, with a band of fleur-de-lis and egg-and-dart moldings. Above the first two stories, the windows were double-hung and aligned with the cast-iron storefront windows on the lower floors. At the third floor, large terra-cotta cartouches surrounded by wreathes appear above the corner of Greene Street and Washington Place and above the two entrances. The tenth story has a round-arched arcade, with the windows boasting Ionic pilasters and keystones at the top of the arch surrounding each window. Above the tenth story is a deep, galvanized iron projecting cornice, supported by brackets. The large building sits on almost the entire lot, although there is a tiny light court at the northwest corner.

KEY STATISTICS

The Asch Building is now known as the Brown Building. Frederick Brown purchased the building in 1911 after it was renovated subsequent to the fire. The New York University (NYU), which was expanding in the neighborhood, began renting space in the building in 1916. In 1929, Brown donated the building to the university, and it was renamed the Brown Building. The building is located at 23–29 Washington Place, at the corner of Washington and Greene Streets, in the Greenwich Village neighborhood of Manhattan. It is one block east of Washington Square Park. It has 10,000 square feet per floor and 10 stories. The structure is steel and iron with brick-and-stone exterior cladding. Although the structure was designed as a factory loft, since NYU has owned it, it has served as classroom and research space. It is presently called the Brown Building of Science and houses biology and chemistry classrooms and labs. On the ninth floor, where most of the deaths from the Triangle fire occurred, NYU presently houses the Center for Developmental Genetics.

CULTURAL SIGNIFICANCE

The tragedy of the Triangle Waist Company fire of March 25, 1911, was not without its favorable consequences. The photographs and articles published by the newspapers, of these young victims and their families, resulted in a widespread public outrage at the conditions these workers endured and the safety precautions that were neglected. The disaster happened on a Saturday evening; on Sunday morning, prayer services were held at synagogues and churches throughout New York. A funeral procession for the unclaimed and unidentifiable bodies was held on April 5, and 80,000 people marched up Fifth Avenue to commemorate these anonymous victims. In addition to the marchers, hundreds of thousands of workers left their place of business to stand along the route in respect for their deceased colleagues. The union gained power as it demanded an industry-wide collective bargaining agreement, increasing pay and reducing hours for all the workers in the garment industry. The owners Blanck and Harris were brought up on charges of manslaughter by the Manhattan district attorney. Although the public was outraged by the actions of the pair, Blanck and Harris were acquitted. The jury found that there was not enough evidence that they were aware that the door to the second fire stair was locked.

The most enduring results of this terrible fire were the legislative actions taken by the city and the state, which served as prototypes for other cities and states in the United States. Members from the Women's Trade Union League (WTUL) began regular inspections of the factories, calling in safety violations to the authorities and reporting them to the newspapers. The WTUL, as well as a number of newly formed groups, pushed for more legislative action for fire safety. The Sullivan-Hoey Act was passed in New York City in June 1911, and as a result, the Bureau of Fire Prevention was established. But the most powerful legislative action was the creation of the New York State Factory Investigating Commission. The commission was chaired by Robert Wagner, the New York Senate Majority leader, and the vice-chair was Assembly leader Alfred E. Smith, who was to become the long-term governor and Democratic candidate for president in 1928. The commission held public hearings in reference to the Triangle fire, and investigated factory conditions. In the end, 36 new laws were passed. These laws included fire safety laws; lighting, ventilation, and sanitation regulations; and laws preventing industrial accidents as well as regulations about the protection of women and children in the workplace. The New York City Building Code was also revised, including rules regarding maximum occupancy and means of egress. These laws and regulations were groundbreaking and were copied by many other municipalities. When President Roosevelt introduced New Deal legislation, he was influenced by the laws introduced in New York State. Robert Wagner, who was Senator Wagner by then, worked with Roosevelt to pass the National Labor Relations Act in 1935 and the federal minimum wage law. Tragic as it was, the Triangle fire served as a catalyst to bring serious workplace safety, fire prevention, and labor laws into existence, and many lives have been subsequently saved because of them.

FURTHER INFORMATION: IMPORTANT PRINT, ELECTRONIC, AND MEDIA RESOURCES

Berger, Joseph. 2011. "Triangle Fire: The Building Survives." *New York Times*. March 22. http://www.nyc.gov/html/lpc/downloads/pdf/reports/brown.pdf. Accessed January 19, 2017.

Harris, Gale. 2003. "Brown Building (Originally Asch Building) Designation Report." Landmarks Preservation Commission. March 25. Designation List 346. LP-2128. http://www.nyc.gov/html/lpc/downloads/pdf/reports/brown.pdf. Accessed January 17, 2017.

Kheel Center, Cornell University. *The 1911 Triangle Factory Fire.* http://www.ilr.cornell.edu/index.html. Accessed January 17, 2017.

New York Times. March 26, 1911. "141 Men and Girls Die in Waist Factory Fire; Trapped High Up in Washington Place Building; Street Strewn with Bodies; Piles of Dead Inside." *New York Times.* https://timesmachine.nytimes.com/timesmachine/1911/03/26/104859694.html?action=click&contentCollection=Archives&module=ArticleEndCTA&region=ArchiveBody&pgtype=article&pageNumber=1. Accessed April 24, 2018.

Stein, Leon. 1962, 1990. *The Triangle Fire.* Ithaca, NY, and London: Cornell University Press.

"Triangle Fire." American Experience. PBS. http://www.pbs.org/wgbh/americanexperience/films/triangle/. Accessed January 20, 2017.

"Triangle Shirtwaist Factory." National Park Service. *National Register of Historic Places Designation Report.* https://focus.nps.gov/pdfhost/docs/NHLS/Text/91002050.pdf. Accessed January 23, 2017.

On March 25, 1911, a devastating fire swept through a sweatshop in downtown New York, killing nearly 150 people, most of whom were women. In the aftermath of the fire, the public became aware through news stories like the one excerpted below, which was published in the *New York Times* on March 26, that the sweatshop owners had failed to take safety precautions because such measures would cut into the profits of their business. Outraged by such a callous disregard for human life, the International Ladies' Garment Workers' Union initiated a massive campaign that forced local and state officials to enact new safety guidelines for businesses and to enforce them strictly. These restrictions led to general reform throughout the United States of workers' conditions.

141 MEN AND GIRLS DIE IN WAIST FACTORY FIRE; TRAPPED HIGH UP IN WASHINGTON PLACE BUILDING; STREET STREWN WITH BODIES; PILES OF DEAD INSIDE

Three stories of a ten-floor building at the corner of Greene Street and Washington Place were burned yesterday, and while the fire was going on 141 young men and women at least 125 of them mere girls were burned to death or killed by jumping to the pavement below. The building was fireproof. It shows now hardly any signs of the disaster that overtook it. The walls are as good as ever so are the floors, nothing is the worse for the fire except the furniture and 141 of the 600 men and girls that were employed in its upper three stories.

Most of the victims were suffocated or burned to death within the building, but some who fought their way to the windows and leaped met death as surely, but perhaps more quickly, on the pavements below.

ALL OVER IN HALF AN HOUR

Nothing like it has been seen in New York since the burning of the General Slocum. The fire was practically all over in half an hour. It was confined to three floors the eighth, ninth, and tenth of the building. But it was the most murderous fire that New York had seen in many years. The victims who are now lying at the Morgue waiting for some one to identify them by a tooth or the remains of a burned shoe were mostly girls from 16 to 23 years of age. They were employed at making shirtwaist by the Triangle Waist Company, the principal owners of which are Isaac Harris and Max Blanck. Most of them could barely speak English. Many of them came from Brooklyn. Almost all were the main support of their hard-working families. There is just one fire escape in the building. That one is an interior fire escape. In Greene Street, where the terrified unfortunates crowded before they began to make their mad leaps to death, the whole big front of the building is guiltless of one. Nor is there a fire escape in the back. The building was fireproof and the owners had put their trust in that. In fact, after the flames had done their worst last night, the building hardly showed a sign. Only the stock within it and the girl employees were burned. A heap of corpses lay on the sidewalk for more than an hour. The firemen were too busy dealing with the fire to pay any attention to people whom they supposed beyond their aid. When the excitement had subsided to such an extent that some of the firemen and policemen could pay attention to this mass of the supposedly dead they found about half way down in the pack a girl who was still breathing. She died two minutes after she was found.

Source: *New York Times* Reports on Triangle Fire. https://timesmachine.nytimes.com/timesmachine/1911/03/26/104859694.html?action=click&contentCollection=Archives&module=ArticleEndCTA&region=Archive-Body&pgtype=article&pageNumber=1

Luna Park

Brooklyn, New York
1903

BACKGROUND

At the debut of the 20th century, American society was transforming. The Victorian doctrine of diligence, self-discipline, and frugality was fading into the past. The culture of mass consumption, with its doctrine of shopping, entertainment, and other leisure activities, was gaining influence. In economist Simon Patten's words, the onset of the "pleasure economy," after centuries of the "pain economy," was a "new basis of civilization." For the first time, there did not have to be a struggle for subsistence brought on by a scarcity of resources. The arrival of the industrial revolution created an abundance that could potentially be shared by all (Kasson 1978, 98). Technology was advancing, and factories began spewing millions of mass-produced, inexpensive labor-saving products. Working-class families were now able to afford these conveniences and therefore had more time to devote to leisure. Economically, as the number of products produced in American factories grew exponentially, a market for these items had to be created. The members of the middle and working classes were anxious to avail themselves of the newest inventions. Sears catalog and the ubiquitous department store provided a litany of new products that were meant for the American consumer. But the availability of mass-produced products was not without its downside. Factories employed hundreds of workers making the same thing every day in a desultory manner, without challenging a spark of imagination. However, even after a long day and a six-day week, these workers had a modicum of leisure time to relax. The opportunity to let off steam after a hard day's work appealed to the public. But where, and how? Reformers in the Progressive era advocated for calm, pastoral pursuits. The novel concept of a public park, innovated by Frederick Law Olmsted in New York's Central Park, encouraged family outings in a bucolic setting away from the city's soot, crowds, and disease. World's fairs, beginning with the Centennial Fair in Philadelphia in 1876, were popular pursuits. Reformers admired these fairs, as long as they were didactic and instructive. The king of all the American world's fairs was the World's Columbian

Exposition, held in Chicago in 1893. The construction of the "White City" bathed in electric lights was meant to instruct and inspire. But it was the Midway, the commercial side of the fair, located apart from the White City, which brought in the biggest crowds. Here the public could ride on the first Ferris wheel, and see a grand sideshow of restaurants, shops, and exhibits. Although the White City's exhibits were free, the Midway's attractions were not. Many of them were sordid, lascivious, and lowbrow. "Little Egypt," who danced a suggestive dance, was one of the main attractions. The Midway in Chicago led the way for additional fairs. The Pan American Exposition, held in Buffalo, New York, in 1901, was one of them, which brought together the founders of Luna Park at Coney Island.

Frederic Thompson, an architect by training, was born in Ironton, Ohio, but was working as a draftsman in Nashville, Tennessee, when he serendipitously fell into the field of promotion. His uncle asked him to improve an attraction at the Nashville fair, which his uncle was invested in. Thompson added a soundtrack recorded on the new gadget, the phonograph. The attraction was a success. Thompson realized that he had the creativity and knack for showmanship that were crucial to this new field. He designed an illusion called "Darkness and Dawn" for the Omaha Trans-Mississippi Exposition in 1898. At this fair, Thompson met another promoter, a man named Elmer Dundy, known as Skip, who had two attractions. Dundy was fascinated with the field, eschewing his former position as clerk of the Omaha Federal Court, where his father was a federal judge. Dundy had an aptitude for finance, a trait that the imaginative Thompson did not possess. Dundy, captivated with Thompson's illusion Darkness and Dawn (nicknamed Heaven and Hell), applied for the concession for the new fair in Buffalo. Thompson also applied for it, but he had neglected to apply for a patent for it. Dundy got the concession. Thompson was so impressed with the wily Dundy that he proposed a joint effort. He had an even better illusion planned that he would share with Dundy if they became partners. The pairing was a match made in heaven. Thompson was a creative genius, but had a drinking problem and no talent for money. Dundy was the manager. Thompson was right—his new attraction called "A Trip to the Moon" was a colossal hit at the fair.

Meanwhile, in Brooklyn, New York, a completely new concept in amusements was getting off the ground. Developers at the beach community of Coney Island, nine miles south of Manhattan, were looking to rebrand it. Although the Manhattan Beach and Brighton Beach sections had a middle- to upper-class clientele in their seaside hotels, the western part of the island, known as West Brighton, had been dubbed "Sodom by the Sea" by the *New York Times* in the 1880s. The political boss John Y. McKane had complete power over the community and allowed it to become a haven for prostitutes, gambling, and criminal behavior. Journalists and reformers targeted the town because of its degradation. When McKane was found guilty of election fraud in 1894 and sent to Sing Sing prison, the opportunity arose to clean up the town. Major fires in 1893 and 1895 that burned down large areas of the resort also contributed to the rebirth of the West Brighton section of Coney Island. Several developers sought to bring in a cleaner clientele, and decided to attract them with an amusement park. The first amusement park was built by Captain Paul Boynton, and was called Sea Lion Park. It had a sea lion attraction, as well as a water slide called "Shoot-the-Chutes," which was very popular. George C. Tilyou, another of the entrepreneurs, built the second park, and he named it "Steeplechase Park" in 1897. His park featured an innovative ride that surrounded the park and emulated a steeplechase, with riders perched on wooden horses that bounced up and down along a track. Visitors liked the ride, as couples could hold onto each other while riding the horse, a delicious encounter not permitted in polite society.

Tilyou invited Thompson and Dundy to open their attraction "A Trip to the Moon" at Steeplechase Park in 1902. Dundy, who was still enthusiastic about world's fairs, did not see the advantage of moving to Coney Island, but Thompson did. Here was a world's fair that was open every summer for all the population to enjoy. They successfully moved the ride from Buffalo to Brooklyn. However, after one year at Steeplechase, Tilyou changed the terms of their contract. Dundy was furious, and threatened to take his business elsewhere. The only other place to go at Coney was Sea Lion Park. Boynton was willing to lease his property to Thompson and Dundy, as he had been faced with financial problems. Thompson and Dundy's deal with Boynton set the stage for the opening of the most innovative and influential amusement park of all time, Luna Park.

CHARACTERISTICS AND FUNCTIONALITY

Frederic Thompson, the imaginative genius of the team, set about to design a park that would amuse and amaze. As a trained architect, Thompson wanted to provide an architectural setting for the park that was bigger than ever before. Theatrical and ebullient, the buildings at Luna Park exuded a joy and unrestrained vitality not found anywhere else. Although he was familiar with architectural nomenclature, Thompson threw tradition to the winds and combined every style of ornament with plenty that he invented himself. He exaggerated features, and littered his towers and arches with playful animals and decorative designs. He spaced his buildings apart so as not to accumulate large crowds of aggravated visitors stacked up on waiting lines. But between each attraction, he provided free features that would entertain visitors while they waited. His vision was the first fully realized park that was drawn up with an architectural master plan. Named after Dundy's sister Luna, it was also dedicated to the first attraction of the partnership, Trip to the Moon. Thompson planned for a budget of $700,000. Dundy had to go to his friends on Wall Street to plead for funding, but he eventually came up with the financing. The duo lived together and lived frugally while planning the park, which took every cent they had. But they were able to open the park on May 16, 1903.

Luna Park opened at 8 P.M. The crowd grew to 60,000, paying a ten cent entrance fee. Because darkness was falling, the 250,000 incandescent light bulbs that were outlining every edge and feature of every building astounded the crowd. For the turn of the 20th-century society, electric light was a new phenomenon, and this riot of lighting was an astonishing feat that took their breath away. Everyone mistakenly believed that "Luna" meant light. One journalist described the interior of the new Luna Park thus: "an enchanted, story-book land of trellises, columns, domes, minarets, lagoons, and lofty aerial flights. And everywhere was life—a pageant of happy people; and everywhere color—a wide harmony of orange and white and gold . . . It was a world removed—shut away from the sordid clatter and turmoil of the streets" (Kasson 1978, 63). The entrance to Luna Park was a massive archway flanked by two tall rectangular towers surmounted by globes. In between the towers was a huge electric light sign that said "LUNA PARK" in block letters. Underneath the sign was a large red sign in the shape of a heart, which stated "The Heart of Coney Island." Once inside the gate, the visitors were greeted by a broad avenue that was named the Court of Honor. To the right was a recreated city of Venice, replete with Venetian buildings, canals, bridges, and gondoliers. On the left were three large buildings that contained the top ride attractions—the Trip to the Moon, the War of the Worlds, and Twenty Thousand Leagues under the Sea. These rides boasted innovative rocking seats that were precursors of the modern attractions created by Disney. Beyond the Court of Honor was a lake that was the terminus for the Shoot the Chutes slides. Boats would tumble down the slide and bounce into the lake as the passengers got sprayed with lake water. The 200-foot tall Electric Tower was located at the center of the lake, lighting up the surrounding region. Circus rings abutted the lake where animals, clowns, and acrobats performed. A band platform and a trained wild animal show were at the opposite end of the lake. Luna Park also contained a variety of ethnological exhibits, with German, Irish, Eskimo, and Hindu villages, Japanese gardens, and a Chinese theater. Boats and a miniature railroad carried visitors through these displays. Elephant displays were a favorite of Frederic Thompson. One of the most infamous of the incidents at Luna Park was the electrocution of an aging but angry elephant named Topsy, who had actually helped build the park. She was killed in a display of Thomas Edison's new technology of electricity. The terrible event was even recorded on Edison's new moving picture cameras.

KEY STATISTICS

Luna Park opened to the public in May 1903. It was opened only in the summer season, from May until September every year. The park was located on the north side of Surf Avenue, between 8th Street, 12th Street, and Neptune Avenue, one block from the beach in Coney Island, Brooklyn, New York. The original park encompassed 22 acres, which included 16 acres from the Sea Lion Park as well as an additional 8 acres adjacent, which had been the home of the infamous Elephant Hotel from Coney Island's earlier days. In 1904, Thompson and Dundy amassed more land for the park, making it a total of 38 acres. The park was an enormous success and continued to attract thousands of visitors for many years. The Great Depression hit the park hard, and it went bankrupt in 1933. Several fires destroyed the park in 1944, with another in 1946, when it officially closed. On the site, an apartment complex was built that was named Luna Park.

CULTURAL SIGNIFICANCE

Luna Park had an enormous influence on the amusement park industry in the United States. Reading the descriptions of the attractions found at Luna Park, it is hard to believe that this amusement park dates to 1903. Many of the concepts were copied by Walt Disney for his theme parks, with Disneyland opening in 1955 and Disney World in 1971. The transformation of American culture to a consumer society with time and money available for leisure activities was on display in these amusement parks where the daily grind of modern life could be whisked away, at least for a few hours. It is true that the working-class visitors escaping the crowds in the Lower East Side tenements encountered just as many crowds in the parks, though without the responsibilities of their typical day weighing on their shoulders. Frederic Thompson, creator of Luna Park, contemplated on the frame of mind of the public when he stated that the visitors "are not in a serious mood, and do not want to encounter seriousness. They have enough seriousness in their every-day lives and the keynote of the thing they do demand is change. Everything must be different from ordinary experience. What is presented to them must have life, action, motion, sensation, surprise, shock, swiftness or else comedy" (Kasson 1978, 66). Unfortunately, Luna Park's founders did not live long after the park was opened. Skip Dundy, the financial wizard, suddenly died in 1907, while still in his forties. Thompson, left to flounder on his own, succumbed to alcoholism in 1919 at the age of 46. However, the park soldiered on, but without the innovation supplied by its founders. In fact, the culture of the times had changed. By the 1920s, there were multiple outlets for amusements available to the consumer public. Motion pictures were ubiquitous; radio, with its variety of musical and talk shows, was available for most homes. The contrast between the daily lives of Americans and the sensation of the

Coney Island attractions was lessened as more entertainment was available to all.

FURTHER INFORMATION: IMPORTANT PRINT, ELECTRONIC, AND MEDIA RESOURCES

Brangham, William. "How a Coney Island Sideshow Advanced Medicine for Premature Babies." *PBS Newshour*. July 21, 2015. http://www.pbs.org/newshour/updates/coney-island-sideshow-advanced-medicine-premature-babies/. Accessed February 5, 2017.

Immerso, Michael. 2002. *Coney Island: The People's Playground*. New Brunswick, NJ, and London: Rutgers University Press.

Kasson, John F. 1978. *Amusing the Million: Coney Island at the Turn of the Century*. New York: Hill and Wang.

Pilat, Oliver, and Jo Ranson. 1941. *Sodom by the Sea: An Affectionate History of Coney Island*. Garden City, NY: Doubleday, Doran & Company, Inc.

Stanton, Jeffrey. "Coney Island—Luna Park." 1998. http://www.westland.net/coneyisland/articles/lunapark.htm. Accessed January 23, 2017.

Sullivan, David A. "Coney Island History: The Story of Thompson & Dundy's Luna Park." Heart of Coney Island. 2015. http://www.heartofconeyisland.com/luna-park-coney-island.html. Accessed January 23, 2017.

Dr. Couney's Incubator Exhibit

Among the bearded ladies, sword swallowers, and freak shows at Luna Park, one of the most surprising shows was the Baby Incubator Exhibit. Dr. Martin Couney, a French-born pediatrician, had become an advocate for using incubators, a new technology that saved the lives of premature babies. He saw them used in Berlin in 1896 and attempted to import them to the United States. However, the technology did not catch on in American hospitals. Realizing that he could save babies' lives if he presented the incubators in a Coney Island side show, Dr. Couney set up shop at Luna Park. For decades, Dr. Couney encouraged local parents to bring their one- to two-pound premature infants to Coney Island, where they were cared for round the clock by qualified physicians and nursing staff. In fact, the level of care for these tiny infants was better than was found in maternity hospitals at the time. Visitors paid 25 cents to view the babies, although parents were not charged for the care. Many people have survived and lived long lives after spending their first several months in Dr. Couney's Incubator Exhibit. Unfortunately, after displaying infants at Coney Island for decades, Dr. Couney died in 1950, in relative obscurity. Incubators were not regularly used in hospitals until after Dr. Couney's death.

Equitable Building

New York, New York
1915

BACKGROUND

Every time New York celebrates one of its championship teams, the city hosts a great parade that marches downtown through the congested blocks of Lower Broadway in the storied "Canyon of Heroes." The financial district of downtown Manhattan is populated by man-made structures, which do form a virtual canyon. The ancient, narrow streets and hulking early skyscrapers still manage to obstruct light and air. The obstruction might have been even worse today, had it not been for the construction of the 40-story Equitable Building, completed in 1915, and the resultant outcry to its bulky mass. The Equitable Life Assurance Society, one of the first and the largest insurance company at that time, was seeking a new home office that would reflect its respected position in the New York financial world. The company, founded in 1859, had developed popular new insurance instruments that were profitable for Equitable as the industry mushroomed after the Civil War. By the 1880s, the company expanded into international markets, employing agents in scores of countries around the world, catapulting it to be one of the most highly valued corporations in the nation.

The burgeoning insurance industry was one of the American innovations of the post–Civil War period. The so-called father of life insurance was Elizur Wright, a reformer and abolitionist who believed in the benefits of the widespread dissemination of life insurance policies in order to protect indigent widows and orphans. The industry existed in the United States and in Britain, but it had been infiltrated by a collection of charlatans and con men who took advantage of the lack of regulations governing the insurance industry. Citizens would buy insurance policies for their families and would find, to their chagrin, that the company had gone out of business when it came time to distribute the funds. Wright was a talented mathematician and enlisted his large brood of children to help him create a raft of actuarial tables that calculated the total assets required by an insurance company in order to remain solvent. Wright's work as a crusader and champion of the industry set in motion numerous reforms in the Commonwealth of

Massachusetts that were soon adopted by other states, propelling the insurance industry into general respectability.

The person responsible for the enormous growth of the industry was another man, one who had the personality of the consummate salesman. In 1859, Henry Baldwin Hyde worked as a clerk in the largest insurance company of the period, Mutual Life Insurance Company, in lower Manhattan. A young man of 25, Hyde had already developed innovative ideas about the industry. Mutual did not allow for life insurance policies to exceed $10,000. The population was expanding and so was their wealth, so many policyholders went to other companies in order to purchase additional insurance. After being fired for making such a revisionist suggestion to the company's administration, the ambitious Hyde immediately rented a space in the same building and put up huge sign for the "Equitable Life Assurance Society of the United States," dwarfing the smaller sign of the larger company occupying the floor below. Through church connections with some of New York's moneyed elite, Hyde was able to aggregate the necessary funds in order to actually establish an insurance company. The ingenious Hyde went on to develop innovative sales techniques as well as expand the company and pioneer the American sales convention. The success of the Equitable company was also influenced by trends in society. The nation was expanding at a furious rate as manifest destiny drove families and immigrants into the western frontiers, and lives became more isolated. Communities were not as strong as in the previous decades as family members who were seeking better opportunities moved away. Life insurance became a new protection for families who had more cash but fewer relatives living nearby. In addition, with the onset of the Civil War, many more fathers and sons took out life insurance policies in order to provide for their families in case they did not survive the war.

The first building constructed for the Equitable Life Assurance Society was built in 1870 and located on lower Broadway in Manhattan's financial district. In 1912, fire destroyed the building. Equitable, which by this time was a colossal insurance giant, desired an impressive structure that would represent the rank and reputation of this prominent company. It was decided that it would replace the lost building with another one at the same location. Construction techniques had changed since the 1870s, and the company was looking to construct a building that would compete with the great new skyscrapers sprouting up in Chicago. The largest architectural firm in the world, the Chicago-based Daniel H. Burnham and Company, designed a building for the site in 1906. The massive building was to soar 62 stories high. However, since the project suffered from delays, it was never built. Burnham died in 1912, and an architect from his firm, Ernest R. Graham, was selected to provide an alternate plan. The Equitable Life Assurance Society's new headquarters was completed in 1915. The huge Equitable

Building represented the power of the life insurance industry at the dawn of the 20th century. It has historical significance for another reason: the hulking mass of this giant building created a stir with the public, as it overwhelmed the surrounding structures and the narrow streets below. The furor created by this building led to a movement to regulate and restrict the design, location, and mass of new structures with regulations that are known as zoning laws. Although the zoning restrictions that were put in place after the completion of the Equitable Building were successful in restraining the blocking of light on the city streets, over the years they had a number of unintended consequences. By the end of the 20th century, zoning laws were ubiquitous but became extremely controversial.

CHARACTERISTICS AND FUNCTIONALITY

The Equitable Life Assurance building is situated on lower Broadway in the financial district of Manhattan. The building was built by the Equitable Office Building Corporation. The architect was Ernest R. Graham, working in the firm of Daniel H. Burnham. The firm was based in Chicago, and Graham used construction techniques and design features that were typical of many of the Chicago-style skyscrapers. However, Chicago was a newer city, and its streets were broad avenues. The financial district of New York was a mix of narrow, short streets where tall buildings cast long shadows. Using typical Chicago building techniques, the frame of the Equitable Building is a steel skeleton, allowing for the 40-story height. The foundation is set on a rock bed, and there is a three-level basement. There is a six-story base and above the base the building is shaped like an "H," with a corridor running through each leg of the "H," forming four office towers. The entire building soars into the air space above, with no setbacks. The exterior of the building is clad in brick, limestone, granite, and terra-cotta. The architectural design of the building has elements of Renaissance Revival and Neo-Classical styles. There is a grand entrance archway at the center of the building on the east and west facades, flanked by Corinthian pilasters. Above the capitals of the pilasters is a one-story classical entablature. Two more stories high, there is another one-story band that encircles the entire building and introduces the H-shaped shaft of the towers. At the top of the building, another decorative element forms a crown, echoing the treatment at the base. Corinthian pilasters flank the double-hung windows on the 31st to 35th floors. The top floors contain simple cornices, and at the 39th and 40th floors large windows form the building's penthouse. The entry arch leads into a magnificent arcade with a coffered ceiling that extends through the building on the east–west axis. Above the archway on both sides of the building is a sign carved in the stone stating "Equitable Building," with a large flagpole mounted at the top of the building's base. The building has shops and banks on the first floor along the interior arcade. The offices above the mezzanine have the identical layout up to the top floors. There is a corridor on each side of the H-shape, running east to west, with offices flanking each side. The Equitable company used several floors and rented out the others to many of the giant corporations of the early 20th century.

KEY STATISTICS

The Equitable Building occupies the entire city block formed by Broadway, Cedar Street, Pine Street, and Nassau Street. Its formal address is 120 Broadway. The building is 40 stories high, rising 545 feet. It has 7 bays of windows along the east and west facades, and 18 along the north and south. There are about 5,000 windows, mostly double-hung. The original building had 10,000 doors and 56 elevators. With 30,000 square feet of office space on each floor, the building totals over one million square feet of floor space. The building exploited its one-acre property more than any other building constructed in New York City. The building maximized the site by the square footage of the total floor area having almost 30 times the total square foot area of the site. Zoning regulations put into place the next year limited the floor area to 12 times the square foot area of the site. The buildings built subsequently may have been taller, but they benefited from setbacks that reduced the floor area. Because of the massive nature of the design, the Equitable Building cast a shadow on the surrounding streets that extended across seven acres.

CULTURAL SIGNIFICANCE

There are two major reasons why the Equitable Building is culturally significant. The first tells the story of the importance of the insurance industry in the first few decades of the 20th century. However, Equitable was not the only great insurance giant to build an impressive building in New York City. The Metropolitan Life Insurance Company also built a beautiful tower at Madison Avenue and 23rd Street, a building that briefly attained the status as the tallest building in the world after it was constructed in 1909. The New York Life Insurance Company also has a prominent headquarters on Madison Avenue, designed by the esteemed architect Cass Gilbert in 1926. Both of these buildings are important landmarks on the Manhattan skyline today. However, the more monumental, less pretty office building that was the Equitable Building made a significant contribution to the appearance of the New York skyline, as well as to the planning of American neighborhoods. Because of the outcry that occurred after the Equitable Building was built, a new type of law was instituted, the first zoning law in the United States. This law, the Zoning Resolution of 1916, established height and setback requirements for all new office towers. Setbacks are design elements that require a building to have a smaller footprint the higher it soars into the air. The Empire State Building, constructed after the passing of the Zoning

Resolution, is a prime example of the use of setbacks. The zoning law also divided the city into separate zones: residential, commercial, and manufacturing. The belief at the time was that industrial areas emitted unhealthy air and water pollution that should not be interspersed with residential or commercial districts. After the Supreme Court validated the constitutionality of zoning restrictions in 1926, zoning laws started to proliferate throughout the country. In New York City, zoning laws created the spires of early 20th-century skyscrapers like the Empire State and the Chrysler Buildings. With the influence of the International Style in the mid-century, buildings such as Lever House and the Seagram Building, among many others, eschewed the setback and instead created large urban plazas surrounding tall, straight, and uniform building slabs. Years later, the effect of these and similar International Style buildings, with the entire tower set back from the street and the consistently underutilized plazas generating a paucity of street life along the sidewalks at pedestrian level, created a backlash. Jane Jacobs was an activist and writer whose most famous and influential work was *The Death and Life of Great American Cities*, published in 1961. She was an opponent of zoning regulations and their effect on urban street life. She fought and won in a fight against the enormously powerful Robert Moses who was planning an urban renewal project that would destroy the neighborhood of her beloved Greenwich Village. Moses had been successful in similar plans several times before, but had not come up against such neighborhood opposition, led by the formidable adversary Jane Jacobs. In her book she describes her impression of a healthy city's street life:

> Under the seeming disorder of the old city, wherever the old city is working successfully, is a marvelous order for maintaining the safety of the streets and the freedom of the city. It is a complex order. Its essence is intricacy of sidewalk use, bringing with it a constant succession of eyes. This order is all composed of movement and change, and although it is life, not art, we may fancifully call it the art form of the city and liken it to the dance—not to a simple-minded precision dance with everyone kicking up at the same time, twirling in unison and bowing off en masse, but to an intricate ballet in which the individual dancers and ensembles all have distinctive parts which miraculously reinforce each other and compose an orderly whole. The ballet of the good city sidewalk never repeats itself from place to place, and in any one place is always replete with new improvisations. (Jacobs 1961, 50)

Another highly controversial aspect of zoning regulations across the country was their influence on suburbanization and racial segregation. Separate zones were created by regional planning boards, with planned suburban districts created farther and farther away from the city's core. Urban areas became districts for the poor and marginalized, whereas middle-class families were given the option to live in safe, quiet, suburban redoubts. Another feature of zoning that was used in the 20th century was the use of density zoning. Neighborhoods were assigned density limits, purportedly so that property values could be maintained. This led to the creation of middle- and upper-income, primarily white neighborhoods in the lower-density districts, and poorer, minority neighborhoods in the higher-density districts. Redlining, and other techniques that encouraged racial segregation, was utilized by banks and real estate agents, which exacerbated the problem. The issue of zoning laws is still being debated as architects and planners have learned to appreciate the dynamism of urban life and denser living. Far-flung suburbs have created a reliance on the automobile, which has had more unintended consequences such as social isolation and the obesity epidemic. As younger millennials strive to relocate to urban centers, the uses of zoning will certainly change. But the ubiquity of zoning laws is not going to go away any time soon.

FURTHER INFORMATION: IMPORTANT PRINT, ELECTRONIC, AND MEDIA RESOURCES

Boorstin, Daniel J. 1973. *The Americans: The Democratic Experience*. New York: Vintage Books.

Jacobs, Jane. 1961. *The Death and Life of Great American Cities*. New York: Vintage Books.

National Park Service. National Register of Historic Places Inventory—Nomination Form. "Equitable Building." http://npgallery.nps.gov/nrhp/GetAsset?assetID=67601cac-4e94-4aad-91a0-d743b12d4336. Accessed December 4, 2016.

Paradis, Thomas W. 2011. *The Illustrated Encyclopedia of American Landmarks*. Leicester: Lorenz Books.

White, Norval, and Elliot Willensky. 1978. *AIA Guide to New York City*. New York: Collier Books.

The 1916 Zoning Resolution

The outcry that occurred after the construction of the Equitable Building in 1915 resulted in a reexamination of the lack of regulations concerning building heights and building mass in New York City. The massiveness of the Equitable Building effectively blocked the

sunlight on the streets on Lower Broadway. City officials were already showing concern for the unbridled development that was occurring along the newly built subway lines throughout Manhattan. There was no city planning department at the time, but in 1913, the borough president of Manhattan was a man named George McAneny, who, among many other talents in the realm of public service, was a proponent of city planning and preservation. He set up a committee in 1913 to study the possible regulation of the height, size, and arrangement of buildings in the city. Until that time, it was only the limits of technology that restricted the height and mass of buildings. With new technologies like steel skeleton construction, elevators, telephones, and other innovations, the limits were disappearing and the buildings were getting higher and higher. McAneny's committee on zoning was therefore prepared to take the leap when the derided Equitable Building was completed in 1915. In fact, after leaving office in 1913, McAneny teamed up with lawyer Edward M. Bassett to write the 1916 Zoning Resolution, the first comprehensive zoning ordinance in the United States. Bassett went on to become a seminal figure in the field of urban planning in the country. The 1916 Zoning Resolution influenced other legislation in many American cities. The regulations in the New York City zoning law led to the designs of many of the iconic New York City skyscrapers, with their signature setbacks, which allowed for light and air to reach the streets below.

Ford River Rouge Complex

Dearborn, Michigan
1917

BACKGROUND

Middletown: A Study in Modern American Culture, the landmark sociological study of life in a small midwestern city, published in 1929, said it all: the ubiquity of the automobile has had an enormous impact on society in the United States. By that year, two-thirds of the residents of the fictional city of Middletown (actually Muncie, Indiana) owned cars. This marked a radical departure from 25 years before, when only the wealthiest and most technologically advanced would even consider purchasing an automobile. The popularity of the automobile had numerous additional consequences. Cities and towns invested in more paved roads, businesses such as gas stations and roadhouse restaurants sprouted up, and real estate development started to extend to the edges of the cities and towns. The continuous growth of the car culture has had enormous impact on American society in the 20th century. Suburban sprawl, air pollution, the obesity epidemic, and the breakdown of community ties have been some of the less positive results of the burgeoning car culture. But in the 1920s, the novel availability of a family car represented a revolution in the middle-class American lifestyle. Families could travel in town or out of town to visit relatives and friends, mothers could drive to pick up their children or shop in the newly invented supermarket, and the plans for a family vacation now seemed almost limitless. The automobile meant freedom to the American family.

How did this fundamental change occur? Much of the responsibility for this revolution in American culture lies with the visionary industrialist Henry Ford. Born in 1863, Ford was the eldest son of William and Mary Ford who had a small farm in a town outside of Detroit, Michigan. The young Henry Ford rebelled against the exhausting labor required to manage a successful farm in the late 19th century. His family allowed him to fiddle with machinery while on the farm, and sent him to Detroit at the age of 16 to seek his fortune in the city. Henry Ford proceeded to reinvent himself as he applied himself to learning the latest engineering technologies. He eventually wound up as chief engineer with the Edison Illuminating Company, the local electrical company. Thomas Edison was his hero, and would ultimately become his best friend in later life. But electricity was not his passion. Ford was fascinated with the new transportation phenomenon called the "horseless carriage." This predecessor of the automobile was in its first stages of development. Many inventors were designing versions of the horseless carriage. Henry Ford was too. He spent his weekends working on his version of the new machine, using bicycle parts. In 1896, he introduced the four-wheeled "quadricycle." This simple machine was the first attempt by Ford to provide a mode of transportation available to the average family. This quest would become the focus of his extraordinarily successful career.

With only several years of education in a rural schoolhouse behind him, Ford was not formally educated. However, he had a talent for understanding the new technologies that were appearing in the late 19th century. This aptitude would serve him well. What also served him well was his talent for self-promotion. Although he had a natural ability to understand the newest technologies, he was rarely the actual inventor. But he knew how to use his folksy manner and his understanding of the use of publicity to promote his ideas in the public sphere. Henry Ford left the Edison Illuminating Company and made several attempts at building an automobile company, without success. He was able to convince wealthy patrons to invest in his new company, but eventually ran into disputes with them. The investors wanted to see a shiny, new luxurious automobile that they would like to drive. Not Henry Ford. He had a vision of a simple car that everyone could afford. He kept tinkering with the product but never produced one. He resented the power of the rich investors and vowed to create his own company on his own terms. In 1903, Henry Ford started his latest company funded by small local investors, which he called the Ford Motor Company, in Detroit, Michigan. His aim was to build a new type of automobile that was simple, reliable, and cheap. He aspired to see America's growing middle- and even working-class families driving a Ford car.

In 1908, Henry Ford introduced the Model T, the product of years of refinement by his team of engineers. This car was the one that Ford had envisioned: economical, simple, and reliable. The price of the original Model T was $850, which was still high for the average family, but much more affordable than the other cars on the market that were sold in the $2,000 range. Ford's vision went beyond the immediate success of the Model T. He fixated on the idea of producing the cars faster and reducing the price even further. In 1910, Ford built a huge new factory complex in Detroit called Highland Park. It was designed by the architect Albert Kahn. In Henry Ford's quest to produce his products faster, he consulted with his staff of engineers who eventually proposed a brilliant innovation. They were inspired by the design of a meat processing plant, where the animal carcasses would travel on an overhead moving conveyor while the workers did the same task over and over as the animal carcasses passed by. By breaking down the work into individual actions, done repeatedly, the production could be speeded up. Ford tried this new method first in the shop that made magnetos, which was part of the ignition system of the car. The assembly line was so successful that Ford insisted on deconstructing the assembly of all the other parts of the car. By the time the assembly line was set up throughout the factory, the total production time for the Model T was reduced from 12 hours and 13 minutes, to 1 hour and 33 minutes, an astounding feat. The price of the Model T was reduced due to the ballooning number of cars rolling off the assembly line. But Henry Ford was not satisfied. Assembly line work is not satisfying and does not require skill. Ford was having trouble retaining his workers who could find jobs elsewhere that were more rewarding at the same pay. He concluded that his dream of making a "people's car" would not be realized if his own workers could not afford to own one. On January 5, 1914, Ford made the radical proposal to more than double the wages of the factory workers, and decrease their hours. On this so-called Five Dollar Day, Ford announced that he would pay his workers $5 per day and reduce their daily hours from nine to eight. Although his profits decreased, Ford's brilliant idea had a number of valuable consequences: he was able to break up the workday into three shifts, he retained his factory workers, and most importantly, he made it possible for his workforce to be able to purchase Ford cars. Henry Ford became an instant celebrity and international hero of the labor movement. However, Ford was no socialist; he was a businessman who understood the most effective way to market his product. Ford's product, the Model T, was so successful that he was able to further reduce the price. By 1924, it sold for $260. And, by 1921, every other car in the world was a Model T.

Henry Ford began to envision a continuous flow for the production of his automobiles, a complete vertical integration of the process. He aimed for a system where all aspects of production were controlled by the Ford Motor Company, including all raw materials. His next venture was to construct a massive production complex in the town of Dearborn, near Detroit, where he could seamlessly bring in all necessary raw materials on an as-needed basis, and transform them into Ford cars. In 1917, Ford again hired the German immigrant architect Albert Kahn. For the next 10 years, Ford and Kahn consulted on every detail of the colossal manufacturing complex that was known as River Rouge, or the Rouge.

CHARACTERISTICS AND FUNCTIONALITY

The River Rouge Complex was the largest factory in the world when it was completed in 1928. It was also the only totally integrated automobile factory, capable of producing all the parts of the automobile from raw materials to finished product. Henry Ford was particularly intrigued with vertical integration because, during World War I, scarcity in certain products resulted in delays in production that Ford despised. In 1915, Ford purchased 2,000 acres along the Rouge River west of Detroit in Dearborn, Michigan. After receiving a contract to produce anti-submarine Eagle boats for the U.S. government during World War I, Ford planned to produce them in his new plant in Dearborn. He built the Dearborn Assembly Plant or B Building in 1918 near a boat slip so that his assembly line could launch the boats straight into the river. However, the war soon ended and the boats were no longer necessary. Ford converted the plant into an automobile manufacturing facility, making Model T and tractor bodies, and after 1927, Model A bodies. The Dearborn Assembly Plant was a massive structure that boasted five aisles that were each 1,700 feet long and contained railroad tracks for moving parts and materials or parts assembly. The one-story structure was expanded to two stories in 1919. The next building to be built at the Rouge was the Dearborn Iron Foundry, completed in 1921. Here 2,000 tons of castings could be poured each day, which were cast into engine blocks. Also built in 1921, the massive power house was able to produce power for both the Rouge plant and the older Highland Park plant. The brick building has eight smokestacks, and the immense power generated by this power house could provide electricity to a city of over half a million people. The gigantic complex also contained blast furnaces; coal, iron ore, and limestone bins; coke ovens; a glass plant; a tire plant; a steel operations building; an engine plant; a tool-and-die building; and an office building.

KEY STATISTICS

The Ford River Rouge Complex is located at 3001 Miller Road in Dearborn, Michigan. The complex presently comprises 900 acres along the Rouge River. As one of the largest factory complexes in the world, there are many remarkable statistics that describe this facility. The complex took over 10 years to complete and cost $269 million. When it opened, the Rouge complex boasted 75,000 employees who worked three shifts as the factory ran 24 hours per day. There were 100 miles of railroad tracks on the site, and 93 buildings. The buildings comprised 6.9 million square feet of floor space. All the structures in the complex were immense; for instance, the Steel Operations Buildings was over a mile long, covering 72 acres. Seven hundred gallons of water were used daily, pumped in from the Detroit River. The complex was virtually self-sufficient. It had its own security force, its own fire department, its own power source, and its own water system. The River Rouge Complex was a small city unto itself.

CULTURAL SIGNIFICANCE

Henry Ford had a profound influence on American society in the early part of the 20th century. His vision of producing a car that all Americans could afford came close to coming true. However, he ultimately despised the effect that his vision had on the country. He even despised his great River Rouge complex after it was completed. Ford was a complicated man. Although an inspiring leader for many of his employees, he was a cruel and manipulative father to his only son Edsel, who desired nothing more than to successfully manage the family business. Although Henry Ford survived into his eighties, his son Edsel died of cancer at the age of 49. Henry was shattered by the blow, even though he had made life miserable for his son during Edsel's entire life. Ford had contempt for bankers and other Wall Street elites. He was an unabashed anti-Semite, even purchasing a local newspaper in the 1920s so he could write opinion pieces that blamed all society's problems on the Jews. This newspaper, the *Dearborn Independent*, was delivered to all the Ford dealerships throughout the country. On the other hand, he hired many immigrants, African Americans, and women for his factories over the years. Although Henry Ford was celebrated for his $5 per day wage and his 40-hour workweek, he was not a supporter of labor issues. He fought unionization of the plant for years, even sending his own thug-like security force to beat up the union organizers. As he aged, Henry Ford developed an increasing disdain for modern American society, a culture that he had a large responsibility for creating. He purchased land near the old family farm and built a restoration he called Greenfield Village, where he displayed artifacts from early technology from the late 19th century, and spent much of his time there in an attempt to recapture his own past.

Henry Ford began his career demonstrating an innate understanding of marketing. He knew how to maximize efficiency and created the ubiquitous assembly line manufacturing method. His visionary ideas concerning a living wage for his workers created a built-in market for his products. He was admired by millions of ordinary Americans as a folksy representative of the working class. His disdain for the rich and powerful made him enormously appealing to the country's common people. But he was, in fact, one of the richest men in the world. And with his wealth he developed an unchecked ego. He began to surround himself with sycophants and yes-men. Even his business acumen failed him, as he insisted on selling only Model Ts for many years after the market for them softened. Ford's biggest competitor General Motors introduced several new concepts in cars, which became very popular. It offered a variety of colors, in contrast to the Model T, which only came in black. It then created the concept of the model year, with a variety of models at differing price points. Both of these new ideas were an anathema to Henry Ford. He finally relented and ceased production of the Model T in 1926, after over 15 million were produced. The new Model A was a success, but the juggernaut that was the original Ford Motor Company was never repeated. Henry Ford finally retired in 1945 and died on April 7,

1947, at the age of 83. His grandson, Henry Ford II, ran the company for the next 15 years.

FURTHER INFORMATION: IMPORTANT PRINT, ELECTRONIC, AND MEDIA RESOURCES

Boorstin, Daniel J. 1973. *The Americans: The Democratic Experience.* New York: Vintage Books.

"Henry Ford." *American Experience.* PBS.org. January 29, 2013. http://www.pbs.org/video/american-experience-henry-ford-film/. Accessed September 22, 2017.

Hyde, Charles K. 1966. "Assembly-Line Architecture: Albert Kahn and the Evolution of the U.S. Auto Factory." *The Journal of the Society for Industrial Archeology* 22 (2): 5–24. Accessed September 10, 2017.

Morgan, Ted. July 13, 1986. "Intrigue and Tyranny in Motor City." *New York Times.* http://www.nytimes.com/1986/07/13/books/intrigue-and-tyranny-in-motor-city.html?pagewanted=all&mcubz=0. Accessed September 22, 2017.

National Park Service. "Ford River Rouge Complex." https://npgallery.nps.gov/pdfhost/docs/NHLS/Text/78001516.pdf. Accessed September 24, 2017.

The Battle of the Overpass

The legendary industrialist Henry Ford is known for inventing the automobile assembly line. He is also credited with conjuring up the innovative notion that by providing a product at a price that his workers could afford he could guarantee sales. To achieve this, he even instituted an eight-hour workday and raised the wages of his workers. Ford was heralded as a champion of the working man. However, Ford did not believe in socialism or in unions. In fact, he ran a strictly autocratic organization, demanding complete control, and he expressed an abhorrence of unionization. In the 1930s, he increasingly relied on his violent band of spies and thugs that constituted Ford's security force led by his right-hand man Harry Bennett. Ford dubbed the group the "Service Department," and he demanded that they enforce top–down control over his factory workers. After Franklin Roosevelt signed the groundbreaking Wagner Act in 1935 that established workers' rights to collective bargaining, the labor movement targeted the automobile industry for unionization. Detroit had traditionally not been supportive to the union movement. However, after a series of sit-down strikes, General Motors and Chrysler relented and allowed the Union of Automobile Workers (UAW) onto their shop floors. Ford remained the holdout, as the "Service Department" goons continued to encourage workers to spy on each other and report any possible union activity.

In 1937, the UAW led by legendary labor leader Walter Reuther made an attempt to enter the plant by commencing a leaflet campaign. After obtaining a permit from the city of Dearborn, Reuther secretly set about to plan a bold move on the grounds of the River Rouge plant. Sensing trouble ahead, Reuther invited local journalists, as well as clergymen, photographers, and representatives of the Senate Committee on Civil Liberties, to attend. They planned to gather at the pedestrian overpass leading to the plant, during the shift change period to hand out prounion leaflets. The labor leaders posed for photographs on the overpass. They were approached from behind by Service Department goons who proceeded to kick and punch the men, giving them a brutal beating. Women who were from the UAW's Ladies' Auxiliary, as well as other spectators watching the event from below the overpass, were brutally beaten as well. A photographer from the *Detroit News* captured the beatings on film. He sent his shocking photos to the newspaper, which printed them and broadcast them to the world on the wire services. The appalling images once and for all commanded worldwide attention to the violence being used by companies to prevent unionization. The "Battle of the Overpass" was a decisive turning point in the American labor movement. In 1941, the Ford Motor Company finally signed its first contract with the United Automobile Workers and Congress of Industrial Organizations. Ford was the last of the "Big Three" automakers to be unionized. In the battle against unionization, Henry Ford had lost.

Grauman's Chinese Theatre

Hollywood, California
1927

BACKGROUND

After World War I ended, the mood of the country had changed. The internationalist agenda advocated by President Woodrow Wilson was roundly rejected by the public after the soldiers returned home from the brutal European war. As historian Frederick Lewis Allen describes, "The torch of idealism that had kindled the revolt of the American conscience seemed to have pretty well burned itself out. People were tired. In particular their public spirit, their consciences, and their hopes were tired" (Allen 1952). The nation turned to isolationism, and the liberal immigration policies of the past were discarded. In 1921, immigration quotas were established, which significantly reduced the number of immigrants allowed into the country. The nation elected a president in 1920 who was the antithesis of the intellectual Woodrow Wilson. Warren G. Harding was a handsome, pleasant, humble man, a Republican senator from Ohio, with little intellectual heft. His motto was "return to normalcy." He died in office after two years, leaving his government with a heap of corruption scandals. His vice president, Calvin Coolidge, was as prudent as Harding was reckless. A man bereft of charm, "silent Cal" was president for another six years. The public was not paying much attention to politics though. It was the "roaring twenties," and the country was searching for a way to have some fun. The economy was growing exponentially, with industrial production increasing 50 percent in the decade between 1920 and 1930. With salaries rising, families had more disposable income. The technological revolution that had been taking place over the last quarter-century finally made many products available to the middle and working classes. More families were now able to purchase an automobile, with the number of registered vehicles quadrupling in the decade following the end of World War I. Labor-saving devices in the home, like the refrigerator and other electrical appliances, were bought on easy-payment plans. Women, who were finally afforded the right to vote in 1920 with the passage of the 19th Amendment to the Constitution, were embracing a new, less restrictive morality. The Victorian constraints were rejected as skirts were shortened, hair was cut short, and corsets were tossed out. Businessmen profited by a dearth of banking regulations, as the economy continued to expand ceaselessly. Even though the laws of Prohibition were passed in 1920, they were flouted almost immediately by the public, which resulted in a more pronounced scorn for the legitimacy of government regulations.

With the country turning inward and with a public itching to spend its disposable income, the 1920s also oversaw the development of the motion picture industry. Moving pictures were invented in the late 19th century and so-called nickelodeons were the first movie theaters, popular in the first years of the 20th century. The nickelodeons were small theaters that played a series of short films for an entrance fee of merely a nickel. These were not luxurious establishments, however, and were sometimes considered slightly seedy. They did introduce the public to moving pictures, however. As full-length films began to be produced, theaters were built that could accommodate filmgoers in more comfortable facilities. The first motion picture production companies were located in New York City, with film production taking place in Fort Lee, New Jersey, since Thomas Edison in nearby Menlo Park, New Jersey, had many patents related to the moving picture industry. A film industry also developed in Jacksonville, Florida, in the early 20th century. The weather was better than in New York, and it briefly boasted the moniker "The Winter Film Capital of the World." There was also an early film industry in Jacksonville, making films with African American casts. Movies were not made in Hollywood, California, until 1910, when D. W. Griffith produced the film *In Old California* there. In 1915, Griffith filmed the racist movie epic *The Birth of a Nation* in California. It depicts the stories of two families during and after the Civil War. Although its filmmaking techniques were groundbreaking, its positive portrayal of the Ku Klux Klan and its racist portrayals of African Americans have made it a controversial film ever since the film's opening day. The National Association for the Advancement of Colored People tried to ban it and protests took place around the country. However, the movie was a great financial success at the box office despite the controversy.

The superior weather and the popularity of westerns promoted the Hollywood location after World War I. With the onset of the 1920s, the movie industry grew rapidly in Hollywood. Movie production companies moved to California to avoid Edison's patent lawsuits, and to take advantage of the abundant sunshine. By the end of the 1920s, there were five major movie studios in Hollywood: Paramount (1914), MGM (1924), 20th Century Fox (founded 1914 as Fox Film Corporation, and merged with 20th Century Pictures in 1935), RKO (1928), and Warner Brothers (1923). Several smaller studios also were founded during the 1920s. United Artists was established by Charlie Chaplin, Mary Pickford, Douglas Fairbanks, and D. W. Griffith in an effort to maintain the artists' control over their films. During this period, all the films were black and white and silent. The first nonsilent film, known as a "talkie," was *The Jazz Singer*, with Al Jolson, made by Warner Brothers in 1927. The film was a huge success and the industry was transformed overnight. The motion picture studio system grew into a big business during the 1920s. Movie stars were given long-term contracts that prevented them from working for rival studios. The in-house publicity department controlled how the stars were marketed. Directors became powerful inside the studio, but also were under contract. The studios maintained their own production, distribution, and even their own theaters as they consolidated control over their interests through vertical integration. By the end of the 1920s, the studio system in Hollywood was in place. The behemoth that is the Hollywood movie industry has produced most of the fiction films made in the United States ever since.

CHARACTERISTICS AND FUNCTIONALITY

The film industry in Hollywood was already a big business when Sid Grauman built the Grauman's Chinese Theatre in 1927. Sidney Patrick Grauman, born in 1879 in Indianapolis, Indiana, was a Hollywood developer and one of the 36 founders of the Academy of Motion Picture Arts and Sciences, the organization that produces the Oscars. He built several movie theaters in Hollywood. The first was the Million Dollar Theatre in downtown Los Angeles. The Egyptian Theatre in Hollywood was his next project. By this time, movie theaters were being built as "movie palaces" that had lavish ornamentation and seated thousands. Grauman's dream was to build a Chinese movie palace. He contacted real estate developer C. E. Toberman to help him get a lease on the property on Hollywood Boulevard. He hired the architectural firm of Meyer and Holler. The architect from that firm responsible for the design was Raymond Kennedy (1891–1976). Grauman owned one-third interest in the property, whereas his colleagues in the industry, Mary Pickford, Douglas Fairbanks, and Howard Schenck, split the rest. The groundbreaking of the project took place in January 1926.

The Grauman Chinese Theatre was designed in the Exotic Revival style. Although most of the decoration is of Chinese inspiration, it is not an authentic style, but a combination of Chinese and other exotic elements. Green copper obelisks in the front and friezes that resemble Greek designs are examples of non-Chinese elements. Grauman requested special permission from the U.S. government to import artifacts from China that he used in the theater. Artisans from China were also brought in to create some of the sculptures that adorn the entrance. The theater is set back from the street with the entrance resembling a gigantic 90-foot-high pagoda. The design was intentionally set back in order to contain the throngs of fans that would crowd the entrance during movie premiere events. It is a transitional space that transports the visitor from the noise and activity of the street to the illusion and grandeur of the theater's interior. The entrance forecourt is surrounded by 40-foot curved walls and turrets with copper tops. There are two red columns holding up the bronze roof. At the top of the columns are a series of wrought iron masks. Rising 30 feet above the set of three double-doors is a tall stone relief carving of a dragon. Two statues of Ming Dynasty guardian lions, called "Heavenly Dogs," that were imported from China guard the entrances on either side. The lobby of the theater has murals depicting life in China. There is a massive Chinese chandelier and columns in red and gold. In a glass case are two wax figures in authentic Chinese costumes. In a third chair, now empty, there was a wax figure of the wife of the former owner of the theater, Rhonda Fleming. Inside the auditorium were originally 2,200 seats. The seats and the carpeting were red. Another gigantic chandelier hung from the center of a starburst design on the ceiling that is decorated with dragons and surrounded by icons portraying scenes from Chinese drama. On the side walls are Chinese lamps and black-and-white murals depicting trees and pagodas.

The most celebrated element of this exterior is the theater's forecourt called the Forecourt of the Stars, where Hollywood stars have placed their footprints and handprints in the concrete since 1927. The concrete paving blocks contain footprints, handprints, and some other features, like Groucho Marx's and George Burns's cigars, in the concrete. The origin of this practice is disputed, although Grauman stated that he accidently stepped on the concrete before it hardened and then invented the publicity stunt. Norma Talmadge is also credited with stepping into the concrete first. But at any rate, the Forecourt of the Stars has become a Hollywood legend, on the schedule of most tourists visiting Los Angeles.

KEY STATISTICS

The Grauman's Chinese Theatre is located at 6925 Hollywood Boulevard in Hollywood, California. The site was owned by Francis X. Bushman, who owned a ranch on that site from 1913 to 1915. The theater had a grand opening on May 18, 1927, one and a half years after the groundbreaking. The opening was attended by thousands of fans trying to catch a glimpse of the stars who were attending. The movie that was shown that night was Cecil B. DeMille's *King of Kings*. A 65-member orchestra and the theater's great organ played. The theater cost $2 million to complete. The theater was renovated in 2013 to accommodate an IMAX theater, and it presently has a capacity of 932.

CULTURAL SIGNIFICANCE

With the onset of television in the 1950s and the Internet in the 1990s, movie palaces have lost their audience. Many of the great movie theaters in the downtown areas have closed. Multiplexes showing a variety of films in tiny auditoriums have replaced the large movie theaters as the public has relocated to car-based suburbs. Although the Grauman's Chinese Theatre has outlasted most of the other movie palaces of the 1920s, it has had its ups and downs through the years. It was the premier theater in Hollywood for years, and hosted many movie premieres, including the premiere of *The Wizard of Oz*, in 1939. During several years in the 1940s, the Chinese Theatre hosted the Academy Awards, until they moved to Shrine Auditorium in Los Angeles. The Oscars have been held in various venues over the years, and are now held in the Dolby Theatre adjacent to the Chinese Theatre. The Chinese Theatre was recognized as a historic-cultural landmark in Los Angeles since 1968. It was owned by the Mann Theatres chain from 1973 to 2001 during which time it was known as the Mann Chinese Theatre. The theater was renovated in the first years of the 21st century for seismic stability. In 2013, it was converted into an IMAX theater, and the seats were reconfigured and the capacity was reduced. The Grauman's Chinese Theatre remains a cultural landmark of the 20th century, representing a period of time in the United States when the country was turning away from international involvement and toward a new type of American entertainment.

FURTHER INFORMATION: IMPORTANT PRINT, ELECTRONIC, AND MEDIA RESOURCES

Allen, Frederick Lewis. 1952. *The Big Change: America Transforms Itself 1900–1950*. New York: Harper and Row.

Betsky, Aaron. November 7, 1991. "Architecture: Mann's Chinese Theatre: Illusion at Its Best." *Los Angeles Times*. http://articles.latimes.com/1991-11-07/news/we-1473_1_mann-s-chinese-theater. Accessed March 3, 2017.

"Chinese Theatre." Los Angeles Conservancy. https://www.laconservancy.org/locations/tcl-chinese-theatre-0. Accessed March 3, 2017.

"Grauman's Chinese Theatre. Seeing Stars—Hollywood Movie Palaces." http://www.seeing-stars.com/theatres/chinesetheatre.shtml. Accessed March 3, 2017.

"History—TCL Chinese Theatres." http://www.tclchinesetheatres.com/tcl-chinese-theater-history/. Accessed March 1, 2017.

Robinson, David. 1968. *Hollywood in the Twenties*. New York: Paperback Library.

Shiel, Mark. 2012. *Hollywood Cinema and the Real Los Angeles*. London: Reaktion Books.

The Grauman's Chinese Theatre in Movies and Television

The Grauman's Chinese Theatre has been highlighted in a number of movies and television shows. The movies include *Singing in the Rain*, *Speed*, and the remake of *Mighty Joe Young*. The television shows include *I Love Lucy* and *The Beverly Hillbillies*.

Woolworth's Store

Greensboro, North Carolina
1929

BACKGROUND

The fabled "five and dime" Woolworth store began its life with the name "The Great Five Cents Store" in 1879 in Utica, New York. The founder was a man named Frank Woolworth, and his ploy to sell goods at either a nickel or a dime proved supremely successful for almost a century. Other chains copied Woolworth's policy, and hundreds of stores with names like Kresge and Kress could be found on the main streets of every American town. Woolworth eventually increased its maximum price, and finally rejected the policy altogether, but continued to expand throughout the nation and throughout the world. Its famous displays of all types of household goods, toys, school supplies, sewing supplies, tools, and so much more made Woolworth's the essential stop for any trip downtown. One more asset in every Woolworth's was the lunch counter. All five-and-dime stores boasted a lunch counter that usually lined the sidewall of the building where lunches, snacks, or just a cup of coffee could be served. The lunch counter gave tired patrons a chance to take a break and rest their feet, and provided the store with its highest profits. Woolworth's home office was located in a magnificent building in downtown Manhattan. The home office allowed the store managers around the country to establish regulations for their stores. And for the states in the South, this meant that the racist Jim Crow rules were in effect. In the South, incongruous as it may seem, African Americans were allowed to purchase at the store, work at the store, work at the lunch counter, and order food to take out at the lunch counter. What they were not allowed to do was to sit at the "whites only" lunch counter and be served.

These Jim Crow rules were enforced throughout the southern states, including at the flagship Woolworth store on South Elm Street in Greensboro, North Carolina. Greensboro was a thriving regional center that had developed after the railroad came through the town in the 1880s. Several colleges were founded in the town. Two historically black colleges and universities were located in Greensboro: Agricultural and Technical College of North Carolina (A&T) and Bennett College for Women. In the fall of

1960, four young freshmen entered college at A&T. They were from various towns and backgrounds but they soon bonded and spent many hours in dorm room "bull sessions" discussing civil rights. These four freshmen, Ezell Blair Jr., Franklin McCain, David Richmond, and Joseph McNeil, were inspired by the call for nonviolent action for civil rights as expressed by Martin Luther King Jr. and Mahatma Gandhi. The freshmen's plans did not gel until after the Christmas holiday when Joe McNeil recounted his experience on the bus returning from his trip home to New York City. He was treated as an equal in the public accommodations in New York. Once in the South, McNeil was denied service in the Greyhound bus stations. The thoughtful, intellectual scholarship student from New York felt that this disparate treatment had to be confronted. The four friends discussed their plan. By February 1, 1960, they were ready to put it into effect.

At four in the afternoon, the four freshmen, dressed in their best Sunday outfits, entered the Woolworth store in Greensboro. They purchased a number of items in the store, and kept their receipts. With the purchases and receipts in hand, the four quietly took seats on the stools at the "whites only" counter and ordered coffee. They were refused service by the waitress and later by the manager himself, but they refused to leave. Sitting quietly but stubbornly, the students remained at the counter until the store closed, half an hour early. They were encouraged by the fact that an elderly white woman sat down next to them and whispered that it was about time someone did this. The next day the four students returned, accompanied by 25 men and 4 women. The students sat quietly and studied, with their textbooks on the counter, while whites crowded into the store and shouted racial epithets. The sit-ins spread throughout the region, due to newspaper and television coverage that was soon on the national news. The protest lasted six months. Woolworth's suffered a large loss in revenue as many locals boycotted the store in support of the sit-in. On July 26, 1960, the Woolworth's in Greensboro quietly desegregated the lunch counter, allowing the black employees to sit there and be served for the first time. Soon most of the lunch counters in North Carolina would be integrated, and the rest of the South followed. This courageous act carried out by four young men became one of the pivotal turning points in the civil rights movement.

CHARACTERISTICS AND FUNCTIONALITY

The building that housed the Greensboro, North Carolina, Woolworth's store was built speculatively by a developer in 1929. The architect was Charles C. Hartmann, who was from New York City. He apprenticed at architectural firm of Warren and Wetmore, where he worked on the plans for the New York's Grand Central Station. Hartmann later went to work for the firm of William Lee Stoddart that specialized in hotel design. One of the commissions Stoddart received was to design the O. Henry Hotel in Greensboro, North Carolina. Hartmann moved to Greensboro to work on the project. In 1921, he was given the commission to design the iconic skyscraper in downtown called the Jefferson Standard Building by the vice president of the Jefferson Standard Life Insurance Company Julian Price, but only if Hartmann would promise to open a practice in Greensboro. Hartmann complied, and spent many years working in the state. The building that housed the Woolworth's store was part of the 1920s' development in downtown Greensboro. Several buildings were built in the Art Deco style in Greensboro. These included the Woolworth's building and the Kress building. The Woolworth's building, a two-story commercial structure, had wide plate glass storefront windows. Spanning the length of the storefront was the iconic red "F. W. Woolworth Co." sign in gold letters. On either side of the gold letters was a diamond shape with a "W" inside of it. Above the sign was the second floor, faced in Indiana limestone with five bays of tripartite windows, with a large window in the center flanked by two narrow windows. Above the windows was an Art Deco narrow frieze spanning the facade. The building was topped by a limestone parapet wall interrupted by notches that contained Art Deco versions of Greek urns, made of granite. Directly under the bronze urns attached to the top of the red sign were bronze acroteria, which were attached to the limestone mullions between the large second-floor window bays. Other elements on the facade of the building included fluted pilasters and medallions. The building, although simple, had various classical elements interpreted in the 1920s' Art Deco style.

KEY STATISTICS

The Woolworth's store was located at 132 South Elm Street in Greensboro, North Carolina. The interior of the store contained 25,000 square feet of retail space and a marble staircase. The lunch counter had a total of 66 stools that faced rose-tinted mirrors. The Woolworth's store has been converted to the International Civil Rights Center and Museum. A section of the lunch counter is on view at the Smithsonian Museum in Washington, D.C.

CULTURAL SIGNIFICANCE

The sit-in that was initiated by four teenagers in Greensboro ignited a movement to integrate public accommodations throughout the South. In 1960, six years after *Brown v. the Board of Education*, the landmark Supreme Court decision that integrated schools, Jim Crow laws were endemic in southern states. The Civil Rights Act would not be passed until 1964. But after the successful sit-in at Greensboro, peaceful demonstrations took place throughout the South. Many students banded together and forced the integration of restaurants and stores through sit-ins. The organization called the Student Nonviolent Coordinating Committee (SNCC) was formed in April

1960 by Ella Baker in Raleigh, North Carolina. These students believed in the nonviolent actions as demonstrated by Mahatma Gandhi. Congressman John Lewis from Georgia was the chairman of SNCC in 1963.

The cultural significance of the Woolworth's lunch counter in Greensboro, North Carolina, is more important than the architectural significance. The counter was a simple laminate; the swivel stools had vinyl seats and chrome backs. They were not unusual or significant. Even the food served at the lunch counter was mediocre. As Joe McNeil stated years later: "Well I went back when I got to school the next September. But the food was bland, and the apple pie wasn't that good. So it's fair to say I didn't go back often." But he knew he could go back any time. And that is how their sit-in protest helped to change the face of the country.

FURTHER INFORMATION: IMPORTANT PRINT, ELECTRONIC, AND MEDIA RESOURCES

"February One: The Story of the Greensboro Four." 2003. Rebecca Cerese and Dr. Steven Channing. *PBS Independent Lens.* http://www.pbs.org/independentlens/februaryone/. Accessed August 20, 2017.

"The Greensboro Chronology." International Civil Rights Center & Museum. https://www.sitinmovement.org/history/greensboro-chronology.asp. Accessed August 17, 2017.

"Greensboro Lunch Counter Sit-In." December 9, 1998. Library of Congress. https://www.loc.gov/exhibits/odyssey/educate/lunch.html. Accessed August 17, 2017.

Manieri, Ray. Old Greensboro Preservation Society. Fall 1979/Winter 1980. For National Park Service. Downtown Greensboro Historic District. http://www.hpo.ncdcr.gov/nr/GF0042.pdf. Accessed August 19, 2017.

Preservation Greensboro. "F. W. Woolworth Co. Building/International Civil Rights Center & Museum." PocketSights. https://pocketsights.com/tours/place/F-W-Woolworth-Co-Building-International-Civil-Rights-Center-Museum-132-South-Elm-Street-4645. Accessed August 19, 2017.

Steinhauer, Jennifer. July 18, 1997. "Woolworth Gives Up on the Five-and-Dime." *New York Times.* http://www.nytimes.com/1997/07/18/business/woolworth-gives-up-on-the-five-and-dime.html?mcubz=0. Accessed August 17, 2017.

The Woolworth Building, New York, New York

The tallest building in the world from 1913 until 1930 was the magnificent neo-Gothic skyscraper, the Woolworth Building in Lower Manhattan. Designed by Beaux-Arts architect Cass Gilbert, the Woolworth Building's stunning Gothic detailing gave it the moniker "the cathedral of commerce." F. W. Woolworth's, the original "five and dime store," had become a commercial behemoth by 1913. The owner Frank Woolworth wanted to build a new headquarters in downtown Manhattan that would display the power and influence of his successful corporation. The 60-story Woolworth Building has been admired for both its beauty and its technological innovations. It has been designated a National Historic Landmark and a New York City Landmark. The upper stories of the Woolworth Building are presently being converted into luxury condominiums.

Empire State Building

New York, New York
1931

BACKGROUND

The 1920s was a time of economic expansion in the United States, so much so that it became known as the "Roaring Twenties." Businesses in New York were booming, and so was the construction industry. Each developer aspired to erect a taller, more impressive building, and the race to build the tallest skyscraper had begun. The Woolworth Building in downtown Manhattan, completed in 1912, was 57 stories high and the tallest building in the world for 18 years. The architect of the Woolworth Building was Cass Gilbert, who worked in the Beaux-Arts style, and the tower had historical allusions in its stunning Gothic design. In the years after the completion of the Woolworth Building, architectural styles were changing, influenced by the French style that was dubbed Art Deco, after the 1925 Paris Exposition Internationale des Arts Decoratifs et Industriels Modernes. American architects began to interpret this decorative style in their designs. The architects who were commissioned to build the new tall buildings utilized aspects of the Art Deco style, and created a new American "skyscraper style." The style had a modern and industrial look, using modern materials like metals, and accentuating the verticality of the tall building. These were not Modernist buildings like the International Style skyscrapers of the 1950s and 60s, however, because they were highly ornamented. Modernist architects like Le Corbusier and Mies van der Rohe eschewed ornament in their designs, unlike the Art Deco architects. The boom times in New York City led to a construction boom in office buildings that was unprecedented until that time. Office buildings were sprouting up throughout downtown and midtown Manhattan. Some of the most prominent ones were the Daily News Building, the RCA Building in Rockefeller Center, and the McGraw-Hill Building, all designed by Raymond Hood, and the Chanin Building and the Metropolitan Life North Building, as well as many others. The most prominent of these 1920s' buildings was the Chrysler Building. Because of the mania for erecting taller and taller spires, two architects entered into an informal contest to build the tallest building. These architects, William

Van Alen and H. Craig Severance, were rivals and former partners. Severance's design was for the Bank of Manhattan and Van Alen's was for the Chrysler Building, and both buildings were competing for the "tallest building in the world" moniker. The intrigue in this story comes when the wily automobile magnate and owner of the Chrysler Building, Walter Chrysler, became obsessed with his building being the tallest. He insisted on hiding the plans for the spire of the building, and hid the actual spire as well. It was constructed secretly and concealed inside the tower, and boosted up through the building at the last minute to enhance the building's height. Chrysler was the winner of the race for tallest building in the world, but not for long. Although the Art Deco spire of the Chrysler Building remains a beloved landmark today, it held the title of the tallest skyscraper only from its completion in May 1930 until April 1931, when the even taller Empire State Building was completed.

The Empire State Building, unlike the Bank of Manhattan or the Chrysler Building, was not built to represent a corporate brand. It was purely a speculative enterprise. The developer was a hugely successful businessman named John Jacob Raskob. Raskob was a self-made man from upstate New York who worked as a young man for a subsidiary of the DuPont chemical industry. Raskob impressed Pierre DuPont, who hired him. Eventually DuPont made him vice president of finance of the E. I. DuPont de Nemours Company in Delaware. Raskob was interested in the automobile industry and invested in the newly formed General Motors Corporation in the early 1900s. He convinced DuPont to invest as well. Both of them made millions from the investment. DuPont became chairman of the board and Raskob became chairman of the Finance Committee. Raskob subsequently befriended a New York politician named Alfred E. Smith, known as Al Smith, a populist Irish Democrat and governor of New York. Although as a wealthy businessman, Raskob voted Republican, he moved to the Democratic Party when he started supporting the campaign of Al Smith. A popular governor, Smith decided to run for president in 1928 against Herbert Hoover. He appointed Raskob to be his campaign manager. Smith was up against a number of tailwinds in his quixotic quest to become president of the United States. He was Catholic and there was a prejudice against so-called Papists that Protestants feared would be too tied to the Pope. In addition, the economy was booming, and voters were leery of any regulations proposed by a Democratic president. Herbert Hoover, the Republican candidate, beat Smith in a landslide. Raskob decided to invest some of his fortune in real estate, as the skyscraper competition continued apace. He dreamed of having the newest, tallest skyscraper and decided to name it the Empire State Building, after the nickname of New York State. He also chose his good friend Smith, a former four-term governor of New York, unsuccessful presidential candidate and presently jobless, to be the president of the newly created Empire State Corporation. For this, Raskob paid Smith a princely salary of $50,000 per year. As a speculative venture, the Empire State Building was not backed by the fortunes of a huge corporation. The idea had to be sold to prospective investors and tenants. Raskob tied the concept of the building to the great state of New York and to the great former governor of New York. He was one of the first developers to heavily advertise the building with promotional brochures. In his brochure called "The Pharoah's Dream," Raskob used flowery prose to describe the yearnings of historical figures to "build a structure nearer to the skies than ever had been built before." Mentioning the pyramids, St. Peter's dome in Rome, the Washington Monument, and the Eiffel Tower, and also New York skyscrapers like the Woolworth Building, the Bank of Manhattan tower, and the Chrysler Building, the brochure ended with these words: "But Empire State is higher than all these. It carries to triumphant completion the vaulting ambition of the Pharaohs, of Pope Julius when he began the building of St. Peters" (Robins 1981, 6). In addition, Raskob, who keenly understood the advantages of effective advertising, used Governor Smith as a celebrity spokesperson. He also utilized public relations by commissioning photographer Louis Hine to take photos of the daring construction workers who worked on the I-beams hundreds of feet above the street. These thrilling photographs were used in the promotional literature and in media coverage and are still seen today. The frenzy of the skyscraper competition was to come to an end, as the stock market crashed two weeks after the project was announced. The project went forward anyway, and was opened on May 1, 1931, only 14 months after the construction was begun.

CHARACTERISTICS AND FUNCTIONALITY

The Empire State Building sits on the former site of the Waldorf Astoria Hotel on 34th Street and Fifth Avenue. The property was part of a farm owned by John Thompson, who sold it to William B. Astor in 1827. The Astor family, the longtime scions of New York high society, owned the property until 1929 when it was sold to the Empire State Corporation. Several members of the Astor family built their mansions on the property during the second half of the 19th century, forming the nucleus of New York's social elite at the time. When William Waldorf Astor chose to relocate to London in 1890, he decided to erect a hotel on the site of his house. His aunt's house was similarly demolished in 1897 and a hotel was built on the property. The two hotels were connected and became the first Waldorf-Astoria Hotel, New York's premier hotel. It lasted until 1929 when the Empire State Corporation purchased the land and the Waldorf-Astoria moved uptown to its present location on Park Avenue. By the 1920s department stores were opening up in the 34th Street area, moving uptown from their former locations on the "Ladies' Mile" between 11th Street and 23rd

Street. Office buildings were also being constructed in the midtown area by this time.

The architect for the Empire State Building was a firm called Shreve, Lamb, and Harmon. The company had worked as consulting architects on the newly finished Bank of Manhattan Building, which had competed with the Chrysler Building as the tallest in the world. It was also known as a firm that knew how to deal with the needs and demands of corporate clients. Richmond Harold Shreve and William Frederick Lamb were both alumnae of the Beaux-Arts firm of Carrere and Hastings, who designed the New York Public Library, among other New York City landmarks. They formed a firm called Carrere and Hastings, Shreve & Lamb in 1920. However, Shreve and Lamb left the firm to form their own firm in 1924 and by 1929, Arthur Loomis Harmon joined the partnership to create Shreve, Lamb, and Harmon. The member of the firm who is acknowledged as the principal designer of the Empire State Building was William Lamb.

Although trained in the classical Beaux-Arts tradition, Lamb was attracted to the Modernist Movement that was beginning to steer away from decorative ornament. In fact, he refused to describe his designs as Art Deco, even though we would call them that today. But the fanciful decorative elements of the Art Deco Chrysler Building did not appeal to Lamb. He had a spare, simple sensibility, which made his buildings seem more forward-thinking and modern in the long term. It also appealed to the businessmen who were developing the project, with time and money at a premium. The end result of the design of the enormous structure was primarily driven by space, time, engineering, and monetary concerns. The architectural program called for completion by May 1, 1931, which it actually bested by a month. This fast tracking of the project meant that it would take only 18 months from first sketches to opening day. The program also required that there could be no more than 28 feet from window to corridor, and that there be the use of limestone on the exterior, and that the project stay on budget. All of these requirements were met.

The Empire State Building has a five-story base that abuts the lot line on the facades facing the street. Because the base is five stories high before the building begins its setbacks, it does not overwhelm the street with its mass. The base has allusions to a group of classical columns with a tripartite design. The base is the horizontal band of storefront windows, the columns are the piers that separate the rows of vertical windows, and the capitals are the smaller windows at the top story of the base. After the building is set back severely from the street at five stories, it rises to the 30th floor with minor setbacks at the 21st and 25th floors. The next setback is at the 70th floor and then a larger one at the 81st floor. The rented commercial space ended at the 81st floor and the next five floors were for the executive suite. The 85th floor had the observatory. Above the observatory is the famous mast that was originally intended to moor dirigibles, but was never used for that. A second smaller enclosed observatory is located at the 102nd floor. The design of the building accentuates the tallness of the structure in its verticality. The main entrance to the building is on Fifth Avenue. There is a central pair of doors, with revolving doors on either side. A three-story high, three bay set of vertical windows rise above the doors, with carved stylized eagles on either side marking the five-story base. In between the eagles above the vertical windows is a sign carved into the stone in an Art Deco font that says "Empire State." Inside the doors is a grand entrance that has a chapel-like feeling with a long, tall, and narrow space. At the end of the space is a piece of artwork installed on the wall that depicts an aluminum image of the Empire State Building, with the map of New York State behind and with rays of a sunrise behind it.

KEY STATISTICS

The Empire State Building is located on Fifth Avenue between 33rd Street and 34th Street. The address is 350 Fifth Avenue. When it was completed in 1931, it was the tallest building in the world and remained so until the North Tower of the World Trade Center in New York was completed in 1970. It is 1,250 feet high and 1,454 feet tall with the television antenna. It has 102 stories, although the usable office space tops out at the 85th floor with the 86th floor serving as the observatory. Another observatory is located on the 102nd floor, and a small balcony is located on the 103rd floor that is accessible only by stairs and is open only with special approval. The views from the observatories are vast—on a clear day, a visitor can see these five states: New York, New Jersey, Connecticut, Pennsylvania, and Massachusetts. There are 1,860 steps from street level to the 102nd floor. The site is approximately two acres. The office space contained inside the Empire State Building is 2.7 million square feet. There are 200,000 cubic feet of Indiana limestone and granite on the exterior, 10 million bricks, and 730 tons of aluminum and stainless steel. There were 473 miles of electrical wire installed when it was built. A total of 3,400 workers were employed to complete the construction of the Empire State Building. In 1945, a B-25 bomber crashed into the building, between the 78th and 80th floors, killing 14 people. King Kong famously scaled the Empire State Building in 1933 in the film *King Kong*.

CULTURAL SIGNIFICANCE

The Empire State Building, although not the tallest building in the world anymore, is certainly one of the most beloved. It was actually voted America's favorite building in an American Institute of Architects poll done in 2007. The simplified version of the Art Deco style has been acclaimed by architectural critics as well. Although immensely tall, it does not crowd the sidewalk because of its numerous setbacks. It was designed before the onset of the International Style's plain boxes that were set away from the property line with wide open plazas, so it holds the street line well and does not leave a gaping hole along the street like so many of the later buildings do. Its major asset is its height and its graceful setbacks that can be recognized for miles around on New York's skyline. It was erected just as the Great Depression began. In fact it was dubbed the "Empty State Building" for the first few years as the owners attempted to lure tenants. The fees from the observatory, which was always immensely popular, paid the bills until commercial tenants could be found. But it was remarkably propitious that the architect, William Lamb, who preferred a simplified, straightforward design, and the developer John J. Raskob, who wanted to build an extraordinarily tall skyscraper, joined forces. The economy was tanking and Lamb and Raskob were compelled to adhere to a severely limited budget. This serendipitous combination of factors created the Empire State Building, which, at over 80 years old, remains the successful office building and admired landmark that it is today.

FURTHER INFORMATION: IMPORTANT PRINT, ELECTRONIC, AND MEDIA RESOURCES

Bagli, Charles V. May 4, 2013. "102 Floors, 10 Million Bricks and Tangled History." *New York Times.* http://www.nytimes.com/2013/05/05/business/empire-state-building-has-a-tangled-history.html. Accessed March 24, 2017.

Empire State Realty Trust. Empire State Building Fact Sheet. http://www.esbnyc.com/sites/default/files/esb_fact_sheet_4_9_14_4.pdf. Accessed March 27, 2017.

Goldberger, Paul. 1979. *The City Observed: New York: A Guide to the Architecture of Manhattan.* New York: Vintage Books.

Pierpont, Claudia Roth. November 18, 2002. "The Silver Spire: How Two Men's Dreams Changed the Skyline of New York." *New Yorker.* https://www.newyorker.com/magazine/2002/11/18/the-silver-spire Accessed March 27, 2017.

Robins, Anthony W. May 19, 1981. "Empire State Building." Designation List 143. LP-2000. Landmarks Preservation Commission. http://s-media.nyc.gov/agencies/lpc/lp/2000.pdf. Accessed March 24, 2017.

Run-Up Event

Every year, the Empire State Building sponsors the Run-Up event. In this event, held annually since 1978, hundreds of runners race up from the lobby of the Empire State Building to the 86th floor observatory. The total number of steps is 1,576 and the length of the run is 1,050 feet, or one-fifth of a mile, straight up. The fastest time recorded for this race was 9 minutes and 33 seconds, won by Paul Crake of Australia in 2003.

Flamingo Hotel

Las Vegas, Nevada
1946

BACKGROUND

The city of Las Vegas, Nevada, is a young city, even by American standards. It was founded on May 15, 1905, when 110 acres in the downtown area were auctioned off by the railroad company, the San Pedro, Los Angeles & Salt Lake Railroad. This new route connected Los Angeles to Salt Lake City, and created a rail shortcut to Chicago. Las Vegas was incorporated as a township on June 1, 1911. The location had a longer history, however. In the arid desert region of southern Nevada, the site of Las Vegas was an oasis. The artesian springs that were found there made it a convenient stopover in the Spanish Trail to Los Angeles as well as for the prospectors who sprinted out west for the California Gold Rush in 1848. The name "Las Vegas" means "the meadows" in Spanish. John C. Fremont, the well-known western explorer, soldier, and politician, made an expedition to the Las Vegas location and camped there in 1844, mapping out the region for the first time. The Mormons set up a fort at Las Vegas in 1855 to protect the mail route from Salt Lake City to Los Angeles. They briefly remained at the fort, growing fruit trees with the artesian water available there, but abandoned it in 1858. One Mormon missionary presciently judged the area as "the land that the Lord had forgotten." Montana senator William Andrews Clark purchased the fort in 1902 to service his proposed rail link to Los Angeles. The new railroad, owned by Clark, made its first run on January 20, 1905. Clark organized the sale of the 1,200 lots, which created the town in 1905. The area that he auctioned off is now what is known as Glitter Gulch, where many casinos are located. The city was virtually a company town in its first years, depending on the railroad as its economic base. It was also a town that reveled in its vice—saloons, casinos, and brothels occupied the area known as Block 16, which was set aside as the red-light district. Gambling was legal in Las Vegas until 1910, when Nevada grudgingly became the last state in the West to outlaw it. Gambling then went underground as it proceeded illegally. In 1921, a nationwide railroad strike prompted the Union Pacific Railroad to relocate its railroad repair yards to another city, an action that resulted in the loss of many of the region's jobs. With the city suffering fiscal woes in the 1920s, the Chamber of Commerce tried to reinvent the city as a resort, building golf courses and hotels. It created an advertising campaign, but it was not successful, as the golf courses were mostly dirt instead of grass due to the arid conditions.

The federal government came to the rescue of Las Vegas in 1929. Plans were finalized by the United States Reclamation Service for the construction of the massive Boulder Dam that was being built in the nearby Black Canyon of the Colorado River. The Boulder Dam, now known as the Hoover Dam, was designed to harness hydroelectric power from the river and provide fresh water in the newly created Lake Mead. The government considered housing the thousands of dam workers in the existing city of Las Vegas but scrapped its plans after it took into consideration the flourishing saloons, gambling, and prostitution trades, which were illegal according to Prohibition laws. The decision was made to build a completely new town for the workers, a town that would be strictly controlled. The newly created town of Boulder City established strict rules that prohibited gambling and drinking. After the work on the dam commenced, the grandeur of the colossal Depression-era project was promoted nationwide, and visitors began to pour into the region to see the great engineering work. The nearest city was Las Vegas, and the hotels began to fill up. In addition, when the workers had time off, they flooded into Las Vegas to escape the stultifying atmosphere in Boulder City. They were looking for fun, and Las Vegas aimed to provide it. Although the city had been ignored in its quest to house the over 5,000 dam workers, it benefited by them just the same. In 1931, the Nevada state legislature passed laws that legalized gambling in the city. Las Vegas continued to embrace its iniquity. Las Vegas further relaxed its laws in 1931 when it liberalized divorce laws. At a time when divorce was frowned upon and took months or years to achieve, Las Vegas introduced "quickie" divorce laws. Here, after a brief stay of six weeks at one of the glamorous dude ranches in the area, a man or woman could obtain a legal divorce. Marriage laws were relaxed as well, with the suspension of the waiting times required by most states. The economic effects of these laws also poured cash into the economy. Las Vegas made it through the Depression in better straits than most other cities, banking its vice-related funds that helped the city expand. It was during World War II that it got another boost from the federal government. Nellis Air Force Base was developed to train B-29 gunners, and later to train fighter pilots. Many members of the Air Force made Las Vegas their permanent home.

The growth of the city led to the expansion of the gambling business. Hotels were built with casinos attached. In 1932, the Hotel Apache in downtown Las Vegas was built, the first with an elevator and a central air-conditioning, a major improvement in a city that often suffers from over

100-degree heat. In 1941, the first themed hotel-casino was built on the Los Angeles Highway, also known as Highway 91 that was to become known as "The Strip." It was called the El Rancho Vegas and was built by a developer named Thomas Hull who had been successful with similar hotels in California. The advantage of the location was that it was outside of the city limits, and was not constrained by the city's tax laws and regulations. It was also cheap, wide open land, where developers could build larger complexes, which would attract the new driving public on their way to Las Vegas from nearby Los Angeles. The El Rancho Las Vegas had a casino, although it was added as an afterthought. The major attraction of the hotel was the large swimming pool that was located prominently near the highway so motorists could not miss it. Another hotel, the Hotel Last Frontier, was added to the Strip in 1942. Like most of the Las Vegas hotels, the Last Frontier boasted a western, frontier theme. Las Vegas portrayed itself as a frontier town, even though it was not. It was founded 15 years after Frederick Jackson Turner famously announced that 1890 marked the end of the frontier in American society. Las Vegas clung to its Wild West image in order to excuse its addiction to its vices. However, by 1946, a new type of hotel was in the works. This hotel would have a totally different style. It was called the Flamingo.

CHARACTERISTICS AND FUNCTIONALITY

The western themed hotels in Las Vegas were known as "sawdust joints" because they had sawdust on the floors. They were designed to appeal to the frontier image that was being promulgated by the city. In the 1940s, some developers began to consider changing the image, and built more luxurious "carpet joints" that featured softer and cleaner carpeting on the floors instead of sawdust. William R. Wilkerson, the publisher of the *Hollywood Reporter* and a nightclub owner from Los Angeles, had a vision. He was a gambler himself, with an unfortunate gambling addiction. Friends suggested that if he owned a casino, he could not lose as much. He envisioned building a casino in Las Vegas. This casino would appeal to the sophisticated crowd that he knew in Hollywood, and they were not interested in frontier-themed sawdust joints. Wilkerson's plan was to build a carpet joint, like none other seen before. He purchased a piece of property on the east side of Highway 91, now known as the Strip. These 33 acres cost Wilkerson $84,000 in 1945. The location was superb—the visitors from Los Angeles would see this property first when driving on the Highway 91. And Wilkerson had big plans—there would be no wagon wheels here. This hotel and casino would have 250 rooms, over twice as many as the other competing hotels. Wilkerson hired a prominent Los Angeles architect, George Vernon Russell. He named the hotel the Flamingo because of his interest in exotic birds. The Flamingo hotel would feature world-class restaurants, a nightclub, a health club, high-end boutiques, a swimming pool, a golf course, and a luxurious casino. It would be air-conditioned. Billy Wilkerson also has been credited with the concept that has become ubiquitous in casinos: no clocks to remind the customers of how much time they are spending there, and no windows to entice the customers back outside. Also, the location of the casino was to be in the center of the building, where guests would be forced to walk through the casino just to get to the registration desk.

Billy Wilkerson was a successful developer; his only flaw was his penchant for gambling. But it was a fatal one. He was able to accumulate two-thirds of the estimated budget of $1.2 million through legitimate sources. He proposed to win the rest of the money playing craps. But he ended up losing $200,000. In desperation, he turned to a New York gangster, Harry Rothberg, who offered him a loan of $1 million. The money was backed by a group of silent partners, also New York underworld figures that included Meyer Lansky, Gus Greenbaum, Moe Sedway, and Benjamin "Bugsy" Siegel. Wilkerson had known Siegel through his ownership of the Hollywood nightclub Ciro's, which was frequented by a bevy of Hollywood stars. Siegel demonstrated an interest in the ongoing construction of the new Flamingo Hotel. He pushed for additional control over the project and fired architect Russell and the interior designer, a man named Tom Douglas. The new architect was Richard Stadelman, and the new general contractor was Del Webb. Siegel eventually took over control of the whole project, with Wilkerson, who was out of money, merely a shareholder. He pushed ahead with the project, spending lavishly. After World War II, building was booming in the United States but building materials were scarce. Siegel had no building experience but he had plenty of access to money due to his successful underworld businesses. He paid extravagant sums for the materials and the tradesmen who were required to complete the hotel. He flew in plumbers and carpenters to complete the work and paid extra on the black market for materials. He even insisted on a separate sewer line for each room. Even though he was forced to scale back the construction program of the hotel significantly, by the end of the project, Siegel found himself over budget upward of $4 million. Wilkerson was eliminated from the project by Siegel totally. The grand opening took place on December 26, 1946. The hotel was not completed, but the opening was held anyway. A winter storm was blanketing the region and many guests did not appear. The opening was a disaster. The rooms were unfinished and the air-conditioning not working. The hotel hemorrhaged money and closed four weeks later. It reopened in March and it was eventually a resounding success. But it was too late for Siegel. On June 20, 1947, while relaxing at his girlfriend's house in Beverly Hills, California, he was shot in the head and killed. Although the murder is officially still unsolved, it is believed that Siegel's mob associates were tired of supporting his profligate spending. They also suspected that Siegel stole from them during the period of the Flamingo's construction.

The Flamingo Hotel was taken over by a group of the mob investors and renamed the Fabulous Flamingo in 1947. Morris Rosen, another of Siegel's mob associates, bought the hotel from Siegel's Nevada Projects Corporation. The silent partners included Meyer Lansky.

The modern Flamingo Hotel design represented a major departure from the previously wild west style of the earlier Las Vegas hotels. It featured large expanses of glass storefront windows with metal framing. No longer was there any wood paneling. The upholstery was pink. The style of architecture was similar to the "Googie" style found in California, named after the Googie coffee shop on the Sunset Strip. The style was modern, with an overhanging roof over the plate glass windows. It had strong horizontal massing. A vertical element was added with the tall, green, rectangular neon sign called a pylon, which was attached to the roof. It announced the name of the hotel "Flamingo" in vertical letters, with a stylized pink flamingo depicted at the top.

KEY STATISTICS

The Flamingo Hotel is located at 3555 South Las Vegas Boulevard, four miles from downtown Las Vegas. The project cost ballooned from an estimated $1.2 million to a final cost of $6 million. The hotel still exists, but it has been changed significantly over its 70 years. There are presently 3,626 rooms, but at the opening of the hotel in 1946, there were only 105.

CULTURAL SIGNIFICANCE

The mobster Bugsy Siegel has been celebrated as the founder of the modern Las Vegas casino. He was a colorful character, a handsome, charismatic mobster who was entranced with glamorous Hollywood and its beautiful stars. Also, he was murdered in spectacular fashion. His murder was covered in lurid detail by the press at the time. A movie was made in 1992 depicting his life and his murder, starring Warren Beatty as Siegel, so the myth continues. However, he was not in fact responsible for the innovations that were introduced in the Flamingo Hotel. The person responsible for those was Billy Wilkerson. Wilkerson had the vision that revolutionized the Las Vegas casino. The western style was eschewed by Wilkerson, as he preferred the California Googie style, a modern California style that emerged after World War II. Wilkerson imagined the casino as a destination, without access to timekeeping, windows, or other distractions. He envisioned a huge resort, with all leisure activities right there, away from the city. His vision has been the norm in ever larger casinos in Las Vegas and throughout the world. The involvement of Bugsy Siegel, however, was also influential. Mobsters developed a significant involvement in the financing of the casinos of Las Vegas during the 1940s and 50s. A two-year investigation by the United States Senate Special Committee to Investigate Crime in Interstate Commerce led by Senator Estes Kefauver into mob ties in Las Vegas exposed the existence of the organized crime syndicate. Las Vegas has grown exponentially since the first casinos were built on the Strip in the 1940s, with the mega-resort-casinos getting grander and more outlandish every year. The Flamingo Hotel was just the beginning.

FURTHER INFORMATION: IMPORTANT PRINT, ELECTRONIC, AND MEDIA RESOURCES

Al, Stefan. 2017. *The Strip: Las Vegas and the Architecture of the American Dream.* Cambridge, MA: The MIT Press.

"The Fabulous Flamingo Hotel History—The Wilkerson–Siegel Years—The History of the Las Vegas Strip." https://web.archive.org/web/20160111084052/http://classiclasvegas.squarespace.com/a-brief-history-of-the-strip/2007/9/23/the-fabulous-flamingo-hotel-history-the-wilkerson-siegel-yea.html. Accessed November 1, 2017.

"History of Las Vegas." 1995–2016. http://www.lvol.com/lvoleg/hist/lvhist.html. Accessed November 1, 2017.

Segregation in Las Vegas

Racial segregation was the policy in Las Vegas hotels in the 1940s. In 1947, African American singer Lena Horne was allowed to stay at the Flamingo Hotel. Lena Horne was the exception who proved the rule. A favorite of Bugsy Siegel, the gorgeous torch singer was allowed to stay at the Flamingo as long as she steered clear of the casino, restaurants, and other public areas. When she checked out, her bedsheets and towels were burned.

Source: http://www.smithsonianmag.com/history/the-vegas-hotspot-that-broke-all-the-rules-165807434/#0t-1drevUJr8XXcTP.99

Northgate Shopping Center

Seattle, Washington
1950

BACKGROUND

The sprawl of the suburbs was spreading at a fast and furious rate in the decades after World War II ended. A combination of factors conspired to bring about this suburban spread. There was a severe deficit of housing options for the returning soldiers and their growing families, due to the Great Depression and the war. Real estate developers came to the rescue, building small tract houses in suburban developments away from the downtowns. With the economy booming, cars were rolling off production lines. The automobile became a necessity for the suburban family. Because of the ubiquity of the family car, parking became an issue for shopping on the main street in the traditional town center. In addition, as the suburbs spread farther away from the city, it became inconvenient to travel downtown to shop and public transportation was inadequate. With the postwar production boom and the Depression over, and with houses to furnish and children to clothe, there was plenty to shop for. Developers saw an opportunity to build shopping centers along the major roads leading to the residential areas. The first "shopping centers" were what is called strip malls. These informal centers were set back parallel to the street with a small parking lot in the front. They were still oriented to the street, similar to the downtown shopping centers of traditional main streets. However, with even more demand for shopping opportunities in these burgeoning suburban areas, a novel idea was pursued. There was plenty of land to develop, and it was not expensive. The developers hired architects who could devise a new shopping scheme, eschewing completely the orientation to the street. This new concept eventually became the American shopping mall.

There have been several so-called fathers of the shopping mall. The first was John Graham, a Seattle architect who was hired by the developers Rex Allison and Ben B. Ehrlichman in 1948. Allison was the president of the Bon Marche department store, a fixture in downtown Seattle. His concept was to provide a shopping center to the newly developed north end of the city, which had been experiencing rapid growth. He formed the development company he called the Suburban Company, and decided to name the center "Northgate Regional Shopping Center" as a symbol of a "gateway to metropolitan Seattle." An enthusiastic announcement of the project was made in the newspaper the *Seattle Post Intelligencer*, on the front page of the Sunday, February 22, 1948 edition. The novelty of this new center was its orientation. Instead of locating it parallel to the street, Graham placed it in the center of the huge 62-acre property. The building could then be surrounded by parking, and customers could park closer to the various entrances. The other innovation was the central "street" in the shopping center. The stores faced each other, and formed a pedestrian street. The mall opened on April 21, 1950.

CHARACTERISTICS AND FUNCTIONALITY

The layout of the Northgate Shopping Center formed the prototype for most of the American shopping malls that have been built in the next half-century. The center pedestrian walkway was lined with stores. There were two large department stores in the center of the mall, and one more at the end. The architect John Graham hoped to encourage shoppers past the mall's smaller stores while walking to the department store at the end of the mall. In fact, later mall designers located the larger stores, called "anchor stores," always at the ends of the mall, in order to force shoppers past the smaller stores in the center. Northgate was the first shopping center to be called "the mall" although its official name was Northgate Regional Shopping Center. At first, the "decorative parkway" at the center of the shopping street was uncovered, although there were covered sidewalks abutting the store entrances. The center of the mall was completely covered some years later. Part of the unique design of the center was the tunnel system located under the building, where trucks could deliver the goods directly to the stores. In addition to the three-story Bon Marche department store, the original mall had an A&P supermarket, Nordstrom's, and a Newberry 5 and 10 cent store. A movie theater opened the following year, which was the first mall movie theater in the country. A building housing a medical and dental facility also opened in 1951. A totem pole, rising 59 feet, was added to the main entrance of the mall in 1952, designed by local sculptor Dudley C. Carter.

KEY STATISTICS

The Northgate Regional Shopping Center (now known as Northgate Mall) is located seven and a half miles north of downtown Seattle. While it is presently in the city of Seattle, when it was built it was outside of the city limits in a community called Maple Leaf. Its location is between NE 103rd Street and E 111th Street and between 1st Avenue NE and 5th Avenue NE. The property for the Northgate Mall was 62 acres when it opened, and the mall had 80 stores. Except for the anchor, the mall had only one story. The movie theater, with a single screen, had a capacity of 1,500. In 1965, Interstate 5 was completed, which serviced the mall and a $10 million expansion was built, adding 25 additional stores. The mall was enclosed for climate control in 1974.

CULTURAL SIGNIFICANCE

The mall holds an essential place in late 20th-century American culture. But Americans have continued to maintain a love–hate relationship with the mall, the king of American consumerism. The mall has had a remarkable history since the 1950s. Besides John Graham, the other man credited with the innovation of the modern design of the mall was an Austrian immigrant named Victor Gruen. Understanding the psychology of human consumer behavior, Gruen designed the first mall that has the salient features of the modern mall. An ardent socialist, Gruen believed that the 20th-century American mall could replicate the walkable street culture he had known in prewar Vienna, and the concept of the Ancient Greek agora, or marketplace. In 1956, Gruen designed the Southdale Mall in Edina, Minnesota. This groundbreaking mall was completely covered and climate-controlled. It was "introverted," with the stores and services facing inward. It also had two stories. This design made it easy for shoppers to make a circular path through the mall on one floor and then the other, ending up exactly where they began so they could return to their cars. Gruen designed a suburban "town center" concept, with a central light-filled atrium boasting fountains, landscaping, and areas for people to gather. The Southdale Mall was an instant success. It was copied ad infinitum in every corner of the country. As the millions of spec homes were built farther away from the cities into the suburbs, hundreds of malls were built alongside them. When Victor Gruen died in 1980 at the age of 76, he was inconsolably disenchanted by what had become of his innovation. He felt that the privately owned malls that had become a fixture in American culture were simply engines for profit. He saw vast acres of parking lots and saw only ugliness. In a speech made in London in 1978, Gruen asserted that he "refused to pay alimony for those bastard developments" (Gladwell 2004). He moved back to Vienna to spend the last years of his life a disillusioned man.

Another factor that contributed to the proliferation of shopping malls throughout the country is a little-known tax policy change. Up until 1954, developers were allowed to set aside income, tax-free, as depreciation, for a total of 40 years. Therefore, the annual set-aside allowed was one-fortieth of the value of the building. The 1954 tax change permitted depreciation at an accelerated 20-year rate. This encouraged development of large shopping centers as a money-making tool. After milking the project tax benefits, the developer would sell the mall at a profit. Records have shown that many of the multitudes of malls that were developed in the late 20th century were not necessarily in the newly populated suburbs. Developers would look for the cheapest land, beyond the suburban developments, to build the new malls. Sometimes they would even build malls in areas that were actually losing population. These real estate investments were made simply for a quick profit. The unfortunate result of all this overdevelopment has been the closing of the least profitable malls throughout the country in the last 20 years.

The other unfortunate result of the explosion of shopping malls throughout North America was the disintegration of the cities' central business districts. As the suburbs grew, and malls were built, the main streets of the nation's towns and cities declined. Middle-class families left the cities and moved to the suburbs. The people who could not afford a house in the suburbs were left in the ever-poorer cities. As racial minorities became the majority in the city, more white flight occurred. The mom-and-pop shops in the downtowns closed. Car culture reigned. The malls, owned by private developers, appropriated the public realm of the city streets and parks. However, the situation has begun to change. With smaller families and a desire for better quality of life, young millennials and some older baby boomers have discovered the downtown's amenities and have relocated to revitalized cities, helping central business districts revive. The overdevelopment of the shopping malls has led to the phenomenon of the "dead mall," left as abandoned scars on the suburban landscape. Some planners and academics are proposing novel uses for these acres of empty buildings and parking lots, as community centers or other community-based facilities. If this works, these former developers' profit centers could at last be used for public service instead of capitalist greed.

FURTHER INFORMATION: IMPORTANT PRINT, ELECTRONIC, AND MEDIA RESOURCES

Esri, Natasha Geiling. November 25, 2014. "The Death and Rebirth of the American Mall." *Smithsonian Magazine.* http://www.smithsonianmag.com/arts-culture/death-and-rebirth-american-mall-180953444/. Accessed February 18, 2017.

Gelernter, Mark. 1999. *A History of American Architecture: Buildings in Their Cultural and Technological Context.* Hanover and London: University Press of New England.

Gladwell, Malcolm. March 15, 2004. "The Terrazzo Jungle." *New Yorker.* http://www.newyorker.com/magazine/2004/03/15/the-terrazzo-jungle. Accessed February 18, 2017.

King, Elizabeth. "The Rise and Fall of the American Shopping Mall." *Broadly, Vice Media.* https://broadly.vice.com/en_us/article/the-rise-and-fall-of-the-american-shopping-mall. Accessed February 18, 2017.

McNerthney, Casey. February 17, 2013. "Northgate—Nation's First Suburban 'Mall'—Announced 65 Years Ago This Week." Seattlepi.com. http://www.seattlepi.com/local/seattle-history/article/Northgate-nation-s-first-suburban-mall-4286441.php. Accessed February 18, 2017.

"Northgate Mall." Mallhistory.com. http://www.mallhistory.com/malls/northgate-mall-seattle-wa. Accessed February 18, 2017.

Wilma, David. August 2, 2001. "Northgate Shopping Mall (Seattle) Opens on April 21, 1950." Historylink.org. http://www.historylink.org/File/3186. Accessed November 6, 2016.

"Dead Malls"

The proliferation of suburban shopping malls in the late 20th century served as the death knell of many American main streets in cities and towns. Families hopped into their cars and drove on the interstate to the mall. This was where they did their shopping, but malls became much more. They developed into privately financed public squares. The streets, the sidewalks, and the public parks of the past were now consolidated into the two stories of the mall, where the young and the old would stroll from one anchor department store to another, or linger at the food court for hours. Many teenagers of the 1960s, '70s, and '80s squandered much of their free time at the mall, hanging out with their friends. But in the 1990s, the situation began to change, with 1986 serving as the apex of the shopping mall construction craze. Some districts overbuilt, constructing malls close to each other in areas that did not have a population to support it. In addition, the new trend was the so-called big box store. These stores, like Walmart, Target, Costco, K-Mart, and others, never attached themselves to the mall anchor spaces. They preferred to build freestanding structures, possibly farther out in the suburbs, with cheaper land and more parking. People were attracted to the bargains offered in these big box stores and flocked to them, ignoring the showy malls with their prettier interiors and higher prices. As the public eschewed the pricier department stores, venerable standbys like Macy's, Sears, and J. C. Penney began to shut their least profitable stores. Without the requisite anchors, the economic doom of many malls was ensured. Malls have suffered an even bigger blow with the onset of online shopping. The 21st century is the age of the Internet. Although Amazon was founded in 1994, it was the second decade of the 21st century that brought online shopping to the forefront and made Amazon the largest Internet company in the world. The number of so-called dead malls littering the suburban landscape is increasing. Whereas the age of the automobile ushered in the advent of the shopping mall, the age of the Internet seems to have spelled its doom.

Sun Record Studio

*Memphis, Tennessee
1950*

BACKGROUND

When World War II ended, an era of prosperity dawned. Millions of postwar marriages led to the baby boom of the 1940s and 50s. The culture became more youth-centered. All of a sudden there was a new focus on a novel age-group—the teenager. Although the term "teenage" was coined in the 1920s, the group that came to be known as teenagers hit the scene in a big way in the 1940s. A 1944 photo essay in the popular *Life* magazine described teen-agers as a distinct group in a world of their own: "It is a world of slumber parties and the Hit Parade, of peanut butter and popcorn and the endless collecting of menus and match covers and little stuffed animals. American businessmen," *Life* proclaimed, "have only recently begun to realize that teen-agers make up a big and special market" (Cosgrove). This growing cohort of young people, neither children nor adults, was developing their own separate culture. They spent more hours in high school where they enjoyed more extracurricular activities. They hung out at luncheonettes and diners with their friends where they played their favorite tunes on the juke box. They had an unprecedented amount of freedom. With this freedom and newly acquired cash in their pockets, teenagers presented a powerful target market.

The music industry had not yet figured out how to exploit this market effectively. Popular music after World War II, listened to by the white middle class, had mutated into an unimaginative assortment of tedious pop singles and novelty songs. The music industry, dominated by a small number of powerful record companies, was ruled by the charts invented by *Billboard* magazine. These charts were divided into three categories: rhythm and blues, pop, and country-and-western. Rhythm and blues, or R & B, was formerly known as "race music," the popular music that was targeted to, and performed by, African Americans. The Jim Crow segregation that permeated American culture before the onset of the civil rights movement was also endemic in the music industry. Popular music that was targeted toward the black population was listed on the R & B charts published by *Billboard* magazine. The charts were compiled from data received from juke boxes in venues that were frequented by African Americans. Hence, white listeners were not often exposed to black popular music. This situation began to change when the Federal Communications Commission decided to allow more local radio stations to be licensed. Before the 1940s, the radio airwaves were dominated by national networks, which were able to control what was played. By providing cities and towns with their own local stations, there could be much more variety in radio playlists. The local stations gained in popularity throughout the country. A number of small local stations, including in the South, began to play black popular music. Once this music hit the airwaves, white people, especially teenagers, began to listen to it surreptitiously. This group of middle-class, white, affluent teenagers represented a huge hidden market for a new type of music. Sam Phillips, a DJ and enterprising entrepreneur with a new recording studio in Memphis, Tennessee, recognized this potential and was one of the major figures who discovered how to exploit this market.

Sam Phillips was born near Florence, Alabama, in 1923 to a family of poor tenant farmers. He developed an appreciation for music as a young child, and an understanding of how both poor blacks and whites depend on the power of music in their daily lives. Phillips made his first visit to the city of Memphis as a teenager on a trip with his family, and he fell in love with the African American blues music he heard on the famous Beale Street. Never able to complete high school due to his father's bankruptcy and subsequent death at an early age, Phillips worked in a variety of jobs. But his goal was to work at a radio station. He found his dream job when he was offered a position as the DJ for WREC in Memphis, which broadcast from the rooftop garden at the posh Peabody Hotel. Although Nashville in eastern Tennessee was the home of the Grand Ole Opry that promoted white country music that originated in the British Isles, Memphis had a culture that promoted both black and white music. This included country and western, bluegrass, blues, gospel, and rhythm and blues. Phillips soon aspired to set up his own recording studio. In January 1950, Sam Phillips opened a business at 706 Union Avenue, near downtown Memphis, which he named Memphis Recording Service, later to be known as Sun Records. Phillips's new dream was to open a music studio where he could record all the types of music that were percolating up through the destitute districts of the Mississippi Delta. Phillips accepted all comers—his business card read the following: "We record Anything—Anywhere—Anytime." Although he made money on paid recordings of weddings, bar mitzvahs, and advertising, his aim was to discover unknown musical talent. He recorded black blues musicians as well as white country and gospel singers. Phillips stated that he felt there were markets for this type of music, especially the blues that were not being reached. Sun Studio did not produce records in the first years. Phillips sent his master recordings to various record companies. But in 1952, he decided that he wanted more control over what got produced, and he started his own record company that he called Sun Records. He relished the idea of a rising sun, a new opportunity, to describe these budding artists. Phillips welcomed many musicians to his studio and his ability to recognize talent ensured that he eventually entertained a litany of the foremost musical talents of early rock and roll. In fact, Phillips has been dubbed the man who invented rock and roll. If he did not actually invent it, he surely discovered it. His list of discoveries includes the blues great B. B. King and rock and country stars Johnny Cash, Roy Orbison, Carl Perkins, and Jerry Lee Lewis. His most famous discovery, however, was the legendary Elvis Presley, who wandered into the studio as a teenager and asked to record a birthday greeting for his mother. Phillips recognized something in his voice and called him back into the studio, with two backup musicians. When he recorded a cover of "It's All Right Mama," a song written by the black Delta blues singer Arthur "Big Boy" Crudup, Phillips thought he had a hit. And when Presley performed at the Memphis outdoor amphitheater Overton Park, behind the popular white country singer, Slim Whitman, the audience went wild. The naturally shy Presley was transformed on stage, as he gyrated and sneered his way through the song. Elvis Presley soon became a national sensation.

CHARACTERISTICS AND FUNCTIONALITY

The Sun Studio, opened by Sam Phillips in 1950, was originally an auto-related business, the Magic Throttle Company, in a part of town that contained that type of business. The storefront building was erected in 1908. It is a one-story brick building, narrow and deep. Although the address is 706 Union Avenue, it faces Marshall Avenue, about 20 feet from Union Avenue. The building next door is attached to the original Sun Studio and has two stories. It is currently used as a visitor's center although during the 1950s it was not part of the Sun Studio complex. The building at 706 is a storefront, and contains two large windows on either side of the central entrance door, which is glass. There is a transom above the door and windows, but it is covered with a wood panel that is painted white. The white paint, which contrasts with the varied earth tone colors of the brick, is continued along the doorway and under the storefront windows to from a base. The brick is variegated, and has a simple stone banding decoration across the front near the top that is repeated at the parapet roofline. Each end of the narrow front facade has a step-up decorative element that is similarly topped with a stone band. There are three neon signs on the facade. Over the door is a large sign with three individual letters in a semi-circle, stating "SUN" in yellow and orange. The storefront windows each have an identical neon sign that states "Memphis Recording Service" in red and blue. Inside the building are three rooms. The first room serves as an office and reception area. It has a pressed metal ceiling. The middle room is the recording studio. The studio has a large, horizontal window facing into the office, and a door. The control room is at the back of the building. Another window faces into the recording studio, linked by another single door. The floor in the control room is raised two feet above the floor of the studio. The window is raised as well. A door leads out of the building at the back to a parking lot. Sam Phillips designed the studio and added acoustical tile to the walls. It was one of the first recording studios that was acoustically designed. Phillips installed acoustical tiles with patterns and at angles that precluded any parallel surfaces in the room. The sound that was created in this unique studio has contributed to the remarkable recordings that came out of Sun Studio during its glory days of the 1950s.

KEY STATISTICS

Sun Studio is located at 706 Union Avenue in Memphis, Tennessee. It was renovated in 1949 by Sam Phillips and his assistant Marion Keisker. The original building for the studio has one-story and is 18 feet wide by 57 feet long. Inside the building, the reception area comprises approximately 200 square feet and is an irregular shape due to the angle of the street. The middle room, the recording studio, is approximately 18 feet wide by 30 feet long. The back room, used as the control room, is approximately 18 feet wide by 13 feet deep. According to his assistant Marion Keisker, the renovation work was all completed by Sam Phillips and Keisker with the money they were able to raise for the project.

CULTURAL SIGNIFICANCE

Sun Record Studio was seminal in the creation of the sound of early rock and roll. Sam Phillips understood how to elicit the raw, unrefined sound that was the hallmark of the fusion of blues, rockabilly, and country, which produced the singular experience of early rock and roll. The new teenaged cohort, increasing in numbers and influence, were ready to hear a new sound that they could claim as their own. When Elvis Presley burst onto the scene in 1954, teenagers embraced the music and the spectacle that Elvis presented. Here was something completely new. Elvis sang songs that were in the tradition of the black blues and gospel. When heard on the radio, most of the listeners assumed that he was an African American singer. But as a white performer, he appealed to the millions of white young people who were searching for something different. Sam Phillips, the visionary music producer, saw that he had a goldmine in his discovery of Elvis. A series of white performers from around the South began pouring in to the Sun Record Studio to try out for Phillips. He was overwhelmed by the interest, and in November 1955, Phillips sold Elvis Presley's record contract to RCA for the princely sum of $35,000. It was the most ever paid for a recording artist's contract, although, considering the phenomenon that Presley became, it seems like a mere pittance today. Presley now had a national stage, and Phillips had the time to develop more new rock and roll artists. His list of discoveries includes Johnny Cash, Carl Perkins, and Roy Orbison. Sun Studio moved to a larger location in 1959 and Phillips lost interest in recording new artists by the 1960s. He went on to open several radio stations, including one that had a staff of only women as administrators and disk jockeys, that Phillips named WHER. However, his overwhelming success was behind him. His vision for combining the multiple talents of the black and white musicians he saw in Memphis became the phenomenon known as rock and roll. With the growth of the recording industry, in addition to the advent of the television with its multiple music shows, rock and roll's audience grew exponentially, both nationally and internationally. As stated in the book *Recasting America: Culture and Politics in the Age of the Cold War*, in the 1950s, music "began to cross previously unsurmountable barriers of race, class, and ethnicity—a time when young artists and audiences transformed the dissonance and noise of urban life into a chorus of many voices . . . they carved out a place in popular culture for a vision of America as a land of a thousand dances" (May 1988). Memphis was the location where this transformation took place, and Sam Phillips with his Sun Record Company was the man who enabled it.

FURTHER INFORMATION: IMPORTANT PRINT, ELECTRONIC, AND MEDIA RESOURCES

Cosgrove, Ben. September 28, 2013. "Teenagers: A 1944 Photo Essay on a New American Phenomenon." http://time.com/3639041/the-invention-of-teenagers-life-and-the-triumph-of-youth-culture/. Accessed October 3, 2017.

Hajdu, David. December 3, 2015. "Sam Phillips: The Man Who Invented Rock and Roll by Peter Guralnick." *New York Times*. https://www.nytimes.com/2015/12/06/books/review/sam-phillips-the-man-who-invented-rock-n-roll-by-peter-guralnick.html. Accessed October 6, 2017.

May, Lary, ed. 1988. *Recasting America: Culture and Politics in the Age of the Cold War*. Chicago, IL: University of Chicago Press.

Menand, Louis. November 16, 2015. "The Elvic Oracle—Did Anyone Invent Rock and Roll?" *New Yorker*. https://www.newyorker.com/magazine/2015/11/16/the-elvic-oracle. Accessed October 3, 2017.

Morgan, Neville (Producer) and Guralnick, Peter (Writer). 2000. "Sam Phillips—The Man Who Invented Rock and Roll." Documentary. A&E Television Networks. https://www.youtube.com/watch?v=tYcadYX-sTyM; https://www.youtube.com/watch?v=Dan6idfM6sI.

National Park Service. "Sun Record Company/Memphis Recording Service." https://www.nps.gov/nhl/find/statelists/tn/SunRecord.pdf. Accessed October 6, 2017.

The Million Dollar Quartet

On December 4, 1956, four musicians walked into the Sun Record Studio in Memphis, Tennessee. The musicians were Elvis Presley, Carl Perkins, Jerry Lee Lewis, and Johnny Cash. The spur-of-the-moment jam session that took place subsequently has become one of the most famous recording sessions in history. It started out as a recording session for Sun's successful rockabilly star Carl Perkins. Sun Record owner Sam Phillips had invited his new artist Jerry Lee Lewis to the session, in order to add some piano to the recording. Elvis Presley, one of Phillips's discoveries who had moved on to RCA Victor Records, happened to stop in that day. Johnny Cash also stopped in, interested in hearing Carl Perkins's new recordings. When the musicians starting jamming, Phillips realized that he had a rare opportunity on his hands. He called his friend at the local newspaper who arrived with a photographer in tow. The session was recorded. The next day an article appeared in the *Memphis Press-Scimitar*, with a photograph of the four musicians, and the headline "Million Dollar Quartet." The one-of-a-kind recording was discovered many years later, and a two-album set was issued in the United States in 1990 with the title *Elvis Presley—The Million Dollar Quartet*. Most of the songs on the recordings are in the country and gospel genre. A musical called *Million Dollar Quartet*, based on this famous jam session opened on Broadway in 2010. It won a Tony Award for Best Featured Actor for Levi Kreis, who played Jerry Lee Lewis.

Lever House

New York, New York
1952

BACKGROUND

With the buildup of industrialization during World War II, the United States had an economy that was ready and able to produce. Unlike the European countries that were decimated by the war's effects, Americans did not fight the war on their own home soil. American factories were prepared to retool from production primarily for the military toward civilian consumer goods. Consumers were primed to purchase new products, weary of dealing with the rationing during the war. Soldiers returned from the war, eager to get married and start families. Jobs were plentiful, and many soldiers took advantage of the GI Bill to attend college. As Americans hunkered down with their families in their new suburban homes, society veered away from the democratic socialism of Franklin Delano Roosevelt and back to a conservative belief in free enterprise. Large corporations were hiring young war veterans for their expanding corporate offices. With the growing demand for consumer goods, corporations were building impressive new headquarters that would house their growing staffs and serve as a public relations icon for their brand. The optimism of the times fueled a strong belief in the positive power of technology. The new materials, products, and designs were reflecting the American belief in science. Even in the world of architectural design, the rational and efficient Modernist designs were appealing to a public that was eager to move into an upbeat and prosperous world, eschewing the heavy ornament of the past. As described by Mark Gelernter, the postwar generation admired the Modernists because they "symbolized a break with the past and seemed to stand for a shiny new age of peace and prosperity." For the corporations, "the visual character of the Modernist style seemed to sum up their own self-images: rational, efficient, the confident possessors of immense power and wealth, and yet not flashy or desirous of individual expression" (Gelernter 1999, 263).

One of the shiniest of the growing corporations in the postwar era was Lever Brothers. A company dating from the late 19th century in northern

England, the Lever Company was started by William Hesketh Lever, with his product called "Sunlight" soap. In 1887, Lever built a model company town in Lancashire that he called "Port Sunlight." The company expanded and grew into foreign markets, including the United States, went public and changed its name to Lever Brothers. It merged with a Dutch company in 1929 to become the multinational corporation called Unilever, although the company used the name Lever Brothers in the United States until the 1990s. By 1950, with many successful soap products on the market, Lever Brothers opted to promote its brand with a new corporate headquarters located in New York City. The company was progressive and had some forward-thinking leaders at the time. The president Charles Luckman, known as the "Boy Wonder of Business," would later leave the business world to become a successful architect on his own. After Luckman left, the newly elected president of the company was Jervis J. Babb, who had served as vice president of the Johnson Wax Company. He worked in Racine, Wisconsin, in the celebrated Johnson Wax tower, designed by Frank Lloyd Wright. He knew that an iconic corporate headquarters could be a valuable advertising tool. In 1949, he hired the firm of Skidmore, Owings and Merrill to design the new building, which would be located on Park Avenue in Manhattan. Recent changes in zoning along a stretch of Park Avenue made it possible to build commercial structures on a previously residential street.

The architectural firm of Skidmore, Owings and Merrill was originally established in 1936 in Chicago as Skidmore and Owings. It received commissions in several parts of the country and proceeded to open offices in various cities, making it one of the first national architectural firms. The partners decided to concentrate on designing only in the "contemporary style" and set about to hire architects who specialized in modern design in order to create a corporate image for the firm. In 1939, they hired John O. Merrill, an architectural engineer. The firm then became known as Skidmore, Owings and Merrill. (The firm is still in business and goes by the name of SOM.) A designer who was hired in the 1930s was Gordon Bunshaft, who became the firm's principal design architect over the next several decades. The firm had an opportunity to design a new town for Clinton Engineering Works in Oak Ridge, Tennessee, during World War II. The federal government was seeking a firm that could design, in total secrecy, a completely new town for 30,000 people. The commission was for the Manhattan Project, the highly classified project to design and build the first atomic bomb. Because of the wide variety of skill sets at the firm, which included surveying, city planning, and engineering, Skidmore, Owings and Merrill was offered the commission. The firm hired a huge staff. The Oak Ridge commission gave the firm the opportunity to prove that it could design and administer large projects. After the war, the firm received several more major commissions. However, the acquisition of the Lever House commission was its most prestigious yet.

CHARACTERISTICS AND FUNCTIONALITY

Lever House is a steel-and-glass structure designed in the International Style. It consists of two simple major geometric elements: a horizontal slab and a vertical slab, clad in green glass. The directors of the company made the decision that they did not want to share any floors of the building with other firms. Therefore, accommodating their 1,200 employees, they did not need to maximize the floor area ratio, which is the maximum height and bulk allowed by zoning restrictions. In fact, the changes in zoning regulations that had recently occurred in New York City allowed the architectural firm to take advantage of the changes and create the building's groundbreaking design. Subsequent to the passing of the original 1916 zoning laws, tall buildings were required to include setbacks, which allowed for more light at street level. The revised regulation allowed buildings to avoid setbacks as long as the building covered 25 percent or less of the property. With only 24 stories, Lever House is not as high as it could have been by law. The tower is turned 90 degrees to the street, an innovation that made Lever House stand out along the avenue. The building next door is the New York Racquet and Tennis Club, designed by McKim, Mead and White in 1916–19. Its solid masonry facade in an Italian Renaissance style fronting directly on the street is in contrast to the light, diaphanous green glass of the Lever House adjacent to it. The design of the building is extremely simple—the only two elements of the building are a 1-story horizontal slab and a 22-story rectangular tower. The horizontal slab is raised up on columns, which give the building a plaza open to the street. Within the one-story slab was the company's dining room, and it contains a courtyard in the center. The exterior is clad in the same green glass as the tower. The tower is a narrow vertical slab set perpendicular to the street. The interior of the tower contained offices for the corporation. The service core and the elevators are located at the western end of the tower, where a masonry shaft is the only part of the building that is not clad in the green glass. The building uses a construction system consisting of a steel frame and reinforced concrete floors. However, the exterior walls are a curtain wall, which is nonloadbearing. The windows are not operable, and the building provided all heating and air-conditioning, which was expected to save on energy costs and was a novel approach at the time. Because of the sealed windows, the architects designed a built-in window-washing gondola, hung from a track on the roof, where window cleaners could descend outside the building in their gondola, cleaning the windows. The concept of the windows and the cleaners was a function of the branding model for the Lever Brothers Corporation, which was famous for making soap products. This building, as a symbol of the company, conveyed a sparkling, green image. It was also clean!

KEY STATISTICS

Lever House, completed in 1952, is an International Style office building located at 390 Park Avenue, between 53rd and 54th Streets in Midtown Manhattan. It contains 290,000 square feet and 24 stories. In the tower, the three topmost stories contain mechanical equipment for the building. The building is 307 feet high. The exterior has large windows in a green glass, which is heat absorbing and transparent. The glass panels are attached to narrow mullions made of stainless steel, which are anchored to the structural frame. The windows are green glass, and between the windows are spandrels that cover the floor slabs. They are also sheathed in a wire glass of the same color, giving the entire building an appearance of a transparent glass-enclosed box. However, at night, the lights inside of the building show the extents of the windows, reducing the monumental effect of the glass wall. There are six elevators. The structural system is a curtain wall, and it was one of the first of this type built in New York City.

CULTURAL SIGNIFICANCE

Lever House was celebrated when it opened in 1952 as "the most handsome and best example of modern architecture in New York," by the *New York Times* architectural critic of the time, who also called it a "sea-colored jewel" (Louchheim 1952). The building represented the corporate brand of Lever Brothers: clean, fresh, optimistic, and new. It was a new style that was embraced by critics, who were entranced by the efficiency, functionality, and technology utilized by architects in the International Style. One person who was not impressed was the iconic American architect Frank Lloyd Wright. He decried the formalism and orthodoxy of the International Style, preferring his own individual, expressionistic designs. The International Style office building, however, became ubiquitous in cities throughout the country, although not always successfully. The Seagram Building, designed by Ludwig Mies van der Rohe, was finished in 1958 and sits across the street from Lever House. It has become known as the masterpiece of the International Style. But Lever House was first and has remained a building that is taught in all architectural history books. The architectural critic Paul Goldberger described the Lever House in his book *The City Observed*, this way:

> [I]t is a building that really did help to make an era. When Lever House was in the planning stage, Park Avenue in the Fifties consisted almost entirely of masonry apartment houses, buildings built out to the street line and carrying a more or less even cornice line

down the avenue. Bunshaft changed everything. He scooped out a block of Park Avenue and inserted two slabs of stainless steel and glass, one set horizontally on columns over an open first floor, the other poised vertically above. The result was not only a change in use of Park Avenue, from a residential street to a commercial one, but a dramatic new model for the office building. Suddenly the tight city was opened up, both at ground level and above. Light poured in, open space flowed around. To a city accustomed to blocks and blocks of limestone and granite, it must have been a dazzling vision of a new world. (Goldberger 1979)

FURTHER INFORMATION: IMPORTANT PRINT, ELECTRONIC, AND MEDIA RESOURCES

Gelernter, Mark. 1999. *A History of American Architecture: Buildings in Their Cultural and Technological Context*. Hanover and London: University Press of New England.

Goldberger, Paul. 1979. *The City Observed: New York: A Guide to the Architecture of Manhattan*. New York: Vintage Books.

Landmarks Preservation Commission. November 9, 1982. "Lever House." Designation List 161. LP-1277. http://s-media.nyc.gov/agencies/lpc/lp/1277.pdf. Accessed March 13, 2017.

Louchheim, Aline B. "Building in the New Style." April 27, 1952. http://www.nytimes.com/1952/04/27/archives/newest-building-in-the-new-style.html. Accessed March 14, 2017.

Roth, Leland. 1979. *A Concise History of American Architecture*. Boulder, CO: Westview Press.

Wiseman, Carter. 2000. *Twentieth-Century American Architecture: The Buildings and Their Makers*. New York, London: W. W. Norton.

Lever House Restoration

The condition of the Lever House, completed in 1952, had suffered throughout the years as the glass elements had broken and been replaced with glass of a slightly different color. As one of the first sealed-glass curtain wall structures, the technology that was utilized was the latest available at the time. However, the iconic green glass curtain wall suffered over the years, with severe deterioration due to weather and material limitations. Water infiltrated behind the horizontal mullions, which resulted in the bowing of the mullions and breakage of many glass panels. In the late 20th century, the firm of Skidmore, Owings and Merrill (SOM) was hired by new owners of the building to renovate it. The original architect of the Lever House was Gordon Bunshaft, a partner at SOM, so it was fitting to engage the same venerable architectural firm to restore the building to its original luster after its many years of wear and tear. The renovations were completed in 2002. The glass curtain wall was replaced by a variety of new materials and modern construction methods that were able to recreate the look of the original curtain wall. These state-of-the-art solutions included stainless steel mullions and heat-strengthened Solex glass. The Lever House's signature green glass facade has now been restored to its original sparkle.

McDonald's

Downey, California
1953

BACKGROUND

The fast-food juggernaut that is the multinational corporation known as the McDonald's Corporation began its life as a modest but innovative drive-up restaurant in San Bernardino, California, a working-class city some 60 miles east of Los Angeles. It was the brainchild of a pair of siblings who had relocated from New Hampshire in the 1920s in the hope of finding work in the growing Hollywood movie industry. Maurice (Mac) and Richard (Dick) McDonald were the sons of Irish immigrant parents. When their father was fired after 42 years working for a local shoe factory, the brothers decided to try to make it in the Hollywood film industry. They both succeeded in working in the movie industry but merely subsisted in low-wage jobs. Saving what money they could, their first entrepreneurial attempt was to purchase a movie theater in the new suburb of Glendora, California. It was during the Great Depression in the 1930s and the brothers were not making much profit on the theater. However, the root beer stand outside of the theater was. So their next great idea was to build a restaurant, and they sold the theater and opened up a restaurant in the town of Monrovia, on Route 66. This food stand they dubbed "the Airdrome" because of its proximity to a small airport. The Airdrome was very successful, and for the first time, the McDonald brothers could start thinking on a grander scale. Looking at the growth of the sales of the automobile and the new roads, they knew that they wanted to attract families who were using their cars. Their next venture was a restaurant in a busy corner of the city, which they called McDonald's Barbeque. Cars would drive up to the parking lot where carhops, waitresses in uniforms, would come up to the car, take the order, and deliver the food back to the car on a tray. This was the typical system in that era in California's new car-centered suburbs. The method was slow and cumbersome, often leading to orders being mixed up. The pretty carhops attracted a dodgy clientele, and teenagers would make it their hangout. But the brothers continued to make a profit through the World War II years.

The postwar building boom hit California. The McDonald brothers saw an opportunity to differentiate themselves from the other roadside venues that were springing up in the area. They analyzed the records of sales and the issues they had confronted. Hamburgers, they discovered, were by far the most popular item on the menu, along with French fries. They were also easier to assemble and less messy than barbeque sandwiches. In addition, they wanted to eliminate the unwelcome attraction of the flirty carhops and their young male admirers. The McDonalds wanted to attract young families instead of teenagers. They sought to streamline the entire operation, in the manner of the famous Ford assembly line. When they heard about the innovative Levitt system on Long Island for building entire suburbs of identical houses on an assembly line, they were further intrigued. Making a risky decision, in 1948 the brothers suddenly shut down the restaurant and followed through with a total redesign. They considered a variety of options. When they were close to finalizing their design, they took the newly hired staff to a tennis court where they drew out the layout of the new restaurant in chalk in full size and had the staff go through the motions of assembling the food. With the most efficient method set in place, they were ready to complete the new restaurant. This restaurant was unique; it was like nothing else in the food industry. Eschewing the carhops who were causing distractions for the clientele, the new McDonald's restaurant boasted male workers only, wearing crisp white uniforms. Service was not provided; the customers had to abandon their cars and walk up to the huge, glass serving window and order their meal, with the sparkling clean kitchen on full display. The menu was now extremely limited. Only nine items were served, with no substitutions. Inside the restaurant, the efficiency of the system was maximized. Dick McDonald even invented a tool that would squirt the exact portion of ketchup and mustard onto each hamburger. Milkshakes were made five at a time in the fancy new contraption called the Multimixer. The brothers created an assembly line system that they dubbed the "Speedee Service System" that saved them money and time, and they passed some of the savings on to the customer. Prices went down, with hamburgers selling for a mere 15 cents, and the food waiting time was almost nonexistent. When the local customers realized that they could get the hamburgers cheap and fast, they flocked to the restaurant. Lines formed but moved quickly. McDonald's was a huge success.

Dick and Mac McDonald were proud of their success and considered selling franchises. They sold a small number of franchises in the California suburbs, with one in Phoenix, Arizona. Dick, who had no formal training, had a vision for a new design for subsequent restaurants. The McDonalds searched for an architect who would understand their concept and translate it into a set of plans. Rejecting a number of local architects, they eventually settled on Stanley Clark Meston in 1952. Meston had experience in designing civic structures, including schools and city office buildings. But his most relevant experience was his apprenticeship with Wayne McAllister, a Los Angeles architect who had designed a number of drive-in restaurants in the 1930s in the Streamline, or "Googie" style. These ultramodern, circular restaurants set California apart from the rest of the country in design. The McDonalds chose Meston and together they came up with the concept of the original McDonald's restaurants.

Meanwhile, the restaurant in San Bernardino was continuing to prosper. The brothers were proud of their Speedee system and they were happy to demonstrate the details of their efficient production method to eager would-be entrepreneurs. They did so when a discouraged multimixer salesman named Ray Kroc wandered in from Illinois. Kroc was having a difficult time selling his product, so he marveled at the McDonald's restaurant's order for eight multimixers. Kroc was further impressed by the success of the venture and the efficiency of the production system. He immediately saw a potential goldmine in franchising the operation. The McDonald brothers were content with the small group of franchises that they had accumulated. They could not see expanding away from the warm and sunny climes of southern California and Arizona. Walk-up windows were not conducive to cold, snowy winters. But Kroc would not be deterred. He begged the McDonalds to let him sell franchises nationwide. The McDonalds relented and drew up a contract with Kroc to allow him to franchise their system, insisting on using Meston's architectural design. With Kroc's business acumen, ruthlessness, and marketing genius, the rest is history.

CHARACTERISTICS AND FUNCTIONALITY

The oldest McDonald's still standing is located in Downey, California. It was the third McDonald's to be built and the second one that used Stanley Clark Meston's iconic design. The design was a combination of suggestions by the McDonald brothers and the architectural experience of Stanley Meston. The idea of the "golden arches" was sketched by Dick McDonald, to be located on either side of the building. He imagined the arches as an iconic advertisement, part of the restaurant's signage, as the beginnings of a branding campaign. The McDonalds understood that on a commercial strip, with the multitude of stores and restaurants, their restaurant would need to be easily differentiated by a passing car. Meston worked with his draftsman Charles Fish and designed two parabolic arches flanking the squat one-story restaurant with the glass walls and the cantilevered roof. The golden arch motif was repeated along the curb as a freestanding sign with the Speedee character, a chubby fellow in a chef's hat who pointed to the restaurant building. All the signage was outlined in red, white, yellow, and green neon to attract customers after dark. The structure had an angled glass front and sides, with a wide overhanging roof at the front that protected the customers from the weather. A dropped soffit above the glass contained another sign stating McDonald's, with the golden arches logo. Customers were free to gaze into the factory-like kitchen, where stainless steel and surfaces of red-and-white ceramic tile looked clean and modern. There was no inside seating or inside accommodation of any kind, only the walk-up windows. This innovative method of serving and unique architectural design were repeated throughout the country after Ray Kroc's franchising program began in 1954. The so-called Googie style of commercial architecture that was popular in the state of California could now be seen nationwide.

KEY STATISTICS

The McDonald's restaurant that still maintains the chain's original design is located at 10207 Lakewood Boulevard, in Downey, California. It was opened on August 18, 1953. The developers were Roger Williams and Burdette Landon, who were associates of the first franchisee Neil Fox. The first franchise was built in Phoenix, Arizona, in May 1953. Williams and Landon found a location in Downey, California, that was one mile from the downtown and surrounded by subdivisions abutting an orange grove. The reason that the restaurant in Downey, California, is still in original condition is that it was not part of Kroc's McDonald's Corporation for many years. It remained under the McDonald brothers' control and therefore was not required to fulfill Kroc's compulsory modernizations. It suffered from low sales by the 1990s and was damaged by the 1994 Northridge earthquake, and was subsequently closed. It came very close to being demolished when the public and the preservation community got together to save the building. It is now the premier tourist attraction in the city of Downey, California.

CULTURAL SIGNIFICANCE

Dick and Mac McDonald had a vision. They had creativity and drive. They saw the future in suburban drive-in restaurants, and they understood the value of creating an iconic building that doubles as a sign. They each had talents, which they combined to craft a novel and efficient food delivery system that provided quality food at a budget price. They were brilliant inventors. But the one thing that they lacked was the killer instinct. Ray Kroc had that instinct. He also had the vision and marketing genius that would make the McDonald's Corporation one of the most powerful companies in the world. After a rocky start in franchising, Kroc decided to purchase the land where the McDonald's were located, which made enormous profits for the McDonald's Corporation. He also took control of all the franchises, standardizing all aspects of the operation, ensuring quality standards throughout the chain. Kroc bought out the McDonalds in 1961, paying the brothers each $1 million with another $700,000 to pay the taxes. In the 1970s Ray Kroc wrote his autobiography, claiming to be the founder of McDonald's, and naming his first McDonald's in Des Plaines, Illinois, as the original one. Dick McDonald, still alive, was furious. Eventually, the McDonald's Corporation spokesman admitted that the McDonald brothers were the pioneers of McDonald's and helped to found the fast-food industry. Ray Kroc is cited as the entrepreneur who is responsible for the McDonald's Corporation.

Fast food has come under scrutiny in the last few decades, as the obesity epidemic has ravaged the United States. Books like *Fast Food Nation*, by Eric Schlosser, and *SuperSize Me*, by Morgan Spurlock, have identified the fast-food industry as a culprit in the added bulk and declining health of many people in this country. In addition, they decry the industrial farming techniques that have been used since the fast-food industry has taken hold. There are so-called food deserts in the country that lack supermarkets that sell fresh food but boast a variety of fast-food chains that are cheap sources of fatty, salty fast food. The innovative creation of the McDonald brothers expanded exponentially by Ray Kroc, has altered the eating habits of the nation, as well as the farming system. Little did they know, when they invented the Speedee Service System for efficient food preparation and delivery, that their little California drive-in restaurant would have such an enormous impact on the country, and the world.

FURTHER INFORMATION: IMPORTANT PRINT, ELECTRONIC, AND MEDIA RESOURCES

Gilpin, Kenneth N. July 16, 1998. "Richard McDonald, 89, Fast-Food Revolutionary." *New York Times*. http://www.nytimes.com/1998/07/16/business/richard-mcdonald-89-fast-food-revolutionary.html. Accessed August 13, 2017.

Hess, Alan. March 1986. "The Origins of McDonald's Golden Arches." *Journal of the Society of Architectural Historians* 45 (1): 60–67. http://www.jstor.org.proxy.library.csi.cuny.edu/stable/990129?seq=1#page_scan_tab_contents. Accessed August 1, 2017.

Hess, Alan. August 14, 2013. "The Oldest McDonald's as Architecture." *Alan Hess on Architecture*. http://alanhess.blogspot.com/2013/08/the-oldest-mcdonalds-as-architecture.html. Accessed August 1, 2017.

Napoli. Lisa. November 1, 2016. "The Story of How McDonald's First Got Its Start." Smithsonian. com. http://www.smithsonianmag.com/history/story-how-mcdonalds-first-got-its-start-180960931/. Accessed August 1, 2017.

Schlosser, Eric. 2012. *Fast Food Nation*. New York: Mariner Books.

The Founder (2016)

The Founder is a biopic that tells the story of McDonald's, the brothers who invented the concept, and the man who took it over, franchised it, and made it an international juggernaut. Released in late 2016, *The Founder* stars Michael Keaton as Ray Kroc, the man who made McDonald's into a fast-food phenomenon. Keaton received positive reviews for his magnetic performance as the hustling salesman Kroc. The movie was directed by John Lee Hancock and costarred Laura Dern as the long-suffering first wife of Ray Kroc, and Nick Offerman and John Carroll Lynch as Richard and Maurice McDonald.

Ruth Peterkin/Dreamstime.com

Fontainebleau Hotel

Miami Beach, Florida
1954

BACKGROUND

Today, the state of Florida is popularly known as the "Sunshine State" and as a retirement and vacation mecca. But it was not until 1896 that the city of Miami in southern Florida began to be developed as a result of the construction of the Florida East Coast Railway. This railroad was owned by Henry Morrison Flagler, a wealthy industrialist who was one of the founders of Standard Oil. Living in New York and hoping to help his ailing wife by relocating to a state with a more favorable climate, Flagler traveled to St. Augustine in northern Florida. With a head for business and plenty of funds, Flagler resolved to build a luxury hotel in St. Augustine and to extend his development to Palm Beach. Annoyed that the area had suffered from a couple of winter freezes, Flagler accepted an offer of land farther south in the Miami area. He built the railroad, opening it in 1896. Flagler was responsible for building the first hotel in Miami, as well as public buildings, schools, housing for workers, and churches, and has become known as the father of both Miami and Palm Beach. The same year that the railroad was completed, 1896, John Collins went to Miami, where he founded the Miami Beach Improvement Company. Collins, with auto parts industrialist Carl Fisher, was responsible for constructing the first bridge to Miami Beach in 1913. Collins cleared the mangrove swamps along the Miami Beach barrier island and cultivated the land. With the land accessible, real estate development took off on Miami Beach, which was officially incorporated as a city in 1917. Fisher was the earliest developer to construct hotels that created the tourist mecca that became Miami Beach. His first hotels were built in the 1920s in the southern section of the city. The economic boom of the 1920s helped the city thrive, but after a hurricane in 1926 and the onset of the Great Depression in 1929, tourism flagged. However, the late 1930s brought another boom to the area, and many new hotels were built. These hotels were designed in the popular Art Deco style. They are part of the revitalization of the South Beach area in Miami Beach today. In the 1940s, the hotels in Miami Beach were used as training headquarters during

World War II, with over 200 hotels leased by the Army Air Corps Technical Training Command. There were 500,000 enlisted men and 50,000 officers trained at the Miami Beach facility.

The northern end of Miami Beach was home to "Millionaire's Row." This was where numerous northern industrialists built winter homesteads. These wealthy families included Carl Fisher, and the owners of Warner Brothers, Russell Stover candies, R. J. Reynolds cigarette company, and others. The estate of the tire magnate Harvey Firestone was built in 1916 and purchased by Firestone in 1923. After Firestone's death, his family relocated to Palm Beach, and the estate was utilized by the army officers during World War II but left abandoned after the war. The city of Miami Beach was flourishing again in the post–World War II economic boom. Visitors to Miami Beach included former service members who were posted there during the war. Transportation to Florida was improved as the commercial airline industry took off and made Miami one of its major hubs. After the war, the interstate highway system brought fast automobile travel to the nation. New hotels were built in the late 1940s, which were larger but still retained the Art Deco and Streamline Moderne styles of the 1930s.

As the hotel section of Miami Beach was developed with larger structures, space for new hotels was at a premium. The New York developer Ben Novack, who was the owner of an existing resort in the Catskills, coveted the opportunity to build a hotel in Miami Beach. Eyeing the Firestone mansion's 14 acres, Novack was determined to secure the property despite the zoning law that prevented the construction of hotels within the "millionaire's row" district. The politically powerful magnates who owned property in "millionaire's row" were not happy to share the neighborhood with the hoi polloi that came to Miami Beach hotels. However, Novack was able to fight the city and had the zoning changed to accommodate large hotels like the one he was planning to build. Novack envisioned a grand, luxurious hotel like none other. He hired a New York–based architect named Morris Lapidus who was a Ukrainian immigrant. Lapidus had been successful in designing retail establishments and show windows. He moved on to interiors of resort hotels, designing the interior of the Sans Souci in Miami Beach in 1949. When Novack hired him in 1952 to design his dream hotel, Lapidus gratefully accepted the commission for an entire complex and not just an interior. He was so excited to receive this opportunity that he proposed an extremely low fee for the project, much to his chagrin, as the demanding and mercurial Novack insisted on so much work from Lapidus that he was forced to raid his own savings. When the hotel was completed, and Lapidus requested more money, Novack refused to pay him. Meanwhile, Novack had collected over three times the money from his outside investors (supposedly to pay the architect) and had pocketed the money. The hotel was opened in December 1954 at a total cost of $13,000,000.

CHARACTERISTICS AND FUNCTIONALITY

Novack's dream project was the Fontainebleau Hotel, named after the French palace of Fontainebleau, which Ben Novack and his wife had visited some years before. Novack liked the name because it sounded "catchy" and wanted to use a "French Provincial" style for his new hotel. His notion of French Provincial was not the authentic style that Lapidus knew. Novack made it plain that he desired "real luxury modern French Provincial," a nonexistent style. Lapidus deduced what Novack had in mind, and came up with a style that he called a mixture of French Renaissance and contemporary design. Lapidus's experience in designing show windows and store interiors helped him with the design of the Fontainebleau, which became a new style unto itself. Lapidus described his resort hotels as providing their guests with an experience of glamor. The interiors of his hotels were designed as stage sets, giving the guests an illusion of being on stage. The design of the Fontainebleau was intended to transport the visitor into a new dimension, beginning with the entrance, which was a driveway that curved around a large fountain. Inside the guests encountered a huge open lobby, with white marble floors accented by black "bow-tie" designs. The columns were marble with gold trim, and the chandeliers were crystal. The renowned "stairway to nowhere" was a floating stairwell that curved up the side of the lobby to a mezzanine that was not used, except to accommodate guests who would take the elevator to the mezzanine, only to descend the stairway, making a grand entrance into the lobby.

The exterior of the Fontainebleau has been called International Style, a style made popular by Mies van der Rohe. It is also known as MiMo, or Miami Modern. Unlike the sumptuous interior, the exterior of the original tower building of the Fontainebleau is simple, with curtain wall construction allowing for wide window expanses and a more open interior. The major feature of the original building, known as the Chateau Building, is the sweeping crescent shape of the tower, embracing the beach, and giving ocean views to the beachside windows. The white banding gives a horizontal appearance. The complex encompasses a complete resort facility, including a free-form pool and cabana complex, multiple restaurants, nightclub, cocktail lounge, and convention facilities. In 1959, an addition was built to the Fontainebleau, designed by the architect A. Herbert Mathes. A legal battle ensued between Novack and the owner of the adjacent property, the Eden Roc, who was a former partner of Novack named Harry Mufson. The architect whom Mufson hired to design his new hotel was Morris Lapidus. Novack was so angry that Lapidus had accepted the commission with Mufson that he asked his new architect to design the new addition with a "spite wall" that would block the sun from the Eden Roc's swimming pool for most of the day. Mufson sued, but lost the case, and the decision stated that he had no legal right to have the sun on his swimming pool. The case,

Fontainebleau Corporation v. 4525, Inc., was a landmark case that has been taught in law schools ever since. Mufson was forced to move his swimming pool to another location at a later date.

KEY STATISTICS

The Fontainebleau Hotel is located at 4441 Collins Avenue, Miami Beach, Florida. The original building of the Fontainebleau is on a lot that extends 700 feet by 500 feet, with Collins Avenue on the west and the Atlantic Ocean on the east. The Chateau Tower is 150 feet high and extends 440 feet wide across the crescent. It is constructed of concrete and block. There are 11 stories in the Chateau Building, with 554 guest rooms. The addition, called the North Tower, has 14 stories. Unlike the Chateau Building, it is rectangular in massing and is 416 feet long. It is also built of concrete and block. It sits on an east–west axis on the property. The Chateau Building had 550 guest rooms and the North Tower added 339 more when it was built.

CULTURAL SIGNIFICANCE

The Fontainebleau Hotel became a symbol for a specific time in the history of the 20th century in the United States. World War II was over, the economy was booming, and optimism reigned. The middle class had more disposable income and the upper middle class was growing. Television was a ubiquitous member of every American family, and the road trip was a summer ritual. Airplane travel became affordable for many families. The visionary developer and his imaginative architect teamed up to devise a new type of resort hotel for a new type of client. The availability of central air-conditioning made the heat of the subtropical climate of south Florida bearable. When the Fontainebleau opened, it made a big splash. It was extremely popular with second-generation Jewish families from the northeast who had become successful in business and had money to burn. This was a time when Jews were not accepted at all hotels and resorts. Hotels, resorts, and clubs often still had "restricted" policies that denied access to Jewish guests. But not the Fontainebleau. (The policies for African Americans, however, remained discriminatory for years. In 1963, Harry Belafonte was the first black performer who was given a room at the one of the luxury Miami Beach Hotels, the Eden Roc Hotel next door to the Fontainebleau.) The hotel also attracted a fast crowd of gamblers, performers, and members of organized crime groups. The most popular show-business personalities of the day always made the Fontainebleau a stop on their tours. The so-called Rat Pack group that included Frank Sinatra, Joey Bishop, Dean Martin, and Sammy Davis Jr. performed regularly at the Fontainebleau for years. Ben Novack had a luxurious apartment at the Fontainebleau where he reveled in the company of these famous celebrities.

The Fontainebleau Hotel was very popular among a large cohort of people. There was one group of people that was not impressed—architecture critics. When the hotel opened, the critics who reviewed the building panned the architecture, calling it kitschy and vulgar. In fact, for many years the architectural establishment virtually ignored Lapidus's work. In 1970, a retrospective of his work was put on at the Architectural League, where Lapidus's designs were roundly criticized. Ada Louise Huxtable, the *New York Times* architecture critic, dubbed Lapidus's designs as "uninspired supershlock." Another critic opined that he appealed to "the great mass of people who don't know the difference between architecture and Coney Island." (Interestingly, Lapidus stated in his autobiography *Too Much Is Never Enough* [Rizzoli 1996] that he was inspired in his designs by his childhood visits to the famous amusement park in Coney Island called Luna Park.) Lapidus defended his work throughout his long life. By the time of his death at age 98, in 2001, his work was going through a reappraisal in the architectural world. Postmodern architects started to appreciate the virtuosity and flamboyant exuberance of his designs. In his obituary in 2001, he is quoted as having said: "I wanted people to feel something. If two people were walking by one of my buildings and one said to the other, 'Did you notice that building?' and the other said, 'What building?' I've failed. But if he looks at it and says, 'Oh my god,' or 'That monstrosity,' I was glad. Because he noticed me" (Rothstein 2001). The resort hotel as envisioned by Morris Lapidus had an enduring influence. The Fontainebleau Hotel went bankrupt in 1977 as Miami Beach suffered a downturn in popularity and the resort hotels were burdened with debts. The resurgence of the midcentury style led to renovations of the great Miami Beach hotels including the Fontainebleau, which is now on the *National Register of Historic Places*. The influence of Lapidus's designs is widespread with the most extravagant and outrageous hotels in Las Vegas making the great Fontainebleau look puny in comparison.

FURTHER INFORMATION: IMPORTANT PRINT, ELECTRONIC, AND MEDIA RESOURCES

CBS Miami. 2012. "Narcy Novack Sentenced to Life in Family Killings Case." http://miami.cbslocal.com/2012/12/17/sentencing-day-in-narcy-novack-family-killings-case/. Accessed February 18, 2017.

City of Miami Planning Department. 2009. "Morris Lapidus/Mid 20th Century Historic District Designation Report." http://mimoonthebeach.com/pdfs/Morris%20Lapidus_Mid%2020th%20Century_FINAL_low%20res.pdf#page=3. Accessed February 9, 2017.

Friedman, Alice T. 2000. "The Luxury of Lapidus: Glamour, Class, and Architecture in Miami Beach." *Harvard Design Magazine* 11: 39–47.

http://www.nyc-architecture.com/ARCH/ARCH-Lapidus.htm. Accessed February 9, 2017.

Glatt, John. 2013. *The Prince of Paradise: The True Story of a Hotel Heir, His Seductive Wife, and a Ruthless Murder*. New York: St. Martin's Press.

Lapidus, Morris. 1996. *Too Much Is Never Enough*. New York: Rizzoli Books.

National Park Service. 2008. "Fontainebleau Hotel." https://npgallery.nps.gov/NRHP/GetAsset/ba895a1a-3110-4396-b7cb-f4dec3dee3f7?branding=NRHP. Accessed February 9, 2017.

Rothstein, Mervyn. January 19, 2001. "Morris Lapidus, an Architect Who Built Flamboyance into Hotels, Is Dead at 98." *New York Times*. http://www.nytimes.com/2001/01/19/arts/morris-lapidus-an-architect-who-built-flamboyance-into-hotels-is-dead-at-98.html. Accessed February 18, 2017.

The Fontainebleau Hotel in Popular Culture

The Fontainebleau Hotel has served as the location for many films and television shows. One of the most well known is the 1963 James Bond film *Goldfinger* starring Sean Connery. Several scenes take place at the Fontainebleau, including the opening aerial shot and the scene where Jill Masterson is famously painted gold. The hotel did serve as the setting for several scenes; however, none of the lead actors actually went there. The lead actors were filmed against a projection screen in Pinewood Studios outside of London, England. The famous scene from the 1983 gangster movie *Scarface* where Manolo, played by Steven Bauer, gets slapped in the face was shot at the Fontainebleau Hotel, although the hotel's name was never mentioned. In addition, several scenes from Whitney Houston's first feature film, *The Bodyguard*, were shot at the Fontainebleau Hotel in 1992. The film included scenes at the hotel's penthouse suite, pool, and nightclub.

Seagram Building

New York, New York
1958

BACKGROUND

The avant-garde artists and architects in Europe in the first decades of the 20th century were true radicals. Rejecting traditional design that included any type of applied ornament, this group embraced the new industrialized culture that was emerging. A school of design called the Staatliches Bauhaus (known as the Bauhaus) was founded in Germany in 1919 by Walter Gropius, a Modernist architect. This school taught a variety of subjects related to design and sought experimental solutions to society's ills. Gropius was an adherent to the controversial theories of the architect Adolph Loos, who had written an essay in 1908 entitled "Ornament and Crime" in which he asserted that ornament was no longer an expression of contemporary culture and that the absence of ornament was a sign of spiritual strength. This essay made its way through the European avant-garde, influencing such Modernist icons as the French architect Le Corbusier and the German architect Ludwig Mies van der Rohe. It served as the foundation for 20th-century Modernist architectural design. The Bauhaus became the center of these design theories. Mies van der Rohe took over as director of the Bauhaus from 1930 until 1933, at which time he was forced out by the Nazis. Hitler considered that the radical theories embraced by the Bauhaus were communistic, overly intellectual, and therefore dangerous. Walter Gropius was invited to relocate to the United States and to teach at Harvard's Graduate School of Design. His work at Harvard and his theories on architecture and Modernism had an enormous influence on American architecture in the second half of the 20th century.

Another Bauhaus alumnus was the German architect Mies van der Rohe. Son of a stone mason, Mies never attended architectural school, although he served as an apprentice to the German Modernist architect Peter Behrens. He also immigrated to the United States, arriving in 1938. He took a position at the Armour Institute in Chicago, which became known later as the Illinois Institute of Technology. The American art world embraced these immigrants as refugees from oppression, which was a valid point at the time.

The dearth of funding for architectural projects that dogged the Depression years led to many architects spending their free time studying architectural theory. The theory of Modernism appealed to them, with its rational design and the idea that the structure of the building should be expressed on the exterior. In addition, the lack of ornament and use of industrial materials resulted in a less costly project, at least in theory. In 1932, several European immigrant architects were asked to participate in a show at the newly opened Museum of Modern Art that highlighted the work of the progressive American and European architects of the day. The show, which traveled the country and produced an influential book, was entitled *The International Style: Architecture since 1922*, giving the name to the style that would predominate in American corporate design for the next half century. The design principles espoused by the creators of this exhibition were listed as a concern with volume as opposed to mass and solidity, regularity as opposed to axial symmetry, and the avoidance of "arbitrary applied decoration" (Wiseman 2000, 150).

Mies van der Rohe was a strict supporter of the Modernist creed that shunned all ornament, and he is known for his assertion that "less is more." In 1956, he was given the opportunity to design most of the buildings at a new campus for the Illinois Institute of Technology. He honed his craft with these spare, almost anonymous low-rise buildings, which could be used for any number of applications, making them adaptable for the university. They were paeans to steel and glass and looked highly industrial. His introduction to bringing his interpretation of the so-called International Style to taller buildings came in 1951 when Mies was given the commission to design buildings in Chicago, two 26-story apartment towers on Lake Shore Drive. These buildings utilized glass and steel, but for the first time, Mies added vertical steel I-beams to the outside of the building to express the structure, although technically they were not structurally necessary. These buildings served as forerunners to the design of the Seagram Building.

The story of the Seagram Building is a tale of high design and corporate branding. The company Joseph E. Seagram and Sons was owned by Samuel Bronfman, a Canadian who founded a liquor company, which bought out Seagrams and incorporated the name in 1928. The company benefited from the illegal sales of liquor during the Prohibition in the United States that lasted from 1928 to 1933. With the markets in the United States opening up, the corporation prospered even more after the repeal of Prohibition. The company wanted to display a corporate presence in the United States, specifically in New York City. Bronfman began to plan a corporate headquarters, and acquired land on the formerly residential Park Avenue north of Grand Central Station, across the street from the newly completed Lever House, headquarters for the British corporation Lever Brothers. He hired the architect Charles Luckman, who had previously been president of Lever

Brothers but had subsequently opened up an architectural practice. Luckman made some proposals. However, Bronfman's young daughter, Phyllis Lambert, an artist living in Paris at the time, caught wind of the proposals and in a seven-page letter, she vociferously protested to her father about the pedestrian design. She ardently believed that the new headquarters should be a representation of the best and most progressive design of the time. In her letter, Lambert asserted to her father, "You must put up a building which expresses the best of the society in which you live, and at the same time your hopes for the betterment of this society" (Lamster 2013). She suggested they consider the most talented architects currently working. They considered Frank Lloyd Wright (too old), Le Corbusier (too difficult to work with), and Mies van der Rohe (just right). Bronfman, impressed with his daughter's savvy, and willing to invest enough capital to complete the project, hired his 29-year-old daughter to be project manager for the design and construction. Lambert successfully managed the project and proceeded to attend architectural school herself at the Illinois Institute of Technology. The Seagram Building was completed in 1958.

CHARACTERISTICS AND FUNCTIONALITY

The Seagram Building is an office building designed in 1954 by Mies van der Rohe, with the help of Modernist American architect Philip Johnson, in the International Style. Bronfman asked for a simple design, but one that would "be the crowning glory of everyone's work, his own, the contractor's, and Mies'." Not a simple task, but one that was fulfilled. The building is set back 100 feet from the front property line and 30 feet on either side, giving the building space to stand out. However, the long side of the tower faces Park Avenue, unlike its neighbor Lever House, which is turned at 90 degrees from the street. It has a large granite-paved plaza, with radiant heating to prevent ice buildup. The plaza contains two reflecting pools on either side of it, on the Park Avenue side. The building has bronze-clad columns at the base with the glass-enclosed first floor interior set back from the facade. The raised base, with the high windowless mechanical story at the top, gives the building a classical feel of a column with a base, shaft, and capital in a very abstracted interpretation. Although the building appears to be a rectangular shaft on the Park Avenue facade, a so-called bustle, a lower tower at the back, and two shorter wings on either side, are hidden from view. The Seagram Building is clad in pinkish-gray tinted glass, and bronze I-beam extrusions, which are applied to the outside of the shaft. This nonstructural use of the I-beam gives the building its monumental verticality. Horizontal bands called spandrels, that separate the glass on each story, are made of Muntz metal, an alloy resembling bronze in color. These spandrels add a horizontal element to the design. At the back of the building on 52rd Street was the Four Seasons Restaurant, designed by Philip Johnson. One of the interesting quirks about the Seagram Building is the design of the window blinds. Mies insisted that the window blinds have only three settings: open, half closed, and fully closed. He hated to see an office building with blinds pulled up to many different heights.

KEY STATISTICS

The Seagram Building is in the International Style, and is the only building designed by Mies van der Rohe in New York City. It is located at 375 Park Avenue, between East 52nd and 53rd Streets. It is an office building that has 38 stories and is 516 feet high, with a tall section at the top that contains mechanical equipment. The "bustle" at the back is ten stories high and the wings are five stories high. The pink granite plaza has a podium that is raised up three wide steps from street level, and parapet walls of verd antique marble. A flag pole is located at the left side of the Park Avenue facade, which is the only asymmetrical element. At the sides of the facade are planting areas with gingko trees. The lobby's walls are covered in travertine. The creed of International Style architecture was simplicity and lack of ornament, which could result in an inexpensive building. However, because of Mies's attention to detail and the luxurious materials that he chose, the simplicity of the Seagram Building came at a high cost. The Seagram Building cost $36 million, a stratospheric price in the 1950s, and a record price for an office building at the time.

CULTURAL SIGNIFICANCE

In 1999, the *New York Times* architectural critic Herbert Muschamp was asked to choose the most important building of the millennium, and his choice was the Seagram Building. Calling it both classical and Gothic, Muschamp discussed the infamous "war of the styles" in design that has been going on for centuries, and asserted that Mies successfully wedded the two styles in his Seagram Building. Classical design was based on ancient Greek and Roman precedents, and it projects balance, symmetry, and rationalism. Gothic design, however, takes the medieval Gothic church as its precedent. It is asymmetrical, intuitive, and appeals to emotion. Muschamp avers that the Seagram Building has both elements in a perfectly exquisite equipoise. With the regularity of its exterior columns, its symmetrical massing, and its allusion to classical columns with a base, shaft, and capital, it recalls classical rationalism. However, the soaring tower, with the lightness of its glass and bronze, brings references to the magnificent height of the Gothic cathedral. Mies van der Rohe designed a building that had perfect proportion and detailing, using sumptuous materials. However, Muschamp's review also mentions the influence of the Seagram Building on the design of the modern glass skyscraper. This, however, has not been as benign. The exquisite details, proportion, and materials that were used in the Seagram Building and the ultimate attention paid by Mies, his design partner Philip Johnson, the planning administrator Phyllis Lambert, and the multiple engineers, landscape architects, and artists who participated in this venture, as well as the infinite budget, all contributed to the perfection of the building. It looked simple and unadorned, but it was not. It looked like it had no ornament, but in fact, the beautiful bronze I-beams that were on the exterior had no structural value; they were merely decorative.

The design of the Seagram Building was copied incessantly, on every corner in every city in America, and even in suburban office parks. It also led to changes in the New York City zoning laws that allowed for the construction of large plazas in exchange for taller buildings, in place of the formerly ubiquitous setbacks. This created a building boom in New York of towers set back from the street, with plazas that were often wind blown, empty, and soulless. Therefore, the casual observer looks at the Seagram Building and sees something that looks achingly familiar. But these replicas did not contain the extravagant materials or the magnificent sense of proportion. They did not have boundless budgets. They were not pretty. Whereas the Seagram Building's plaza was inviting to passersby, the new ones were often vacant and bleak. Therefore, as architectural critic Paul Goldberger states that the Seagram Building's influence created a "sense on the part of society at large that contemporary architecture was a faceless, styleless art." However, he further asserts that the Seagram Building itself is "true not to the rules of an abstract system but only to itself, like all great works of art." All others were mediocre copies.

FURTHER INFORMATION: IMPORTANT PRINT, ELECTRONIC, AND MEDIA RESOURCES

Gelernter, Mark. 1999. *A History of American Architecture: Buildings in Their Cultural and Technological Context*. Hanover and London: University Press of New England.

Goldberger, Paul. 1979. *The City Observed: New York: A Guide to the Architecture of Manhattan*. New York: Vintage Books.

Lambert, Phyllis. 2013. *Building Seagram*. New Haven, CT, and London: Yale University Press.

Lamster, Mark. April 3, 2013. "A Personal Stamp on the Skyline." *New York Times*. http://www.nytimes.com/2013/04/07/arts/design/building-seagram-phyllis-lamberts-new-architecture-book.html. Accessed March 12, 2017.

Landmarks Preservation Commission. October 3, 1989. "Seagram Building, Including the Plaza." Designation List 221. LP-1664. http://s-media.nyc.gov/agencies/lpc/lp/1664.pdf. Accessed March 13, 2017.

Muschamp, Herbert. April 18, 1999. "Best Building; Opposites Attract." *New York Times Magazine.* http://www.nytimes.com/1999/04/18/magazine/best-building-opposites-attract.html. Accessed March 17, 2017.

Roth, Leland. 1979. *A Concise History of American Architecture.* Boulder, CO: Westview Press.

Wiseman, Carter. 2000. *Twentieth-Century American Architecture: The Buildings and Their Makers.* New York and London: W. W. Norton.

Why Did the Great Architect Ludwig Mies van der Rohe Only Design One Building in New York City?

It could be that he had a hard time qualifying as an architect in order to practice in New York, which has strict professional licensing laws. Mies did not have an architectural license in New York or a degree in architecture. The New York Department of Education demanded that he prove he had at least a high school education. Incensed, Mies temporarily walked off the job until his German school could send the proper documents. He also had trouble with the New York City Buildings Department regulations, who insisted on his using more fire-resistant materials.

TWA Flight Center

Queens, New York
1962

BACKGROUND

In the decades following the end of World War II, the United States entered a period of economic expansion and growth. The Eisenhower Interstate Highway System, authorized by the Federal Aid Highway Act of 1956, was connecting towns and cities throughout the country, allowing for automobile travel and the creation of ubiquitous car-centric suburbs. Television was in virtually all American homes by the end of the 1950s, linking homes from coast to coast, where families would watch the same nationally broadcast television shows. It was a period of optimism, and the economic boom fueled technological advancement. The expansion of the airline industry was also an example of the growth that occurred in the mid-20th century. For the first time, passengers could travel by jet across the country within five hours. The term "Jet Age" described the onset of the ultrafast jet engine, used for the first time in passenger planes. The commercial airline industry was growing so fast that airports could not be constructed fast enough to accommodate the need. But the commercial aviation industry was still relatively young. Airplanes were a new invention at the beginning of the 20th century. When the Wright brothers made their first flight at Kitty Hawk, North Carolina, it was December 17, 1903. The Wright brothers entered the aviation manufacturing industry in 1909 when they opened the Wright Company. By World War I, however, the United States had not kept up with other countries such as France in airplane manufacturing. The military needs of World War I prompted the United States to expand the industry, and by the end of the war, thousands of airplanes had been built, as well as many more airfields. New designs were also invented during World War I. The American aviation industry had been created. With the conclusion of the war, a new use for airplanes was devised—airmail. In 1918, airmail service was inaugurated by the U.S. Post Office. It was a boon to commercial development across the country, as the speed of delivery of the mail was accelerated. In addition to the airmail service, pilots used the surplus airplanes from the war to barnstorm and participate in airshows. The public was entranced with these magical vehicles, and fell in love with the airplane. However, the incident that was the most captivating to the American people in the 1920s was the 1927 flight of Charles Lindbergh from New York to Paris. It was the first solo nonstop transatlantic flight in history. Americans adored "Lucky Lindy," and the press coverage of the event led to an expansion of the small airplane industry, known as general aviation. The first time that the federal government regulated the airline industry was with the Air Commerce Act of 1926, which established the Aeronautics Branch of the Commerce Department. The regulations involved air safety and airways, and promoted aviation and airports. The next expansion of the industry came at the onset of World War II. For the first time, federal funding was used to develop airports, airways, and airport traffic control, primarily for defense purposes. These federal responsibilities were continued after the war was over. The technological advances and the production capabilities that the war provided influenced the growth of the postwar aviation industry. Jets were invented during the war as fighter planes, but the technology would revolutionize the commercial airplane industry as jets were introduced as passenger airplanes. Airports were transformed as well. The earliest airports consisted of a small building, containing a waiting area for the airplane. Tickets were not even sold at the airport—they were sold at ticket offices in the city, where passengers were provided transportation to the airport. After World War II, airport design was changed as airports accommodated more passengers. Tickets were sold on site, waiting areas were expanded, and restaurants were added. It was in the 1950s that the concept of the departure lounge was invented, where ticketed passengers relocated to a lounge near the gate, and services were relocated there as well.

After World War II, the commercial aviation industry grew rapidly. Even before the war, in New York City, Mayor LaGuardia constructed the New York City Municipal Airport, known as LaGuardia Field, or LaGuardia Airport, in 1939. Mayor LaGuardia did not favor using Newark Airport, which was opened in 1928, because it was actually in New Jersey, not New York. He made further plans for a larger airport in 1941. This airport was on the grounds of the Idlewild Golf Course in Queens. Although construction was begun in 1942, commercial flights did not begin to use the airport until 1948. Although its name was officially New York International Airport, it was known as Idlewild until the name was changed to John F. Kennedy Airport in 1963. The airport took years to build, as several master plans were created and then discarded. The city turned over the management and operation of the airport to the Port Authority in 1947. With another master plan in place in 1954, the concept was selected to construct unit terminals for the vast airport, not one gigantic terminal building. This was dubbed "Terminal City." The plan consisted of an International Arrivals Building, with seven airline terminal buildings in the surrounding acres. The plan also included an 11-story control tower, roadways, parking facilities, and a central plaza with a reflecting lagoon. The largest airlines were selected for the individual terminals. These large corporations relished their opportunity to build iconic structures that would forever be associated with their brands, although the concept would not be as successful as predicted considering the changed landscape of the industry over the next half century.

The airline called TWA, or Trans World Airlines, was one of the most prominent commercial airlines by the 1960s. It was the only airline with both domestic and transatlantic routes at the time. The airline was a creation from a number of earlier mergers, and the name was originally Transcontinental & Western Air, Inc., which was changed to Trans World Airlines in 1950, also known as TWA. The airline's principal stockholder from 1939 to 1960 was the famous businessman Howard Hughes. TWA was offered a terminal site at one end of the International Arrivals Building. Its chief competitor, Pan Am, was offered the terminal at the opposite end. The TWA president Ralph S. Damon hired the architectural firm of Eero Saarinen & Associates to design the building. Damon's vision of this terminal was described as "a building that starts your flight with your first glimpse of it and increases your anticipation after you arrive" (Landmarks Preservation Commission 1994, 5).

CHARACTERISTICS AND FUNCTIONALITY

The architect that was selected for this project was a Finnish immigrant, the son of two talented artists who had emigrated from Finland in 1923. Eero's mother was Loja Gesellius Saarinen, a textile designer. His father was a prominent architect named Eliel Saarinen. Eliel was already known for projects in Finland, and also for several projects at the Cranbrook School and Academy of Art in Michigan. Eero studied art at Cranbrook and was particularly interested in sculpture. He studied at the Academie de la Grand Chaumiere in Paris, but later received a bachelor's degree in architecture at Yale. Although Eero Saarinen became famous for his architecture, he continued his fascination with sculpture. His architectural designs demonstrate that fascination. He was also a successful furniture designer, and collaborated with the acclaimed midcentury furniture designer Charles O. Eames. Saarinen's most famous works are the Jefferson National Expansion Memorial (known as the Gateway Arch) in St. Louis (designed in 1948 and completed in 1964), the Dulles Airport Building in Chantilly, Virginia (1958–1962), and the TWA Flight Center at Kennedy Airport, which was begun in 1956 and completed in 1962. Saarinen's untimely death at 51 in 1961 meant that he did not live to see the completion of three of his most famous projects.

The architectural style that was prevalent during this period was the Modernist, rectilinear International Style, based on the designs of the celebrated

German-born architect Ludwig Mies van der Rohe, often known as Mies. This pared-down style, using glass curtain walls and steel framing, was identified by his adage "less is more." Saarinen, a sculptor at heart, was not a believer in the International Style. His designs were expressionistic and sculptural in concept. Deemed "architecture parlante," which means "speaking architecture" in French, this type of architecture expressed its function metaphorically through its design. The TWA Flight Center resembled a gigantic bird taking flight. The architect, however, never admitted that the design represented a bird literally. He insisted that the building's design was an abstraction of the idea of flight. The main terminal, also called the head house, consists of four thin-shell concrete roofs, supported by broad curvilinear concrete piers that flow up to the roofs in a sculptural fashion. The concrete shells soared above huge window walls, giving the facade an impression of two arching wings. The center roof shell drops down to a center point that resembles a hawk's beak. The roof shell vaults allowed for an open interior layout unfettered by walls or columns. The side window walls gave the interior a light-filled openness that allowed for passengers to see the comings and goings of the airplanes outside. The interior was also filled with curved elements, which made the building appear all of one piece. Signs, air-conditioning ducts, clocks, and other interior elements were designed by Saarinen as curved sculptures to complement the avian theme. When entering the main terminal, a visitor was confronted with a soaring, bright space, clad in white marble with accents of solid red carpet. Curving staircases rose up to restaurants and meeting rooms under the wings of the roof, where the light streamed in through the gigantic windows. After passing the ticket counters, the visitor could descend into a sunken waiting area in the center of the structure, with a massive, sculptural information desk. In addition, two long corridors extended out on either side from the main building to the boarding gates. This type of terminal design was called a satellite system.

KEY STATISTICS

The TWA Flight Center is located at Terminal 5 at what is now known as John F. Kennedy International Airport in Queens, New York. It sits on seven and a half acres. It did not open until May 1962, although the firm Saarinen and Associates was originally commissioned in 1955. The budget for the project ballooned from $9 million to $15 million. TWA was committed to the project, however, and did not demand redesign due to budget constraints. The TWA terminal was the last of the group of terminals planned for "Terminal City" in the airport's master plan. The International Arrivals Building and the Eastern Airlines, American Airlines, United/Delta Airlines, and the Pan Am Airlines terminals were all finished before the TWA terminal. As the airport was forced to expand due to the growth of the industry, the owner of the airport, the Port Authority, announced a 10-year expansion plan, which would allow accommodation for the larger jumbo jets, and even the supersonic jets that were being planned. The terminal area was expanded from 635 to 837 acres by eliminating a runway and some taxiways. The decorative lagoon and reflecting pools were eliminated as more availability of parking became an issue.

CULTURAL SIGNIFICANCE

Hailed as an icon of the Jet Age, the futuristic TWA Flight Center became a beloved landmark soon after it opened. The architecture critics of the period celebrated it as a tour-de-force. Although some critics who were wedded to the anonymous aesthetic of the International Style chided Saarinen's work for its idiosyncratic expressionism, many saw its sculptural qualities and soaring interiors as a paean to the nascent jet-based aviation industry. The TWA terminal has been compared to Pennsylvania Station, which was demolished the same year that the TWA terminal opened, and to Grand Central Station, which has been lovingly restored. They all represent icons to modes of transportation. Unfortunately, because of the rapidity of technological change, the TWA Flight Center was virtually outdated by the time it was opened. By 1967, the launch of the Boeing 747 made many of the individual JFK terminals obsolete. That year, TWA announced that it would expand its terminal to accommodate jumbo jets and additional passenger traffic. The changes in the airline industry, with greater numbers of passengers, the growth of the departure lounges, increased security measures, and deregulation, have made the 1960s' vintage TWA terminal inadequate today. The beautiful, fully realized design of the TWA terminal could not be easily altered. TWA suffered bankruptcies during the 1990s and was eventually purchased by American Airlines in 2001. The Flight Center was closed that year. It was at risk for demolition after that, although there was an outcry from the architectural community. In 1994, the TWA Flight Center was declared a landmark by the New York City Landmarks Preservation Commission. JetBlue Airways has built a modern terminal, called T5, that abuts the Flight Center. In December 2016, MCR Hotels announced a project that includes the original Saarinen terminal being restored. Its plans are to build a 505-room, 6-story hotel adjacent to the terminal. Included in the plans is the reuse of the iconic building with a reception desk, restaurants, a nightclub, event space, and food court, with expected completion in 2018. The original tubes to the gates will be reused for connections to the JetBlue terminals and the hotel rooms. One of the firms commissioned for this construction/renovation project, Beyer Blinder Belle, was responsible for the shining restoration of the Grand Central Station in Manhattan. The TWA terminal, with its landmark status, will be enjoyed for many years to come. In the words of Thomas Fisher, from *Progressive Architecture Magazine*, "whatever the drawbacks in the original design or the limitations in current capacity, the TWA terminal remains one of the best works of architecture" (HABS No. NY-6371, 13). The idea of mid-20th-century air travel and its concomitant concept of romance are embodied in Saarinen's TWA Flight Center at the JFK Airport.

FURTHER INFORMATION: IMPORTANT PRINT, ELECTRONIC, AND MEDIA RESOURCES

"Air Travel in a Changing America/America by Air." 2007. Smithsonian Air and Space Museum. https://airandspace.si.edu/exhibitions/america-by-air/online/jetage/jetage04.cfm. Accessed January 30, 2017.

"Aviation in American History." Guidelines for Evaluating and Documenting Historic Aviation Properties, *National Register of Historic Places Bulletin.* https://www.nps.gov/nr/publications/bulletins/aviation/nrb_aviation_II.htm. Accessed January 30, 2017.

Dunlop, David. 2016. "Symbol of Jet Age Is Bound for a New Era." *New York Times.* December 7, 2016, p. A23.

Fiederer, Luke. 2016. "AD Classics: TWA Flight Center/Eero Saarinen." *ArchDaily.* http://www.archdaily.com/788012/ad-classics-twa-flight-center-eero-saarinen. Accessed January 30, 2017.

Gelernter, Mark. 1999. *A History of American Architecture: Buildings in Their Cultural and Technological Context.* Hanover and London: University Press of New England.

Historic American Buildings Survey (HABS) No. NY-6371, "Trans World Airlines Flight Center, John F. Kennedy International Airport, Jamaica Bay, Queens (subdivision)," Queens, New York. http://lcweb2.loc.gov/master/pnp/habshaer/ny/ny2000/ny2019/data/ny2019data.pdf. Accessed January 27, 2017.

Landmarks Preservation Commission. July 19, 1994. "Trans World Airline Flight Center at New York International Airport." Designation List 259. LP-1916. http://s-media.nyc.gov/agencies/lpc/lp/1915.pdf. Accessed January 27, 2017.

Roth, Leland M. 1979. *A Concise History of American Architecture.* Boulder, CO: Westview Press.

Wiseman, Carter. 2000. *Twentieth-Century American Architecture: The Buildings and Their Makers.* New York and London: W. W. Norton.

Howard Hughes

One of the most intriguing and controversial figures of the 20th century was the businessman Howard Hughes. His fortune was made in the movie industry and the aviation industry. He was the principal owner of TWA Airlines for many years. Hughes was very well known in Hollywood and he dated a number of famous actresses. He later became an introvert and eccentric recluse. Part of his life was portrayed in the 2004 Martin Scorsese film *The Aviator*, starring Leonardo DiCaprio.

Watergate Complex

Washington, D.C.
1964–1971

BACKGROUND

The term "Watergate" has become a symbol of government malfeasance, with the suffix "-gate" used to describe a multitude of government scandals. Although the Watergate affair took place in the 1970s and many of the original participants are gone, the term endures in the American lexicon. As a historical term, the name Watergate refers to a series of actions that brought down the Nixon presidency. However, Watergate is also the name of a huge complex of buildings in Washington, D.C., that has its own controversial history. Therefore, the story of Watergate comprises two parallel tales, involving both a landmark building and a historic series of events. The history of the Watergate complex began in an underutilized 9.4-acre industrial site along the Potomac River in the Foggy Bottom section of the capital. Formerly home of the Washington Gas Light plant, by the early 1960s, it was known primarily as the address of a popular restaurant called the Water Gate Inn. Following a major rezoning plan published in 1958 and amended in 1961, the city of Washington, D.C., newly allowed for large mixed-use private developments known as planned unit developments, or PUDs. A private developer could use this zoning provision to build a large superblock that would contain a variety of uses. This virtual town, which included a diversity of high-rise apartment types, as well as a hotel, office building, and a variety of amenities like shops and restaurants, would be surrounded by landscaped open space for the use of its occupants. The idea was to entice middle- and upper-income Washington residents to stay in the city and not relocate to the suburbs. The Washington Gas Light company site was purchased by a development company based in Italy called Societa Generale Immobiliare, or SGI, in June 1960. SGI, partially owned by the Vatican, was known in Italy as a successful apartment developer, and was looking to expand into the United States. SGI hired an Italian Modernist architect named Luigi Moretti to design the massive complex. Moretti himself had a controversial background. He had been Benito Mussolini's favorite architect, and was briefly imprisoned as a fascist during World War II.

Moretti advocated for a modern approach to the design of the Watergate complex. Washington, D.C., was chock full of low-rise neoclassical buildings, and Moretti believed that the city needed an example of more contemporary design. The city was concerned that the high-rise buildings would overwhelm the iconic structures in the Washington mall area, and required a reduction in maximum height for the towers. Although there was some pushback against the modern proposal, the city eventually approved of the plans for the complex. The Watergate complex was completed in 1971. It was an immediate hit with the Washington elite, becoming home to many of the most famous denizens of the capital social scene.

As the Watergate mixed-use complex gained cachet in the capital, Richard Nixon was preparing for his run for reelection as president of the United States. He had been elected in 1968, beating his opponent Hubert Humphrey, who was dogged by his support of the Vietnam War while serving as vice president under Lyndon Johnson. The prolongation of the Vietnam War was generating unrest throughout the nation, as protests grew larger and support waned. Nixon was becoming agitated by the chaos he saw on the television. The blockbuster *New York Times* scoop known as the "Pentagon Papers," leaked by Henry Kissinger's former aide Daniel Ellsberg, described the thinking behind many of the decisions made within the White House concerning Vietnam. Nixon feared that there was additional information ready to be published about his administration's decisions concerning Vietnam. He was developing a paranoia about leaks that was infecting his entire administration. He issued a secret executive order that allowed his administration to perform break-ins, spy on, and tap the phones of ordinary Americans. Nixon believed, and stated, that "If a President does it, it is not illegal." However, the powerful FBI director J. Edgar Hoover, in his fourth decade as director of the FBI, refused to carry out the orders of the president. Nixon then proceeded to form a secret "Special Investigative Unit" in the White House in 1971. These so-called "Plumbers" were given the task of stopping leaks, using any means necessary, including wiretapping, kidnapping, leaking false news to the press, and using other "dirty tricks" that could hurt his opponents in the Democratic Party as the presidential election campaign got under way. The Plumbers were sent to California to break into the office of the psychiatrist of the hated leaker Daniel Ellsberg, in a quest to discover derogatory information about Ellsberg. Although nothing useful was found, the technique proved appealing, and the Plumbers planned another break-in, this time at the headquarters of the Democratic National Committee, located at the Watergate office building. After several unsuccessful attempts, the Plumbers were able to break into the office in late May 1972 and install telephone-bugging devices and take photographs of donor lists. Not satisfied with the results, Nixon's top aides who were running this unit planned another break-in several weeks later, on June 17,

1972. The burglars met at the Watergate Hotel to plan the heist. However, the break-in was thwarted when the Metropolitan Police discovered them inside the headquarters at 2:30 A.M., alerted by a Watergate security guard.

The break-in at the Watergate led to immediate attempts to cover it up by the Nixon White House. The task of covering up the White House's role in the break-in was assigned to John Dean, the president's counsel. The fallout from Watergate continued for two more years, although Nixon was reelected in 1972 by a landslide against his Democratic opponent George McGovern. The *Washington Post* team of Bob Woodward and Carl Bernstein began investigating the affair, aided by information secretly delivered by the acting FBI associate director W. Mark Felt, whose code name was "Deep Throat." The Senate Select Committee on the Investigation of the Presidential Election Campaign of 1972 set up hearings led by Senator Sam Ervin, in May 1973. A special prosecutor, Archibald Cox, was selected by Attorney General Eliot Richardson with the task of investigating the break-in and the subsequent cover-up. When it was discovered that the president taped all conversations in the Oval Office, the special prosecutor and the Senate Committee subpoenaed the tapes. Nixon fought the release of the tapes. As a last resort, Nixon demanded that the Attorney General Eliot Richardson fire Cox. When he refused, and Deputy Attorney General William Ruckelshaus also refused, they both resigned, in what has become known as the "Saturday Night Massacre" on October 20, 1973. The solicitor general, Robert Bork, was left with the task of firing Special Prosecutor Archibald Cox. The end result of this bloodbath was the call for impeachment of President Nixon. The House Judiciary Committee began an impeachment investigation, with hearings beginning on July 27, 1974. Three articles of impeachment were submitted for the following crimes: obstruction of justice, abuse of power, and contempt of Congress by refusing to release the tapes. The Supreme Court eventually ruled against President Nixon and his claim of "executive privilege" and allowed for the release of the tapes. Nixon was heard on a tape recorded on June 23, 1972, demanding that his aide H. R. Haldeman order the CIA to get the FBI to impede the Watergate investigation, based on the bogus claim of national security. This "smoking gun" tape was the last straw. On August 9, 1974, Richard Nixon resigned from office.

CHARACTERISTICS AND FUNCTIONALITY

The Watergate Complex is a mixed-use development along the Potomac River. It consists of six interconnected buildings of varied uses. The first building to be completed was Watergate East, an apartment building with 13 stories and has a curved facade with a long extension on one side. The next buildings that were completed, in 1966, were the office building at 2600 Virginia Avenue and the Watergate Hotel. These were the buildings that were involved in the Watergate break-in. These buildings form a T shape, with the office tower on the top of the T and the hotel at the stem of the T. The office building has 11 stories and the hotel has 12 stories. The Watergate West apartment building was completed in 1967. It is at the north end of the site and has a rounded projecting corner at the narrow site boundary that has been compared to the prow of a ship. The final buildings constructed at the Watergate were Watergate South and 600 New Hampshire Office Building, which were completed between 1969 and 1971. They are 12 stories high and form an unusual semicircular shape in the form of a C. All the buildings in the complex share similar design elements. They are all built of reinforced concrete. Unornamented white concrete bands alternate with the dark windows and balconies, giving the buildings a strongly horizontal appearance. All the apartment buildings have deep balconies, but the office buildings have uninterrupted wide bands of windows, which give all the buildings a similar look. The complex has many curved elements, which have a streamlined appearance, analogous to a cruise ship. Within the complex is a sunken shopping mall and underground parking garages. The buildings only comprise one-third of the property. The rest of the property is occupied by the landscaped areas and several swimming pools.

KEY STATISTICS

The Watergate complex is located on a 9.4-acre triangular property bordered by the Potomac River and the Rock Creek Parkway on the west, New Hampshire Avenue on the southeast, and Virginia Avenue on the northeast. Watergate West, 2600 Virginia Avenue office building, and Watergate East face Virginia Avenue. The office building at 600 New Hampshire Avenue is also along the street. The curved facade of Watergate South and the Watergate Hotel are sited in the center of the property along the Rock Creek Parkway. The engineering for the multiple curves of the buildings in the complex is said to be one of the first uses of CAD, or computer-aided design, in the United States. The landscaping of the complex was designed by the landscape architect Boris Timchenko.

CULTURAL SIGNIFICANCE

There is much to say about the significance of the Watergate complex in Washington, D.C. First, the complex is considered one of the masterpieces of the celebrated Italian Modernist architect Luigi Moretti. It is the only building he designed in the United States. It is also the first use of the PUD concept in urban planning, providing a complex with multiple uses within the same property, which became highly successful. As a Modernist design, it stands out among the many neoclassical buildings in Washington, D.C. When you see it, you recognize it right away, with its ship-like curves and horizontal bands. However, those who are not living in the District will not necessarily know the complex called Watergate. But they will certainly know the scandal. The Watergate affair and its effects on society are still being felt. Every political scandal that appears gets the suffix "-gate" attached to it. The public disappointment with President Ford's pardon of Nixon may have led to the election of a Democrat, Jimmy Carter, in 1976, as well as many Democrats to Congress in the election of 1974. Campaign finance laws were passed as a result of Watergate. The Ethics in Government Act regarding politicians' financial disclosures was also passed, and the Freedom of Information Act was expanded as a result of the Watergate scandal. The country was profoundly disturbed by the disregard for the rule of law that was displayed by Richard Nixon and his closest aides. In the words of John Dean, counsel to the president under Richard Nixon, the Watergate scandal represented a "cancer on the Presidency."

FURTHER INFORMATION: IMPORTANT PRINT, ELECTRONIC, AND MEDIA RESOURCES

Lindsay, Drew. October 1, 2005. "The Watergate: The Building That Changed Washington." *Washingtonian*. https://www.washingtonian.com/2005/10/01/the-watergate-the-building-that-changed-washington/. Accessed July 21, 2017.

Moeller, G. Martin, Jr. 2012. *AIA Guide to the Architecture of Washington, DC*. Baltimore, MD: Johns Hopkins Press.

National Park Service. Watergate, Washington, DC. http://www.watergate50.com/preservation/2005_hNRHPregAp.pdf. Accessed July 25, 2017.

Watergate (documentary series). 1994. BBC and Discovery. Directed by Mick Gold, produced by Paul Mitchell and Norma Percy. https://www.youtube.com/watch?v=fRCih5rUiVQ. Accessed July 24, 2017.

The Watergate Hotel

The Watergate Hotel was a hit when it was opened in 1967. After the burglars checked into and then ate at the hotel before breaking into the Democratic National Headquarters in 1972, it became even more popular as a tourist attraction. However, the years were not kind to the hotel and it closed a decade ago and remained closed until 2016. A $125 million renovation restored the hotel to its original midcentury design, and it is now open and ready for guests once again.

Sears Tower (Currently Known as the Willis Tower)

Chicago, Illinois
1973

BACKGROUND

The genesis of Sears, Roebuck and Company was in a tiny settlement in Minnesota, where Richard Warren Sears, a 22-year-old freight agent for the railroads, fell into some good luck. Without any resources of his own, he had the foresight to turn a chance incident into a fortune. A package of watches was sent to a local jeweler from a manufacturer in Chicago. When the jeweler refused them, Sears decided to try his hand at selling them himself. He knew that there were thousands of other freight agents along the telegraph line, and he offered to sell them the watches, pocketing $2 for each. Sears had a genius for merchandizing, and understood that the newly passed federal law that instituted standard railroad time made it crucial for businessmen and farmers to always have the correct time. These small businessmen depended on the railroads to transport their goods. Before the standardization of time zones, local regions used their own times based on the sun, which made setting railroad schedules nearly impossible. Sears sold his company, the R. W. Sears Watch Company, after only two years in 1889 for $72,000. He soon was back in business, though, with a partner named Alvah Curtis Roebuck, who was mechanically inclined, and had an ability to repair watches that the company sold. Sears opened up a business in Minneapolis, and soon relocated to Chicago. His expanded mail-order business now competed with the popular Montgomery Ward catalog, selling all types of goods. Sears was a born salesman, and wrote the copy for the catalog, which soon developed into hundreds of pages. His catalogs were required reading for the population that resided along the railroad lines in isolated communities in the newly settled Midwest. Sears sold everything from patent medicines, which contained opium, to entire house kits. For families in the expanding communities of the Midwest, they could pick out the house design they liked and the required lumber and materials for the construction of the house would be shipped to them. Tens of thousands of houses in the United States were built using Sears catalog homes. The Sears, Roebuck and Company catalog remained a staple in American homes for decades. In 1908, Sears retired (Roebuck had left the company years before), and Julius Rosenwald took over. By the 1920s, with the country becoming less isolated, the company made the decision to concentrate on brick-and-mortar stores. The growth of the suburbs after World War II led the company to open stores in malls throughout the country. By 1969, Sears, Roebuck and Company was riding the crest of the booming economy and had profits to burn. It was ready to build a corporate headquarters in Chicago that would serve as a symbol of the immensely successful retail giant.

The largest retail corporation in the world was Sears, Roebuck and Company, a company that had ballooned in growth since its inauspicious beginnings as a one-man watch company in 1886. By the 1960s, Sears employed 350,000 employees and had outgrown its headquarters in Chicago. It considered relocating to the suburbs as many corporations were doing at that time, but the Chicago mayor Richard J. Daley, who understood the potential positive impact a new Sears building could have on the city, proposed a property at the western edge of the Loop that could accommodate the kind of massive structure that Sears was looking to build. The chairman of the board at Sears was a man named Gordon Metcalf. He realized that the company needed an iconic building that represented the power of the Sears corporate brand at the time. He hired the architectural firm of Skidmore, Owings and Merrill (SOM), one of the premier designers of Modernist office buildings in the 20th century. SOM had recently completed the celebrated John Hancock Building in Chicago, completed in 1968. SOM assigned the project to Bruce Graham, who had designed a number of skyscrapers, including the Hancock Tower. Graham was a Colombian American who had studied architecture at the University of Pennsylvania and proceeded to move to Chicago where he sought out the design counsel of the legendary Modernist architect Mies van der Rohe. After working for two years in the firm of Holabird, Root and Burgee, Graham joined the Chicago office of Skidmore, Owings and Merrill, and became a partner in 1960. His design credits include many projects in Chicago. He is known for his knack for designing buildings that maximize the usable space and keep costs down. His partner in many of his designs was the Bangladeshi American structural engineer named Fazlur Khan, who was responsible for many of the design innovations that were used in the Sears Tower, as well as many subsequent skyscrapers.

CHARACTERISTICS AND FUNCTIONALITY

When it was completed in 1973, the Sears Tower was the tallest building in the world and remained so until 1998 when the Petronas Twin Towers in Kuala Lumpur were completed. The Twin Towers of the World Trade Center in New York City were the tallest for a brief three years before the Sears Tower was built, and before that, the venerable Empire State Building held the title after its completion in 1931. In the 1920s, there was a competition to build super tall skyscrapers. The Empire State Building was the culmination of that push into the sky, but with the intervention of the Great Depression, World War II and the postwar concern that supertall buildings were inefficient, nothing had been built that surpassed the great height of the Art Deco masterpiece until 1973. The reasons that the "tallest building in the world" moniker could once again be used for a new structure were due to the use of new technology and innovative structural techniques that were available. There is a story about the design innovation told by the architect Bruce Graham. Apparently, the chairman of the board at Sears, Gordon Metcalf, did not care for the design of the Hancock Tower. That tower has exterior cross bracing, which appears as gigantic diagonal beams spanning large expanses of the exterior of the structure. These beams are indeed structural and are required to stabilize the building for the high wind loads that are present in Chicago, which, after all, is known as "the Windy City." Unfortunately, the beams are obvious, not only on the outside, but through the windows on the inside, partially blocking the view. Graham was working with his friend the engineer Fazlur Rahman Khan when he took out his fresh pack of cigarettes, tapped the bottom and a knot of cigarettes popped out at different levels. Graham suggested that they build a structure consisting of a number of tubes rising to different heights. Although the two had designed a number of single-tube buildings, Graham thought that a bundle of tubes would also be effective. He called it a cigarette structure. All the staggered tubes were self-supporting, and tied together they created a stiff structure that resisted the heavy wind loads. Although Graham remarked that he suggested the bundled tube concept, Khan, the structural engineer, is credited with inventing the structural system used in the Sears Tower, which he continued to use in subsequent skyscraper projects. It was certainly a collaborative effort.

The unique design of the Sears Tower was based on a nine-unit three-by-three grid at ground level that formed a square, similar to a tic-tac-toe board with a frame around it. These nine units actually served as nine separate skyscraper structures. The square tubes rose from the ground to various heights. The nine tubes at the massive ground all rose to the 49th floor. At the 50th floor, only seven tubes continue to rise to the 65th floor. At the 66th floor, five tubes continue up to the 90th floor in the shape of a cross, and only two tubes rise to the ultimate height of 108 floors. The Federal Aviation Administration limited the height of the building at 108 stories for air traffic safety reasons. The original plan also called for a hotel on the site, which would have made a base of fifteen tubes instead of nine, but the idea was scrapped. The bundled tube structure was efficient in its use of materials as less steel was required, which made it very cost-effective. The style of the building is Modernist, as Graham was influenced by the Modernist icon Mies van der Rohe. There is virtually no ornament on the Sears Tower;

it is a "bold and muscular interpretation of the Miesian glass box" (Grimes 2010). The Sears administration's program for the building included large open floor plans for the Sears staff, which would be located on the lower floors. The upper floors were smaller in footprint and could be leased out to smaller business entities as tenants, which made the entire building less expensive for Sears to operate. The building also contained an observation deck on the 103rd floor. There is a large Alexander Calder sculpture in the lobby.

KEY STATISTICS

The Sears Tower is located at 233 South Wacker Drive in the West Loop section of downtown Chicago. It is 1,450 feet high, with 108 stories. With the additional two television antennas on the top of the building, it rises to 1,750 feet. The total square footage inside the building is 4.5 million. The frame is structural steel, and the exterior is clad in a lightweight skin of black aluminum and bronze-tinted glare-reducing glass. The building cost $150 million to complete in 1973, and the construction took only three years. There are over 16,000 windows in the building, and six roof-mounted robotic window-washing machines. The building accommodates over 12,000 occupants and has 104 elevators. Like all supertall structures, the Sears Tower was designed to sway in the wind. The typical sway is only six inches, although it was designed to withstand a sway of up to three feet. The view from the observation deck allows visitors to see four states on a clear day—Illinois, Indiana, Michigan, and Wisconsin. Although the Sears Tower was the tallest skyscraper in the world when it was completed, it now stands as the 12th tallest in the world and the 2nd tallest in the United States, eclipsed by New York's new One World Trade Center, also known as the Freedom Tower.

CULTURAL SIGNIFICANCE

The Sears Tower is culturally significant as an iconic skyscraper that represents Chicago. It is a wildly popular tourist destination that supports long lines to access its observation deck and newly opened "Ledge" attraction. When construction was begun in 1970, the United States had just landed men on the moon. Technology was revered, and the new innovation of the bundled tube construction was another indication of the progressive advances of science in an optimistic age. American ingenuity seemed to know no bounds. The tower also represented an American icon of the merchandizing industry. Whereas Sears, Roebuck and Company saw enormous success in the first years of the 20th century, and through the middle of the century, the 21st century has brought a severe decline to the great Sears empire. The building was sold in 1994, when the merchandizing giant relocated to the Chicago suburbs. As an extremely successful office building in a hot market, Sears actually made more profit that year in the sale of the building than it did in its merchandizing sales. Although it is still limping along, Sears is no longer the leader in American merchandizing that it once was. When an English insurance broker leased several floors of the building in 2009, it was renamed the Willis Tower, after Willis Group Holdings, Ltd. The appellation has not been universally accepted, however, and many Chicagoans continue to call the building the Sears Tower.

FURTHER INFORMATION: IMPORTANT PRINT, ELECTRONIC, AND MEDIA RESOURCES

Charles River Editors. 2017. *The Sears Tower: History of Chicago's Most Iconic Landmark.* Middletown, DE: Charles River Editors.

Gelernter, Mark. 1999. *A History of American Architecture: Buildings in Their Cultural and Technological Context.* Hanover and London: University Press of New England.

Grimes, William. March 10, 2010. "Bruce Graham, Chicago Architect Who Designed Sears Tower, Dies at 84." *New York Times.* http://www.nytimes.com/2010/03/10/arts/design/10graham.html. Accessed April 14, 2017.

History and Facts—Willis Tower. http://www.willistower.com/history-and-facts. Accessed April 10, 2017.

Miller, Donald L. 1996. *City of the Century: The Epic of Chicago and the Making of America.* New York: Simon & Schuster.

The Skyscraper Center. Willis Tower. https://skyscrapercenter.com/building/willis-tower/169. Accessed April 10, 2017.

A View on Cities. Sears Tower. http://www.aviewoncities.com/chicago/searstower.htm. Accessed April 14, 2017.

The Ledge—Willis Tower's New Skydeck Attraction

In 2009, a renovation to the Willis Tower's observation deck included construction of a series of glass bays that extend from the building on the 103rd floor. These glass boxes give the visitor a hair-raising view out to the surrounding city and countryside, and straight down 1,353 feet. The attraction has been a successful addition to the already popular Skydeck Chicago.

World Trade Center Twin Towers

New York, New York
1973

BACKGROUND

The narrative of the heartbreaking story of the World Trade Center twin towers began with a successful attempt by one of the most famous of America's prominent business clans to revitalize the declining financial district in Lower Manhattan in the late 1950s. David Rockefeller, grandson of the founder of the Standard Oil Company, John D. Rockefeller, and youngest of the five powerful Rockefeller brothers, spearheaded the construction of a new headquarters for his company, Chase Manhattan Bank, in 1957. The area around Wall Street in Lower Manhattan, the oldest section of New York City, was falling behind in development to Midtown Manhattan. Banks and other large corporate headquarters were relocating uptown, abandoning downtown Manhattan. David Rockefeller recognized the historic significance of the city's downtown financial district and convinced the leadership of the bank to build a new headquarters that would become an architectural icon in an area that had not seen major new development since the Great Depression. One Chase Manhattan Plaza, a Modernist skyscraper designed by the renowned firm Skidmore, Owings and Merrill, proclaimed the Lower Manhattan financial district still relevant in New York's elite business circles. Rockefeller, however, understood that constructing one major building in a neighborhood would not guarantee the area's continuing viability. He knew that more development in the downtown would be necessary to ensure that Chase Manhattan Plaza did not become an expensive white elephant.

David Rockefeller had a vision. His uncle Winthrop W. Aldrich was a proponent of world trade as an avenue to world peace, and in 1946 he was appointed by the governor of New York State, Thomas E. Dewey, to head a new state agency called the World Trade Corporation. His mission was to build a complex called the World Trade Center. Although his plans were not successful at the time, his nephew David Rockefeller, now president of Chase Manhattan Bank, pursued his uncle's vision with unalloyed vigor. Rockefeller had a dual purpose: he was determined to create a World Trade Center, and he was likewise committed to reviving the financial district. He set up an organization he called the Downtown Lower Manhattan Association that would promote development in the downtown area. Rockefeller also worked with the Port of New York Authority (a bistate agency that was responsible for the construction and maintenance of local airports, bridges, tunnels, and ports that was later known as the Port Authority of New York and New Jersey) to devise a plan to build a center of world trade in Lower Manhattan. A plan was created to build this new center on the west side of downtown Manhattan directly across from the east side location of the Wall Street district. This neighborhood, beginning in the 1920s, was a disheveled community locally known as "Radio Row." The old storefronts and warehouses were not part of the glitzy Wall Street crowd. They were a variety of electronics stores selling used and new radios, televisions, and phonographs as well as parts for them. The shops were favorites for the local do-it-yourselfers. The neighborhood did not have the political clout to survive, however, and, despite local protests and lawsuits, the neighborhood was demolished through eminent domain in the early 1960s. The Port Authority hired a well-known American Modernist architect named Minoru Yamasaki to design the complex. Yamasaki had designed a number of smaller office buildings as well the infamous Pruitt-Igoe public housing project in St. Louis that was demolished in 1972 as an example of a totally failed experiment in housing for the poor. Yamasaki engaged the architectural firm of Emery, Roth & Sons to produce the construction drawings, and the firm of Worthington, Skilling, Helle and Jackson as engineers. The construction for the complex was begun in 1966.

CHARACTERISTICS AND FUNCTIONALITY

The World Trade Center complex contained seven office buildings. The twin towers, however, were the most famous, consisting of the North Tower and the South Tower. The construction of the gigantic towers required a number of modern construction innovations. First, the location of the towers on the west side of Lower Manhattan did not benefit from the bedrock called Manhattan schist that was found under most of the island. The land under the Trade Center had been landfill, with half of the property on land that had once been the Hudson River. The bedrock was 65 feet below grade. The engineers, led by Jack Kyle of the Port Authority staff, devised a solution called the slurry trench method for keeping the water from the river at bay. A three-foot-wide trench was excavated down to the bedrock in 22-foot sections, and a slurry of water and bentonite (a type of clay) was pumped into the trench. A cage of reinforced steel was lowered into the trench. Reinforcing tiebacks were attached to the cage and anchored to the bedrock on the outside of the wall. Later, concrete was pumped in from the bottom and the slurry was forced out from the top. As the concrete set, a wall was formed. When the enclosing wall was complete, it formed a protection from the river that was dubbed "the bathtub." This wall allowed for the excavation that was required to build the foundation for the towers. The three million yards of fill that was excavated from the World Trade Center site was donated to the city of New York on a site across West Street in the Hudson River, creating additional land in Lower Manhattan. The land sat idle for years alongside the complex, but was developed in the 1980s and 90s into the new neighborhood called Battery Park City.

Another innovation for the World Trade Center was the unique elevator design. One of the major drawbacks of building a giant skyscraper was the number of required elevators. An elevator shaft takes up space inside the building, and tall buildings required a series of elevator shafts that carried passengers to groups of floors within the building. With a mega skyscraper, the number of separate elevator shafts would occupy an unacceptable amount of usable interior space. The engineers of the World Trade Center devised an efficient elevator design called the "skylobby" system. Based on the familiar New York City subway system with its fast express trains and slower local trains, two intermediate skylobbies, at the 44th and 78th floors, were built. Passengers would have to change elevators at either the 44th or the 78th floor, after a very fast ride, and transfer to a local elevator that would deliver them to their particular floor. By designing the elevators this way, the same shafts could be reused. In each of the two towers, there also was a superfast express elevator that reached the 107th floor. This was where the observation deck was located in the South Tower, and the restaurant called Windows on the World was located in the North Tower.

The third innovation in the design and construction of the twin towers was the structural support system. The design of these massive towers made use of a clever structural technique. The central core of each building, consisting of the elevator shafts and the fire stairs and other services, contained a series of structural columns. In addition, the exterior of the towers had structural columns as well. From the outside, the visible lines that went up the outside of each building were not only decorative; they were aluminum-clad steel structural columns. By designing the towers in this way, the interior of each floor was completely flexible and open for use without the pesky columns that were typical of most other office buildings. Because of the massive columns at the core and the periphery, the floor structure was designed to be of minimal strength. The floor structure consisted of open web trusses sprayed with a fireproof coating, which held up each floor but had no redundant strength. Although technically strong enough to hold up the building under normal stresses and loads, the floor trusses were not overdesigned as many floors in the earlier skyscrapers had been. The structural system was adequate. It even was designed to withstand a Boeing 707 hitting it. How could the engineers predict what would befall the towers after the onset of the 21st century?

KEY STATISTICS

There were seven buildings in the World Trade Center complex, encompassing the giant twin towers and five low-rise buildings surrounding them. The center was located on a so-called superblock (the existing streets within the huge block were eliminated by the complex). The block was bounded by Vesey, Liberty, Church and West Streets on the west side of Lower Manhattan. The property was a total of 16 acres. The twin towers were 1,368 and 1,362 feet tall, making them the two tallest buildings in the world from 1971 to 1973 when they were surpassed by the Willis Tower (also known as the Sears Tower) in Chicago. The twin towers of the World Trade Center each had 110 stories, with a total of 10 million square feet, and accommodating 50,000 workers. The innovative express elevators in the towers carried 55 people and traveled 1,600 feet per minute. Because of the unique structural system that supported the buildings with columns in the central core and on the exterior facades, the interior space was completely open, with 65 feet of space on two sides and 35 feet on the opposite sides. The columns on the outside of the towers were only 22 inches apart, which made for narrow glass window openings. In total, there were 21,800 windows in each tower. In order to lessen the sway of the towers caused by wind, 11,000 dampers, similar to shock absorbers, were installed in each tower. Office workers were not disturbed by the movement of the towers when working in the open office environment. However, when venturing into the fire stairs in the central core on a windy day, the eerie creaking sound of the building swaying could be heard.

CULTURAL SIGNIFICANCE

The World Trade Center complex was completed in 1973. The coming fiscal crisis hit New York City extremely hard and the first years of the Trade Center were an economic disaster for the Port Authority. The 10 million square feet of space was a lot to fill, and private businesses did not have the extra profits to use on high World Trade Center rent. The 1970s saw the twin towers occupied by the owners, the Port Authority of New York and New Jersey, in the North Tower, and the offices of the State of New York in the South Tower. Additionally, the response from the architectural critics and the intelligentsia was withering. Paul Goldberger of the *New York Times* called the complex boring, banal, pretentious and arrogant. *Harper's* magazine called it "The World's Tallest Fiasco" (Glantz and Lipton 2003, 116). Local critics called them David and Nelson, after the Rockefeller brothers who promoted the project. The barren windswept plaza, peopled by absolutely no one, seemed like the ultimate proof of the total miscalculation in the zoning change that allowed for taller buildings in exchange for open plaza space. In the 1970s, it seemed like a giant white elephant, a colossal mistake. It was not until the 1980s, with the economy booming again and the financial district bursting at the seams that the complex attracted firms from the financial industry and rents rose. Nevertheless, out-of-towners were perennially fond of the twin towers, and the observation deck and Windows on the World continued to rake in profits. Eventually, even the recalcitrant critics softened their views about the complex. Goldberger admitted that they became a benign presence on the skyline, something that you could see from all over, like a medieval cathedral spire. He called them "minimalist sculpture." The fact that the towers were offset, with the footprint of the towers not aligned with each other, made them interesting to see from different angles. When the sun shone on the aluminum exterior columns, the towers glowed. The initial criticism of the complex lessened as the World Trade Center became a familiar element of the city skyline. It was not until September 11, 2001, that the towers of the World Trade Center became more than a controversial complex, beloved by some and tolerated by others. They instantly became martyrs, like the 2,600 souls who tragically succumbed in the attack at the World Trade Center. The glorious September morning that the two planes plowed into the two towers and changed the world made the twin towers the first skyscraper martyrs. The horrifying pancaking fall of one tower after another on that fateful day represented a loss that was, in Mayor Rudolph Giuliani's words, almost too hard to bear. The minimal structural support built into the floor trusses may have contributed to the fall of the towers. Of course, so did the enormous amount of jet fuel that started the fire that melted the tower's structural elements. We may never know all the details. However, the world of skyscraper design has been permanently altered by the tragic results of the attack. But we do know that the new One World Trade Center tower conforms to scores of new structural and security requirements that were not even considered when the original World Trade Center was designed and built in the 1960s and '70s. A comment made by Ada Louise Huxtable, the architectural critic of the *New York Times* in 1966, when the design of the complex was first announced, was eerily prescient: "Who's afraid of the big, bad buildings? Everyone, because there are so many things about gigantism that we just don't know. The gamble of triumph or tragedy at this scale—and ultimately it is a gamble—demands an extraordinary payoff. The Trade Center towers could be the start of a new skyscraper age or the biggest tombstone in the world." How could Ada Louise Huxtable guess that the twin towers would become a gigantic tombstone? The loss of the towers has indeed introduced a new skyscraper age with a myriad of new security and structural requirements. The skyscraper age lives on, although the original twin towers tragically do not.

FURTHER INFORMATION: IMPORTANT PRINT, ELECTRONIC, AND MEDIA RESOURCES

Glantz, James, and Eric Lipton. 2003. *City in the Sky: The Rise and Fall of the World Trade Center*. New York: Times Books, Henry Holt and Company.

Goldberger, Paul. 1979. *The City Observed: New York*. New York: Vintage Books.

Goldberger, Paul. September 24, 2001. "The Skyline: Building Plans." *New Yorker*. http://www.newyorker.com/magazine/2001/09/24/building-plans. Accessed June 4, 2017.

Huxtable, Ada Louise. May 29, 1966. "Who's Afraid of Big, Bad Buildings?" *New York Times*. https://timesmachine.nytimes.com/timesmachine/1966/05/29/140000432.html?pageNumber=92. Accessed May 12, 2017.

Port Authority of New York and New Jersey. History of the Twin Towers—World Trade Center. https://www.panynj.gov/wtcprogress/history-twin-towers.html. Accessed June 4, 2017.

Roth, Leland M., and Amanda C. Roth Clark. 2016. *American Architecture: A History*. Boulder, CO: Westview Press.

Tyson, Peter. April 30, 2002. "Twin Towers of Innovation." *Nova Online*. http://www.pbs.org/wgbh/nova/tech/twin-towers-of-innovation.html. Accessed May 21, 2017.

9/11, Its Aftermath, and the Subsequent "War on Terror"

On September 11, 2001, 19 men who were part of the Islamic extremist network associated with Al Qaeda, hijacked four commercial airliners and attempted to fly them into targets in the United States. Included in those targets were the iconic World Trade Center towers in New York City. The horrifying result of this attack, the worst in U.S. history, was the deaths of 2,996 people, including the 19 hijackers. The attacks in New York were the worst: 2,606 people died as the two giant World Trade Center towers both fell straight down, each floor tumbling down onto the next one, incinerating thousands with the fiery jet fuel that engulfed the buildings. Americans watched in abject horror as the enfolding disaster was broadcast live on their televisions nationwide. What began as a glorious fall day in New York ended in a tragedy that would alter the way the United States handled itself, both at home and in the world. The reaction to these sudden attacks led to a surge in paralyzing fear and patriotic fervor in the country. President George W. Bush announced a "war on terror" in the days after the attacks. A massive bombing campaign was commenced targeting the Taliban and Al Qaeda and its leader Osama bin Laden in Afghanistan. In October 2001, President Bush signed into law the USA PATRIOT Act, which bequeathed vast power to the federal government to conduct secret searches and surveillance. Soon after, the United States was accused of using torture techniques with the captured Taliban and Al Qaeda militants who were sent to a newly built prison in Guantanamo Bay in Cuba and other "black sites" around the world. In 2002, the Bush administration loudly claimed that Iraq had procured weapons of mass destruction and was pursuing nuclear weapons. Members of the Bush administration also accused Iraq of having been involved in the 9/11 attacks, which was later proven to be completely false. The United States, nevertheless, invaded Iraq in March 2003. The grueling wars in Afghanistan and Iraq have turned into the longest in American history. Islamic extremists, who were not in Iraq in 2003, moved in after the United States left a power vacuum in the country, as the militant group called ISIS took over cities in northern Iraq. Islamic terrorism has evolved, becoming a more dispersed, but just as dangerous, international force. The USA PATRIOT Act, enacted weeks after the 9/11 attacks, is still in force. What happened on that fall day in 2001 is still affecting the United States and the world.

Walt Disney Concert Hall

Los Angeles, California
2003

BACKGROUND

Driving through downtown Los Angeles, a visitor may arrive at the corner of Grand Avenue and First Street. Here, among the variety of rectangular modern office towers, the visitor would be astonished to see a gleaming, billowing silver sail-like structure bursting out of the corner property. This stainless-steel clad building, so unlike anything seen before, is the Walt Disney Concert Hall. It was designed by the architect Frank Gehry, one of the world's most famous living architects. Gehry was born in Toronto, Canada, in 1929, to working-class Jewish parents. His name at birth was Frank Owen Goldberg. His family relocated to Los Angeles when Frank was a teenager, hoping, like so many others, to improve their economic conditions in the "golden state." After high school, Frank initially attended Los Angeles City College. Not sure what professional course to pursue, Gehry had always had an interest in the arts, he eventually opted to attend architecture school at the University of Southern California School of Architecture, from which he graduated in 1954. In 1956, he attended the Harvard Graduate School of Design, studying city planning. He was not impressed with the stodgy, elitist vibe there and did not complete the course. It was the same year that Gehry changed his name from Goldberg to Gehry. He had felt the sting of anti-Semitism throughout his life and wanted to be accepted on his own terms. Returning to Los Angeles, Gehry worked for several architectural firms and then launched his own firm in 1962. Gehry received a number of commissions during this time, but made his name on two lines of innovative furniture designs called Easy Edges and Experimental Edges that utilized unexpected materials like corrugated cardboard. Using the profits he gained from selling his furniture line, Gehry then set out to renovate his own house in Santa Monica, California, in 1978. This house, a 1920s-era bungalow, was transformed by Gehry with a groundbreaking design that gave the architect his first taste of notoriety. Taking the traditional bungalow design and splitting it open, the house looked like it had been exploded into the yard. Gehry utilized inexpensive building materials. The design captivated the architectural critics, who identified it with the new architectural movement called deconstructivism. This project led to other residential design commissions for Gehry. His unique designs gained notice, and by the 1980s, Gehry was receiving larger commissions for public works. By the 1990s, Gehry's work had matured and his trademark sculptural forms brought him even more success, with Gehry winning the ultimate architectural accolade, the Pritzker Prize, in 1989.

In 1987, Walt Disney's widow Lillian Disney donated $50 million to build a concert hall in her late husband's name. Gehry was selected after a design competition to design the hall. He began work on the design, enlisting the help of the Japanese acoustical engineer Yasuhisa Toyota. The design of the hall proceeded slowly, and by 1994, the project came to a halt due to a ballooning budget and a lack of funds. In 1996, the Disney family revived the project, eliciting funds from a variety of sources. The Guggenheim Museum in Bilbao, Spain, had just been completed to rave reviews. Gehry's fame intensified, and interest in the Disney project returned. Gehry reworked the design, tightening the plan and using more economical materials. The result, which opened in October 2003, at a final cost of $274 million, is the masterwork that is the Walt Disney Concert Hall today.

CHARACTERISTICS AND FUNCTIONALITY

The Walt Disney Concert Hall is directly across the street from the Dorothy Chandler Pavilion, a more mundane, 1960s-era concert hall that was the home of the Los Angeles Philharmonic before the opening of the Disney Hall. It is part of the Los Angeles Music Center, which includes the Disney Hall, the Chandler Pavillion, the Mark Taper Forum, and the Ahmanson Theatre. The exterior of the Disney Concert Hall is clad in stainless steel that evokes billowing sails in gleaming silver. The Bilbao Guggenheim has a similar shining exterior, but it is clad in titanium, a much more costly material. At the corner of First Street and Grand Avenue is a grand staircase that leads up to the entrance. It is a street-friendly building, with a café and bookstore at street level. It also encourages discovery by visitors on foot. It has a large public garden that has a Gehry-designed fountain in the shape of a rose, which is dedicated to Lillian Disney and contains shards of her beloved Delft china. Gehry named the fountain "A Rose for Lilly."

Once inside, the silvery effect turns to gold. The interior walls are clad in a warm, gold-toned Douglas fir. Within the huge lobby, Gehry carved out a space that serves as a small performance or lecture space. This space is also open to the public. Inside the lobby, the gigantic air-conditioning ducts resemble tree trunks covered in Douglas fir. The layout of the concert hall itself is unusual. The seats envelop the stage on all four sides, giving the hall an intimate, democratic air. Above the stage is the focal point of the hall, the pipe organ, whose pipe enclosures are arranged in a jubilant array that resembles a pile of French fries standing up, or as Paul Goldberger in the *New Yorker* described, "like a stack of lumber that has just exploded." The ceiling of the hall curves "like a gargantuan version of the canopy on a four-poster bed" (Goldberger 2003). There are skylights in the hall that are partially hidden and give light to the space during the day. The seats in the hall are covered in a colorful wildflower-designed fabric. One of the most successful aspects of Gehry's design is the acoustics inside the hall. Working closely with Yasuhisa Toyota, Gehry made sure that the curves and materials utilized in the hall provided the best acoustics possible. An inveterate model maker, Gehry built a model on a 1:10 scale, which included model occupants in all the seats. He tested the acoustics with Toyota, ensuring that the results could be scaled up tenfold for the final space. The curves of the space are convex, an outward curve that will disperse the sound. Gehry knew that acoustics engineers had discovered that concave curves tend to trap the sound and lead to poor acoustical results.

KEY STATISTICS

The Walt Disney Concert Hall is located at 111 South Grand Avenue on the corner of Grand Avenue and First Street in downtown Los Angeles in the neighborhood called Bunker Hill. The property sits on 3.6 acres, and the building contains 293,000 square feet. The capacity of the concert hall is 2,265. The hall is the home of the Los Angeles Philharmonic. The enormous organ has 6,134 pipes. Although the building was commissioned in 1987, funding and other issues delayed its completion until 2003. It was opened on October 23, 2003.

CULTURAL SIGNIFICANCE

The Walt Disney Concert Hall has become an icon of the city of Los Angeles in its short lifetime. It has also become the masterpiece of the renowned architect Frank Gehry. Its sculptural exterior and its acoustically magnificent interior have made this venue a must-see for the Los Angeles visitor. The neighborhood of downtown Los Angeles, which had suffered from urban decay for years, is reviving. Property values have improved, and the new Broad Museum, named for the philanthropist Eli Broad, opened in 2015 and is located adjacent to the concert hall. It was designed by the prominent architectural firm Diller, Scofidio + Renfro, designers of the new High Line Park in New York City. The famous Guggenheim in Bilbao, also designed by Frank Gehry, almost instantly made the small Basque city into a tourist destination, with the so-called Bilbao effect. The city fathers of Los Angeles were hoping for something like that to happen in their city. It seems to be on its way.

Gehry's romantic, expressionistic style would never have made it off the drawing board if it had not been for the invention of computer-aided design

(CAD) and powerful computers. In fact, the individualism of Gehry's work, designed from his initial freehand sketches, was not even possible with the existing CAD programs. The drawings created by Gehry's imagination were so complicated that contractors could not understand what was required, and bid the projects at outlandishly high prices. Gehry's colleague Jim Glymph discovered a program called CATIA (computer-aided three-dimensional interactive application) that was being used by the French aerospace industry to design fighter planes. Gehry's reinterpretation of this program has allowed him to use computers to take his vision from his models to the contractor and manufacturer. The program utilizes a tool that traces the model and converts it into a three-dimensional image. The additional advantage of this program is that the data produced in the complex working drawings could be sent directly to the manufacturers, where exact computations could be made, and pricing could be estimated. Gehry, who does not use computers himself, has also launched a software firm, selling his invention to other architects. He has become known as an architect who can design a complex, expressionistic building, and still come in on time and under budget, which is a rare skill.

FURTHER INFORMATION: IMPORTANT PRINT, ELECTRONIC, AND MEDIA RESOURCES

"Frank Gehry's High-Tech Secret." October 6, 2003. *Bloomberg Business Week.* https://www.bloomberg.com/news/articles/2003-10-05/frank-gehrys-high-tech-secret. Accessed February 27, 2017.

Goldberger, Paul. September 29, 2003. "Good Vibrations." *New Yorker.* Conde Nast Publications. http://go.galegroup.com.proxy.library.csi.cuny.edu/ps/i.do?&id=GALE|A106518159&v=2.1&u=cuny_statenisle&it=r&p=AONE&sw=w. Accessed February 26, 2017.

Jones, Rennie. October 23, 2013. "AD Classics. Walt Disney Concert Hall/ Frank Gehry." *ArchDaily.* http://www.archdaily.com/441358/ad-classics-walt-disney-concert-hall-frank-gehry. Accessed February 27, 2017.

McGuigan, Cathleen. August 18, 2003. "A Mighty Monument to Music: Frank Gehry's Swooping, Soaring Walt Disney Concert Hall Is the Architect's Masterwork—And the Mirror of This Own Restless Energies." *Newsweek.* http://onesearch.cuny.edu/primo_library/libweb/action/display.do?frbrVersion=2&tabs=detailsTab&ct=display&fn=search&doc=TN_gale_ofa108321611&indx=6&recIds=TN_gale_ofa108321611&recIdxs=5&elementId=5&renderMode=poppedOut&displayMode=full&frbrVersion=2&vl(62436675UI0)=any&query=any%2Ccontains%2Cwalt+disney+concert+hall&dscnt=0&search_scope=everything&scp.scps=-scope%3A%28CUNY_BEPRESS%29%2Cscope%3A%28SI%29%2C-scope%3A%28AL%29%2Cprimo_central_multiple_fe&onCampus

=true&vid=si&queryTemp=walt+disney+concert+hall&institution=SI&tab=default_tab&vl(freeText0)=walt%20disney%20concert%20hall&group=GUEST&dstmp=1488138072814. Accessed February 26, 2017.

Muschamp, Herbert. October 23, 2003. "Architecture Review; A Moon Palace for the Hollywood Dream." *New York Times*. http://www.nytimes.com/2003/10/23/arts/architecture-review-a-moon-palace-for-the-hollywood-dream.html. Accessed February 22, 2017.

"The Bilbao Effect"

Frank Gehry, one of the most renowned living architects, has been labeled a "starchitect" because of his unconventional designs, celebrity status, and name recognition. The Walt Disney Concert Hall in Los Angeles is one of his most recognized buildings. However, he is also celebrated for one of his earlier buildings, the gleaming titanium-clad Guggenheim Museum Bilbao, which was established in 1997. By the late 20th century, the city of Bilbao in northern Spain was becoming a faded industrial backwater, and it was searching for a transformational project that would bring in tourist dollars to improve the economy. The Guggenheim Bilbao project did just that. Millions of tourists have made Bilbao a stop on their European tour in order to see this iconic building. "The Bilbao Effect" is a phrase used by architectural critics to describe attempts by cities to bring in economic and cultural revitalization through commissioning a celebrated architect to design a cultural institution that boasts an attention-grabbing design. Cities like Denver have been successful with their new art museum designed by Daniel Libeskind. Los Angeles is hoping that Gehry's Walt Disney Concert Hall will have the same effect on the city's faded downtown neighborhood.

One World Trade Center

New York, New York
2014

BACKGROUND

When those two fuel-laden planes crashed into the two towers of the World Trade Center on that sparkling September morning in 2001, the citizens of the city, the country, and the world felt as though they had been struck as well. The subsequent anguish and pain suffered by the surviving families and the nation made the subject of the redevelopment of the site an excruciatingly sensitive topic. The fact that many of the remains of the dead were never found made the land at "Ground Zero" a permanent cemetery in the minds of many. But the real estate developer Larry Silverstein, who had just signed a 99-year lease with the owner, the Port Authority of New York and New Jersey, a few weeks before, was receiving an insurance payment to cover his loss, which had certain requirements according to the language of the policy. What has eventually been designed and constructed on that hallowed site has been influenced by the politics and investments of a powerful group of stakeholders, which included the leaseholder Silverstein, the state and the city of New York, the Port Authority of New York and New Jersey, the Transit Authority, the architects and engineers who received the commissions, and of course the powerful family groups that were grieving their loss. The result has had mixed reviews, but the fact that the tower has been completed and has drawn millions of visitors to the site can be seen as an accomplishment in itself.

When the debris was finally cleared from the so-called pile where the twin towers once stood, the summer of 2002 was about to begin. Underground fires that continued to burn as well as the careful search for remains of the victims delayed the work. When the site was cleared, many voices were heard with differing opinions about the desired end product of the redevelopment of the site. Two architectural competitions were held. The first one provided no satisfactory designs, so a second one was advertised. Many famous international architectural firms participated in the competition. One wanted to replace the old buildings in kind to convey a statement of strength. Another made the new buildings into a skeleton of steel latticework that resembled a permanent portrayal of the corpse of the two towers. The winner of the second competition for the overall plan for the site in 2003 was the Polish-born and Bronx-raised architect named Daniel Libeskind. His design was hailed by the critics but despised by the leaseholder Silverstein. There were a total of six tall buildings on the site, with the focal point a towering skyscraper with an asymmetrical mast at the top that was meant to recall the upraised arm of the Statue of Liberty. Engineers questioned the integrity of such a design, as the wind loads at the top of the building would be substantial. Silverstein rejected the entire design, although he retained the overall site plan provided by Libeskind. However, unfortunately, the resulting complex lacks any building designed by the competition winner Daniel Libeskind. Larry Silverstein went ahead and hired a prominent architect from the New York firm of Skidmore, Owings and Merrill (SOM) named David M. Childs to redesign the central tower. What had been known as the Freedom Tower was now named One World Trade Center. The design was released in 2009.

One of the signature aspects of the Libeskind site plan was the inclusion of the World Trade Center memorial. As usual, many groups had many opinions about the design of the memorial within the site. Some family members wanted to see the entire site given over to a memorial. Others in the finance and development field sought a complete redevelopment of the 16 acres as a commercial business district in order to prove that the commercial core of the city remained undaunted by the attack. Libeskind's plan was to retain the footprint of the two towers as a memorial, redeveloping only the remainder of the site. This judicious plan was accepted as a compromise that respected the tragic history of the attack but acknowledged the persistence of the business life of the city. In 2004, another competition was held to design the memorial using the site identified by Libeskind. Fifty-two hundred architects submitted entries for this competition, the largest in history. The winner of the competition was an architect named Michael Arad who was working for the city's beleaguered Housing Authority, lending unexpected prestige to the local civil service workforce. His minimalist design that literally reflects the footprint of the two towers as deep voids, which he called "Reflecting Absence," has been acclaimed by critics and visitors alike.

The outcome of the Freedom Tower, known as One World Trade Center, was more problematic. Childs reworked the plan to accommodate the wind loads as well as the myriad of security concerns that accompanied the design program. Soaring costs and political fights led to a number of design changes that altered the final appearance of the tower. However, by 2014, the tower was completed.

CHARACTERISTICS AND FUNCTIONALITY

The One World Trade Center tower functions as an office building. Many critics have derided the building for not including multiple uses within its walls. There are only a few restaurants or other retail establishments, and no theater spaces, opera houses, and apartments within the structure or on the entire site. The explanation for this dearth of amenities is that the insurance policy that paid for the building required that the complex be replaced in kind, with 11 million square feet of commercial office space. The tower is in the shape of an obelisk, influenced by the iconic Washington Monument in Washington, D.C. The unusual design is chamfered, consisting of eight enormous isosceles triangles that taper as they rise to the top. In so doing, the footprint of the floors changes from a square at the bottom, to octagons in the middle to a rotated square at the top. The symmetrical exterior appears faceted like a cut gemstone. The tallest floor is the same height as the original twin towers. The building is clad in glass with a steel frame but the interior core consists of a concrete mass that rises up to the highest floor like an interior flagpole. It contains all the services of the building, including staircases, elevators, and ductwork, leaving the space around the core available for office space. The structure has been designed to resist wind loads as well as gravity loads. The tragedy of the "pancaking" fall of the twin towers has been attributed to the light structural trusses that supported the floors with minimal strength. This building has no such flaws. In addition, in 2005, the Police Department of the City of New York demanded that the building be fully protected by a fortified base to prevent against car bombs. In fact, the first 15 floors of the building, serving as a concrete bunker enclosing the mechanical systems, is a windowless pedestal designed to protect the base of the building. In order to give circulating air to the mechanical equipment contained inside, the base is covered with fins made of laminated glass, some of which can be open to let in air. The original design by David Childs called for a tall mast at the top of the building, which would bring the height of the building to the called-for 1,776 feet, in recollection of the year of the Declaration of Independence. At the base of the mast was to be a radome, which is an enclosure of the mast. When the developers decided that the radome was too expensive to build and maintain, the architect expressed disappointment. A number of design features that were called for in the original design had been altered or eliminated due to cost constraints.

The alter ego of the gigantic One World Trade Center tower is the World Trade Center Memorial. Abutting the soaring tower puncturing the sky are the two deep voids that puncture the earth. Designed by architect Michael Arad and landscape architect Peter Walker, the memorial serves as a civic square, a memorial park. The two voids that literally replace the locations of the two twin towers are enormous waterfalls. The black, square holes feature water spilling from the top to the bottom along all four sides. At the center of the bottom of the holes is another square void, where the water rushes into the earth. The tranquil sound of the running water, with the accompanying coolness emanating from the void, draws the visitors up to the edge. Along the parapet wall, in bronze panels along the edge, are the engraved names of the victims who perished on 9/11. They are arranged in related groups, not in alphabetical order, so that they would be remembered as they were in life. At night the names are lit from beneath, giving an additional mysterious aura to the victims' remembrance. The area around the voids contains a simple design of swamp white oak trees, backless benches, and light poles. The September 11 Museum is an underground space that is located next to the memorial. The pavilion entrance was designed by the Danish architectural firm Snohetta. The museum itself was designed by the Davis, Brody, Bond architectural firm, and opened in 2014. It contains over 10,000 artifacts from the site and many oral histories from the survivors, as well as a piece of the slurry wall, or "bathtub," that held back the water of the Hudson River in the foundations of the original World Trade Center towers.

KEY STATISTICS

The One World Trade Center tower is located on the northwest corner of the 16-acre site, bounded by West Street on the west, Vesey Street on the north, Washington Street on the east, and Fulton Street on the south. It contains 104 stories, and rises 1,776 feet including the spire, making it the tallest skyscraper in the Western Hemisphere. There are 3 million square feet of office space in the building. There are 70 elevators in the building. In making the building as safe as possible, several features were added that exceed building code requirements. The interior staircases are extra wide, and there are dedicated staircases for firefighters' use exclusively. The elevators, as well as the staircases, are located in the central concrete core of the building. In addition to the safety features, the building attained LEED (Leadership in Energy and Environmental Design) CS Gold certification from the Green Building Council, making it the most environmentally sustainable project of its size in the world. The observatory at the top of the tower opened in May 2015. It has a 360-degree view of the surrounding city.

CULTURAL SIGNIFICANCE

The redevelopment of the World Trade Center site after the tragedy of September 11, 2001, has been a fraught exercise from the very beginning. Now that over 15 years have passed, the city and the nation have begun to come to terms with the aftermath. With emotions running sky-high at the time, some of the ideas for the redevelopment of the site could now look incredibly dated. Fortunately, the various voices involved in the project came to a compromise that will most likely endure. The One World Trade Center tower has been disparaged by the critics consistently, as mediocre, impersonal, touristy, stunted, and bland. However, the ever-popular observation deck has attracted millions of eager visitors to its magnificent view and its supersonic elevator ride. Remember, even the twin towers were excoriated by critics for years, as the public grew ever fonder of the towers and their place on the New York City skyline. Some critics now compare the old towers favorably to the new one, as the lure of nostalgia is wont to do. However, the city goes on, the tourists keep coming, and the vibrancy of the 16-acre site on the lower west side of Manhattan will go on.

FURTHER INFORMATION: IMPORTANT PRINT, ELECTRONIC, AND MEDIA RESOURCES

Betsky, Aaron. August 13, 2012. "One World Trade Center's Decent into 'Meh.'" *Architect Magazine*. http://www.architectmagazine.com/design/one-world-trade-centers-descent-into-meh_o. Accessed June 10, 2017.

Dunlap, David W. June 12, 2012. "1 World Trade Center Is a Growing Presence, and a Changed One." *New York Times*. https://cityroom.blogs.nytimes.com/2012/06/12/1-world-trade-center-is-a-growing-presence-and-a-changed-one/. Accessed June 11, 2017.

Dupre, Judith. 2016. *One World Trade Center: Biography of a Building*. New York, Boston, and London. Little, Brown and Company.

Goldberger, Paul. September 12, 2011. "Shaping the Void—How Successful Is the New World Trade Center?" *New Yorker*. http://www.newyorker.com/magazine/2011/09/12/shaping-the-void. Accessed June 10, 2017.

Kamin, Blair. October 18, 2014. "One World Trade Center 'A Bold but Flawed Giant.'" *Chicago Tribune*. http://www.chicagotribune.com/news/columnists/ct-one-world-trade-center-review-kamin-met-1019-20141017-column.html. Accessed June 10, 2017.

Kimmelman, Michael. May 28, 2014. "Finding Space for the Living at a Memorial." *New York Times*. https://www.nytimes.com/2014/05/29/arts/design/finding-space-for-the-living-at-a-memorial.html. Accessed June 11, 2017.

Kimmelman, Michael. November 29, 2014. "A Soaring Emblem of New York, and Its Upside-Down Priorities." *New York Times*. https://www.nytimes.com/2014/11/30/nyregion/is-one-world-trade-center-rises-in-lower-manhattan-a-design-success.html?_r=0. Accessed June 10, 2017.

"One World Trade Center." Port Authority of New York and New Jersey. http://www.panynj.gov/wtcprogress/index.html. Accessed June 10, 2017.

Roth, Leland M., and Amanda C. Roth Clark. 2016. *American Architecture: A History*. Boulder, CO: Westview Press.

The Ten Tallest Skyscrapers in the World

The tallest skyscrapers in the world comprise a list that has to be regularly updated. What was once the tallest may not even make the list today. For instance, the Willis Tower (formerly the Sears Tower) in Chicago has fallen to 17th on the list, with the Empire State Building in New York coming in at a lowly 37th place. The new One World Trade Center in New York is 6th on the list, but boasts of the symbolism of its 1,776-foot height, referring to the nation's birthday. Here is the list of the ten tallest skyscrapers today. All the buildings are in Asia or the Middle East, with the exception of One World Trade Center.

1. **Burj Khalifa**
    Dubai, United Arab Emirates
    2,717 feet high
    Built in 2010

2. **Shanghai Tower**
    Shanghai, China
    2,073 feet high
    Built in 2015

3. **Abraj Al-Bait Clock Tower**
    Mecca, Saudi Arabia
    1,971 feet high
    Built in 2012

4. **Ping An Finance Centre**
    Shenzhen, China
    1,965 feet high
    Built in 2017

5. **Lotte World Tower**
    Seoul, South Korea
    1,819 feet high
    Built in 2016

6. **One World Trade Center**
    New York, New York, USA
    1,776 feet high
    Built in 2014

7. **Guangzhou CTF Finance Centre**
    Guangzhou, China
    1,739 feet high
    Built in 2016

8. **Tianjin CTF Finance Centre**
    Tianjin, China
    1,739 feet high
    Built in 2017

9. **Taipei 101**
    Taipei, China
    1,667 feet high
    Built in 2004

10. **Shanghai World Financial Centre**
    Shanghai, China
    1,614 feet high
    Built in 2008

Domestic Architecture

First Houses

Fallingwater

Cabrini-Green Homes

Levittown

Seaside

First Houses

New York, New York
1935

BACKGROUND

When millions of destitute immigrants arrived on the America's shores in the late 19th century, they needed a place to live. To accommodate this growing demand, developers saw an enticing profit opportunity. They snatched up properties on the Lower East Side of Manhattan where they constructed buildings that were as tall and deep as technologically possible. The first tenements, built specifically to house poor immigrants, were so gigantic that they occupied 90 percent of the typical 25-foot-by-100-foot New York City lot. These behemoths were six-story walk-ups, and contained up to 18 rooms on each floor, with only the front and back rooms having any natural light and air. With public transportation virtually nonexistent at the time, families sought to find housing close enough to easily travel to work. By the beginning of the 20th century, the middle class had relocated to better neighborhoods as the Lower East Side became home to hordes of immigrant families crammed into a teeming slum. Eventually realizing that the conditions in these tenements led to outbreaks of disease and fires, the city of New York passed several laws over the decades meant to ameliorate the housing conditions endured by these destitute families. Fire escapes were added, shared toilet facilities were required, and interior windows were added in the apartments in order to bring some natural light into the space. However, by the 1930s, an estimated 2 million New Yorkers still occupied 67,000 tenements. Some landlords refused to make the costly upgrades to their buildings and would evict their tenants and rent out only the first floors as commercial spaces. There were few options for families that were barely getting by and the tenement remained the only alternative for most newly arrived indigent immigrants.

By the onset of the Great Depression, housing conditions for the poor in New York City had hardly improved. With the unemployment rate skyrocketing, the poor were suffering more than ever. The Hoover administration did not believe in government intervention in real estate. Federal dollars were used only as fiscal incentives to encourage private development.

However, things started to change after Franklin Delano Roosevelt was elected in 1932. Roosevelt was cognizant of the deteriorating housing situation and in fact mentioned the plight of the urban and rural poor in his second inaugural address when he acknowledged that one-third of the nation was ill-housed (Wright 2008, 131). One of Roosevelt's programs, under the New Deal's National Industrial Recovery Act, passed in 1933, was the Public Works Administration (PWA). This program included a Housing Division, which was the first federal program that directly sponsored the construction of housing around the country, either through loans or grants to the developer or through direct project development. The PWA Housing Division was responsible for developing over 50 projects by 1937. Government intervention in real estate was considered by many as a slippery slope to socialism. But with the country in such a desperate state, many accepted the reforms proposed by Roosevelt's New Deal as necessary to kick-start the economy and help despairing Americans who were suffering from the ravages of the Depression.

New York State also contributed to the reform efforts in housing. In 1934, it passed the Municipal Housing Authority Act. This law permitted municipalities in the state to form public authorities. These quasi-public entities were then given the right to float public bonds in order to sponsor housing developments paid for by government funding. The creation of the Municipal Housing Authority Act led to the immediate formation of the New York City Housing Authority (NYCHA) in 1934.

The first project in New York City sponsored by NYCHA was given the unimaginative name of "First Houses." However, the name was significant: it was not only the first public housing built in New York City, but also the first public housing development constructed in the United States. It was paid for through funding provided by the federal government's Federal Relief Administration. The property was purchased from Vincent Astor, grandson of the scion of the New York real estate industry John Jacob Astor. Vincent Astor owned many tenements on the Lower East Side and was a believer in the policy of "slum clearance" that would provide for improved housing conditions through public funding of new construction. He sold 38 of his properties to the Housing Authority at the price of $189,281.31, a discounted price that was less than half of the properties' assessed valuation. NYCHA issued tax-free bonds that financed the purchase. There were two properties that were not owned by Vincent Astor in the group. The owner, Andrew Muller, refused to sell. He then proceeded to seek an injunction against NYCHA to stop the demolition of his property, and challenged the constitutionality of the condemnation of the buildings in 1935. A landmark case was handed down in 1936 in the New York State Court of Appeals, which stated that the use of eminent domain was constitutional as long as it was being used as a public benefit, that is, slum clearance, which was beyond the scope of the private sector to remedy. The labor for the construction of the project was provided through the federal government's work relief program. The unemployed workers who were paid by the Works Progress Administration were successful in getting the project completed. However, they did run into resistance from local labor unions, who objected to the use of nonunion labor. The project ran into cost overruns and delays, primarily due to the fact that the existing buildings, which were originally planned to be renovated, were in such poor condition. The final cost tripled from the original budget of $350,000. However, the completion of First Houses was a great coup for the city of New York. The project was dedicated in December 1935, with a throng of well-wishers who included Eleanor Roosevelt, Robert Moses, Governor Lehman, and Mayor LaGuardia, among many others. The proceedings were broadcast on radio nationwide. President Roosevelt sent his greetings to the thousands of New Yorkers who had gathered to celebrate the completion of this novel improvement to housing for the poor.

CHARACTERISTICS AND FUNCTIONALITY

The plan of the First Houses served as an experiment in design. It was an innovation in slum clearance, with an attempt to utilize the existing tenements in order to construct a new type of model housing. The architect, Frederick L. Ackerman, was a respected architect who had studied other public housing efforts in England and had worked on model housing development designs in Radburn, New Jersey, and Sunnyside Gardens in Queens. He was an advocate for quality low-income housing. The initial plan for the construction of First Houses involved a renovation of the existing tenements. The idea was to demolish every third tenement in the row, thereby allowing natural light and air on the side walls of every unit. This practice had been successful in projects in Britain, and was thought to be a solution to future slum clearance projects in New York. However, when the third tenements had been removed on the block, the builders discovered that the remaining two tenements were too fragile to stand on their own. They were, after all, already at least half a century old, and were shoddily constructed to begin with. In the end, the project was mostly rebuilt, with only three of the eight buildings using any of the old material, with structural steel required on each floor and for the staircases. However, the demolition of the old structures provided bricks that were reused and what was left over was sold, providing income for NYCHA. The project remained a type of renovation, though. One of the stipulations of the funding from the federal government was that the project be a renovation of existing tenements.

The buildings facing Avenue A are four stories high and in between the buildings, where the third tenement was located, is a one-story commercial structure. The buildings facing East Third Street are five stories high and have open access where the third tenement originally stood. The access to each of these structures is not facing the street, but is from the back. At the back of all the buildings is a paved courtyard. The windows are double-hung with six over six sashes. The buildings are very plain. The only decoration of the unrelieved brick fronts is three raised brick courses at the corners above the top row of windows. There are also four small recessed panels above the top row of windows that line up with the raised brick courses. These simple decorations are influenced by Art Deco design. The most appealing aspect of these buildings is the extended courtyard that runs behind the buildings. It boasts trees, benches, and charming concrete sculptures designed by artists who were employed by the New Deal Federal Artists Program. The sculptures include horses, a bear, a dog, and a dolphin. Separating the courtyard from the next property is a one-story brick wall with decorative concrete panels that depict more whimsical animals including a gazelle, seagull, rabbit, pigeon, cat, goat, turkey, and fox. The apartments are three or four rooms each. All the units had private bathrooms, which was a novel idea to the long-suffering tenants of the tenements. They also had steam heat and full kitchens. They did not have elevators, as opposed to the later, taller public housing projects. However, they did have wide staircases.

KEY STATISTICS

First Houses occupies an L-shaped lot located on Avenue A and East Third Street in Manhattan. The addresses of the units are 29–41 Avenue A and 112–138 East 3rd Street, comprising 1.2 acres. Although referred to as the Lower East Side, the neighborhood is now considered the East Village. Each apartment contained a full kitchen with a stove and a refrigerator and room for a dinette set, a living room with about 180 square feet, and one or two bedrooms of about 130 square feet each. There was a bathroom in each apartment that included a toilet and a bathtub. Tenants from the tenements nearby did not have these luxuries. Each room, including the kitchen and bathroom, had a window, an amenity not often found in New York apartments even today. The buildings had laundry rooms and a community room. It was originally planned to house 122 families, who paid an average monthly rental of $6 per room, a rent that included amenities. The buildings are four stories high on Avenue A and five stories high on East Third Street.

CULTURAL SIGNIFICANCE

The landmarked housing project called the First Houses is an unassuming set of brick apartment buildings lining East Third Street and Avenue A in Manhattan. They are surrounded by a number of later projects built by the New York City Housing Authority. But they are significant for a number of reasons. Yes, they were the first—the first in New York and the first in the country. They were an experiment. The ubiquitous New York

City tenements provided unacceptable housing conditions for thousands of indigent families. The First Houses project was designed as a solution to the tenement house issue. And it remained a solution. It served the public successfully for over 80 years and is still a little star in the constellation of housing projects overseen by NYCHA. The houses were wildly popular at the time they were opened. Almost 4,000 applications were received for 122 apartments. Tenants were very carefully screened by a committee of social workers. They had to fit a specific profile. They were typically the working poor. All were white, which is not surprising considering the times. To accommodate African Americans, another project was constructed the following year in Harlem. The Housing Authority was very concerned that the First Houses, its initial project, be successful. Building housing for the poor with public funds was a risky venture at that time. The advocates for public housing not only wanted to provide adequate accommodations but also wanted to prove that the poor would appreciate the quality housing that was provided for them. Public housing has been a contentious issue in the decades since the First Houses was built. Although the New York City Housing Authority has been the largest and most successful public landlord in the country, there are still many serious issues in today's housing projects. Nonetheless, there is a waiting list of a quarter million people waiting for apartments in 334 developments throughout the city. Some projects have been more successful than others. Designs that took over large properties to create "superblocks" with tall towers surrounded by open space proved to be problematic, and a number of projects in other American cities were eventually demolished. But the blueprint for the First Houses project, with its small size and its location within a neighborhood and abutting the street, has proven itself to be a winner.

FURTHER INFORMATION: IMPORTANT PRINT, ELECTRONIC, AND MEDIA RESOURCES

Gray, Christopher. September 24, 1995. "Streetscapes/Public Housing; In the Beginning, New York Created First Houses." http://www.nytimes.com/1995/09/24/realestate/streetscapes-public-housing-in-the-beginning-new-york-created-first-houses.html. Accessed December 28, 2016.

Landmarks Preservation Commission Nomination. "First Houses." LP-0876. November 12, 1974. http://www.neighborhoodpreservationcenter.org/db/bb_files/74-FIRST-HOUSES.pdf. Accessed January 13, 2017.

Plunz, Richard. 1990. *A History of Housing in New York City*. New York: Columbia University Press.

Smith, Lindsey. January 2, 2015. "Happy 80th Birthday to America's First Experiment in Public Housing." http://bedfordandbowery.com/2015/01/

happy-80th-birthday-to-americas-first-experiment-in-public-housing/. Accessed December 28. 2016.

Wright, Gwendolyn. 2008. *USA: Modern Architectures in History*. London: Reaktion Books.

Eleanor Roosevelt, in Her Speech at the Dedication of the First Houses on December 3, 1935

Eleanor Roosevelt, in her speech at the dedication of the First Houses, stated, "Low-cost housing must go on in the United States, but it will not go on unless this is a success . . . Now the question is, will the tenants do their part to make this experiment successful."

Source: Smith, Lindsey. January 2, 2015. Bedford and Bowery.com. http://bedfordandbowery.com/2015/01/happy-80th-birthday-to-americas-first-experiment-in-public-housing/.

Fallingwater

Mill Run, Pennsylvania
1939

BACKGROUND

It was 1935, the depths of the Great Depression, and America's most famous architect had been suffering from the worst professional and personal period of his life. It was true that some of his difficulties were self-inflicted. In 1909, Frank Lloyd Wright left his wife and six children in Oak Park, Illinois, outside of Chicago, to travel to Europe to connect with the wife of one of his early clients, Mamah Cheney, with whom he had developed a romantic relationship. His wife, Kitty, refused to divorce him. He felt creatively drained and he longed to spend time with Mamah. Wright took time off from his professional career while in Europe and produced several publications containing drawings and photographs of his prior work, which influenced the modern European architectural movement. However, when Wright returned to the United States, society in Chicago refused to accept him with his mistress and he retreated to a rural location in Wisconsin where he built a home that he called Taliesin. Heartbreak seemed to dog Wright, and in 1914, an employee at the estate went on a killing spree, murdering seven people including Mamah and two of her children, subsequently setting fire to the complex. Devastated by the loss, Wright rebuilt Taliesin. The years of the 1920s were financially disastrous. Wright received few commissions, and the commissions he did receive remained on the drawing board. His home at Taliesin burned down again and he was mired in financial woes due to divorce litigation and bankruptcy. The brilliant, idiosyncratic architect of the early-20th-century "prairie style" seemed to be past his prime. However, his personal life was looking up. He finally received a divorce from his second wife and he married Olga Lazovich, who outlived him, and gave Wright a more stable home life. With Olga's organizational skills, Wright set up a Taliesin Fellowship in his home in Wisconsin, where he launched an architectural school and apprenticeship program. One of his students was a young man named Edgar Kaufmann Jr. from Pittsburgh, Pennsylvania. Through Edgar Jr. Wright met the man who would become the proud owner of the most beloved and celebrated house ever designed by Wright.

Edgar Kaufmann, Sr., was the owner of a very successful department store in downtown Pittsburgh. Although he lived in the Pittsburgh area, he also owned land in the wooded hills southeast of the city, where he enjoyed escaping Pittsburgh's summer heat and sooty air. After meeting Wright, Kaufmann was impressed with Wright's genius and asked him to design a country hideaway for the family near a waterfall on his property. Wright visited the site only once, and proceeded to retreat to his office in Wisconsin to draw up the plans. When the plans were completed, the Kaufmanns were surprised to find that Wright's plans revealed a daring design that placed the house right on top of the waterfall. Edgar, Sr., had expected to see a pleasant country house with a view of the waterfall. Instead, he got a modern masterpiece that incorporated the waterfall into the house. The design was the ultimate example of Wright's theory of "organic architecture," that is, architecture that appears to grow directly out of the landscape in an organic way. The Kaufmann house, that Wright dubbed "Fallingwater," was designed to be an integral part of the landscape, with the waterfall providing a constant, soothing sound for the residents relaxing directly above it. This house would soon boost the sagging career of Wright right back into the highest firmament of America's greatest architectural talents.

CHARACTERISTICS AND FUNCTIONALITY

The house designed by Wright deep in the woods of western Pennsylvania was conceived as a tree house. Wright placed it right in the forest perched above the small waterfall called Bear Run. Its structure also resembled a tree, with implausibly deep cantilevers stretching out from a central stone core. The house seems to grow right out of the site, as the broad cantilevered patios hover over the waterfall. The central sandstone core of the house is anchored into a natural rock formation from which the concrete cantilevers extend. The series of concrete cantilevers are shaped like trays, with the upturned edges of the trays serving as low parapet walls for the terraces. There is a stunning interplay between the vertical rough stone elements and the smooth concrete horizontal elements, connected by the horizontal bands of windows. The sandstone used as the core was quarried on the site and cut into thin slabs of various lengths. The concrete was reinforced with steel to buttress the long spans that were supported on only one end. Wright's use of color on the exterior was also a crucial factor in the design. To complement the natural colors of the trees and stone, Wright selected two paint colors for the exterior: ochre for the concrete cantilevers and Cherokee red as an accent on the window frames.

Fallingwater is not a large house, consisting of only a living room, three bedrooms, and service rooms that include a small kitchen. The dining area is part of the huge living room. Wright was a master manipulator in his designs, and in Fallingwater, he brought visitors into the house through a narrow, dark entry after which they would be greeted by a glorious, 48-foot-wide living room space with continuous bands of windows that bring the outside in. Wright always altered the ceiling heights to alter the mood. In his low-priority spaces like the entry or interior corridors, the ceilings were uncomfortably low. He thought that these spaces were unpleasant necessities and he wanted to encourage visitors to move through them as quickly as possible so that they could enjoy the light and space of the main living spaces. The living room space has a variety of ceiling heights and materials that identify different uses for the areas within the gigantic space. The central focal point of the room is the massive asymmetrical stone fireplace. In front of the fireplace is an outcropping of a boulder found on the site. Wright was a great fan of fireplaces; he considered the hearth to be the heart of the home and he used them in almost every room. The second floor has a master bedroom, a master study, and a guest room. The third floor has another bedroom and study and was used by their son Edgar Jr. All the rooms of the house have connecting terraces looking out over the waterfall and stream. These terraces comprise the famous cantilever trays. In 1939, Wright was contracted to design a separate guest house and servants' quarters for Fallingwater on the hill above the main house. He incorporated the design of the guest house to add onto the artistic composition of the house. The guest house was reached through a curving walkway, which was covered by a cantilevered concrete canopy, which recalls the concrete terraces of the main house. Wright demanded total artistic control when he designed a building, and this house was no different. He often designed all the elements of the building, including the furniture. The furniture he designed for Fallingwater was almost exclusively built into the walls, so the clients did not have the option of relocating it, thereby ruining the artistic vision of the architect. In the case of Fallingwater, the exquisite black walnut veneer Wright selected can still be seen in built-in furniture throughout the house.

KEY STATISTICS

Fallingwater is located in Mill Run, Pennsylvania, in Fayette County in the hills southeast of Pittsburgh. It was designed and built between 1936 and 1938, with the guest house added in 1939. The house has a total of 5,330 square feet, of which 2,445 square feet are dedicated to the outdoor terraces. The guest house adds an additional 1,700 square feet. The entire site of the Fallingwater estate is 5,000 acres and is called the Bear Run Nature Reserve. The cost of the house was above budget. Originally budgeted for $30,000, the final cost was $155,000. Wright collected a fee of $8,000. The design of the house relied on many locally found materials. Native sandstone was used in the walls, piers, and chimney core. The floors were also made of native sandstone. The cantilevers were reinforced concrete.

CULTURAL SIGNIFICANCE

Frank Lloyd Wright's house that he named Fallingwater has become known as his masterpiece. It has been placed on a number of "must see" lists and is dubbed one of America's favorite buildings by the American Institute of Architects. Wright's sputtering career got a huge lift by the acclaim that was afforded the country house in Pennsylvania. Wright made it to the cover of *Time* magazine in January 1938 after Fallingwater was completed. The renowned architectural historian Vincent Scully deemed that the house is "one of the complete masterpieces of twentieth-century art." The house is perfectly partnered with its natural site, and demonstrates Wright's respect for nature that he espoused in his theory of "organic architecture." However, it is also Wright's personal interpretation of the Modernist ethos. When Wright went to Europe, he was not pleased with the cold, rational designs of the Modernist giants like Gropius, Le Corbusier, and Mies van der Rohe. Ever the romantic, he excoriated International Style buildings as they began to crop up all over the United States, and refused to adhere to any architectural style but his own. However, looking closely at Fallingwater, you see that this is a Modernist building. Certain views of Fallingwater look like a version of European 1920s' Modernist designs, with broad bands of unornamented concrete cantilevers forming bold asymmetrical lines separated by dark voids. It is stunning from every perspective, from the typical photo view showing the cantilevers over the waterfall to the magnificent, warm walnut and stone interiors, to every carefully thought-out detail throughout the house. After the death of Edgar Kaufmann in 1955, the house was left to his son Edgar Jr., who then entrusted it to the Western Pennsylvania Conservancy in 1963, which is still in charge of the property. The constant flow of visitors, totaling upward of 5 million since its opening to the public in 1964, has proven that the house still has broad appeal.

FURTHER INFORMATION: IMPORTANT PRINT, ELECTRONIC, AND MEDIA RESOURCES

"Fallingwater Facts." 2017. Fallingwater. http://www.fallingwater.org/38/. Accessed July 2, 2017.

"The Life of Frank Lloyd Wright." Frank Lloyd Wright Foundation. http://franklloydwright.org/frank-lloyd-wright/. Accessed July 2, 2017.

Lind, Carla. 1996. *Frank Lloyd Wright's Fallingwater*. Portland, OR: Archetype Press.

Love, Kenneth. 2006. *Saving Fallingwater*. Documentary. Kenneth A. Love International.

Pitts, Carolyn. January 26, 1976. "Fallingwater: National Register of Historic Places Inventory—Nomination Form." National Park Service.

http://www.dot7.state.pa.us/CRGIS_Attachments/SiteResource/H000868_01J.pdf. Accessed July 2, 2017.

Roth, Leland M., and Amanda C. Roth Clark. 2016. *American Architecture: A History*. Boulder, CO: Westview Press.

Upton, Dell. 1998. *Architecture in the United States*. Oxford: Oxford University Press.

Wald, Matthew L. September 2, 2001. "Rescuing a World-Famous but Fragile House." *New York Times*. http://www.nytimes.com/2001/09/02/us/rescuing-a-world-famous-but-fragile-house.html. Accessed July 2, 2017.

Necessary Renovations to Fallingwater

In 1997, a graduate student in engineering from the University of Virginia did a study on the structural support of Frank Lloyd Wright's renowned house in Pennsylvania called Fallingwater. Rumors had persisted that the wide concrete cantilevers had insufficient reinforcing steel to hold up the daring terraces, which were supported on only one end. Wright had specified all the reinforcing steel, although contemporary engineers had protested that it was not enough. In fact, when the house was built and the forms were removed from the concrete, the cantilevers immediately sank by 1.75 inches. The study done by the graduate student showed that the house was still deflecting, so an engineering firm, Robert Silman and Associates, that specialized in that type of work was hired to investigate. The house was found to be in severe danger of collapse. Temporary bracing was placed under the cantilevers as the engineers studied what type of solution could be found. A total of $11.5 million was raised, and by 2001, work on the renovation of the structure was begun. The interior of the great living room had to be totally removed and saved in order to reach the four main beams that supported the cantilevers. The solution was a new method called "post-tensioning," which involved high-strength cables that were strung along either side of the beam, attached by blocks of high-strength concrete. The cables were tightened at the ends, which gave added strength to the beams. None of this work is visible, so the great masterpiece looks exactly the same. When it was completed, the interior was replaced after all the parts had been restored. Today, the house looks as good as it did when it was built 80 years ago.

Cabrini-Green Homes

Chicago, Illinois
1942–1962

BACKGROUND

The Near North section of Chicago is located in walking distance to the Loop, Chicago's central business district. It is also a few blocks from the Gold Coast, Chicago's most luxurious neighborhood, replete with high-end shopping and million-dollar mansions, townhouses, and condos. However, the Near North, as close as it was to the bustling Loop and the glitzy Gold Coast, was not known for its glamour. It was known for its murder rate. The neighborhood was dubbed "Little Hell" or "Little Sicily" in the first decades of the 20th century, with a mostly southern Italian and Sicilian population. This was an isolated and poor population, many of whom worked in the steel mill located in nearby Goose Island in the Chicago River. Crime was so endemic in this neighborhood that the corner of West Oak Street and Milton Avenue had a list of over 100 unsolved murders, giving the location the nickname "Death Corner." The residents of this district were frightened by the organized crime and the blackmailing schemes of the so-called Black Hand that threatened them with death if they squealed to the police. This lawlessness of the Little Hell neighborhood only worsened with Prohibition and the alcohol rivalries perpetrated by the gangs of Al Capone and Giuseppe "Joe" Aiello. This violent neighborhood ultimately would be replaced by another place of isolation and crime, which became known as Cabrini-Green, an infamous housing project that would also eventually be demolished.

CHARACTERISTICS AND FUNCTIONALITY

In 1934, in the depths of the Great Depression, housing was at a premium in the city of Chicago. The newly formed Chicago Metropolitan Housing Council produced a plan to rebuild 36 square miles of downtown Chicago, clearing the slums and industrial enterprises in order to make room for new development and put Chicago's idle construction workers back to work. The destruction of the Near North's Little Hell neighborhood was part of the plan. With the passage of the federal Housing Act in 1937, funding became available to clear slums and build public housing in urban areas hit hard by the Depression. The city of Chicago began acquiring land in the Near North for its new housing project. The project initially was planned as a 920-unit development in a large swath of land adjacent to the Montgomery Ward headquarters and warehouses. The city was not able to acquire all the land, and the project was reduced in scope to 586 units on 16 acres, bounded by Chicago Avenue, Larrabee Street, Division Street, and Hudson Avenue. Half of the existing properties were purchased by the city, and the rest was condemned by eminent domain. In 1942, the crumbling district was razed, and the first section of the Cabrini-Green public housing development was built. This initial segment of the project was called the Frances Cabrini Homes, named after Mother Cabrini, the first American to be canonized by the Catholic Church. These homes were a low-rise development. The first tenants in these townhomes were workers who were contributing to the war effort, a requirement enforced by federal guidelines during World War II, although some low-income families were also housed there. The architects for this part of the development were a group consisting of Henry Holsman, George Burmeister, Maurice Rissman, Ernest Grunsfeld Jr., L. R. Soloman, G. M. Jones, K. M. Vitshum, I. S. Loewenberg, and Frank McNally. The cost was $6,333 per unit, which was rather high for the time, but the acquisition of the land had raised the cost significantly. There were both two- and three-story buildings in the project. The three-story buildings were located along the edges of the property and consisted of a first floor garden apartment with a separate entrance on the interior side of the building. The upper two floors had entrances on the street side and had exterior stairs going up to the second floor, making a two-story townhouse. Both units had separate entrances, without any interior corridors, and there was a small yard for each unit. Each unit also had its own heating plant. These first projects were planned to be as maintenance-free for the Housing Authority as possible. The project included a mix of races, with 75 percent white residents and 25 percent African American residents. They were screened so as to only accept the "worthy poor," denying any families with poor job history, credit rating, or arrest records.

The second set of buildings to be erected in the Cabrini-Green project was called the Cabrini Extension, built in 1957. These red-brick mid- and high-rises, with 1,900 additional units, became known as "the Reds." The architect for these buildings was A. Epstein and Sons. The final set of buildings in the Cabrini-Green project was called the William Green Homes, built in 1962. These buildings had another 1,000 units, and became known as "the Whites" because of their reinforced concrete exterior. They had exterior open-gallery corridors that made them the most dangerous and crime-ridden of the projects. The architect of these buildings was Pace Associates. All the buildings that were erected after the initial low-rise Frances Cabrini Homes were in the model of Le Corbusier's "tower in the park" concept. The Modernist ideals had taken hold in architectural design, and tall, isolated apartment buildings with their characteristic "superblocks" reigned, which destroyed much of the street grid. By the 1960s, the Cabrini-Green project contained a total of 3,600 apartments and 15,000 residents. The racial makeup of the project changed by the 1960s. With the influx of southern black families into Chicago after World War II, as part of the Great Migration, the city of Chicago had to house thousands of new residents. White districts in the city refused to allow the construction of public housing. By the 1970s, the Cabrini-Green development was virtually all African American. The Chicago Housing Authority's rules on maximum incomes within the projects made the most stable of households move out. So what was left was the poorest of the poor.

KEY STATISTICS

The Cabrini-Green Homes were located in the Near North district in central Chicago, on land bordered by Clybourn Street and Halsted Street on the north, North Larrabee Street on the west, Chicago Avenue on the south, and Hudson Street on the east. They were built and maintained by the Chicago Housing Authority. Nearly all the buildings that comprised the development have been demolished. Only some of the original low-rise buildings that were constructed in 1942 remain. The mid- and high-rise buildings were demolished between 1995 and 2011.

CULTURAL SIGNIFICANCE

The unhappy ending of the Cabrini-Green Homes was caused by a multitude of factors. The fact that the mid- and high-rise structures have all been demolished whereas the oldest section, the low-rise townhouses, though rundown, still remain says something about the effectiveness of the "tower in the park" idea for public housing. Nationwide, many of the giant high-rise public housing projects have been demolished. In addition, the Chicago Housing Authority has been accused of systemic mismanagement in all its projects, due to the rampant corruption in Chicago politics and the subsequent patronage jobs at the Chicago Housing Authority that were most often doled out to the least qualified. The initial low-rise units had an integration policy with a quota for African Americans and a screening process for applicants. However, federal rules were changing and income limits were lowered for acceptance into the projects. The influx of poor blacks from the South in the 1960s and the dearth of available housing in other parts of Chicago where white residents adamantly resisted integration made projects like Cabrini-Green warehouses for the most indigent African Americans. Factories were leaving the city, and over 350,000 industrial jobs disappeared in Chicago between 1953 and 1999. White families abandoned the city as they took advantage of the policies of the Federal Housing Administration (FHA), which encouraged them to purchase inexpensive homes in the suburbs. Racist policies such as redlining, which were actually written into the federal law as the city mapped out districts that would benefit from the FHA mortgages, prevented even upwardly mobile African Americans from purchasing a house in the expanding suburbs. These unfair advantages afforded to white families made paying a mortgage cheaper than renting. With the help of the FHA, the growing value of the house was a wealth builder for the family. However, it was not that way for the families living in the Chicago projects. As the projects began to descend into the depths of despair, the Chicago Housing Authority responded by reducing maintenance and leaving apartments vacant. This led to more criminal activity as gangs took over empty apartments. The superblocks created a virtually walled-off community that was off-limits to the white middle class. Police avoided the area; schools went downhill, as the neighborhoods surrounding the projects lost population. Isolated and poor, the tenants of the Cabrini-Green projects were left to fend for themselves.

The Cabrini-Green housing project became a symbol of the failure of public housing policy in the United States. As many of the high-rise projects fell into disrepair, Cabrini made national headlines in its notoriety. After the assassination of Martin Luther King Jr. in April 1968, riots accelerated the downhill slide of the Cabrini-Green projects. The killing of two white police officers in 1970 put Cabrini in the headlines once again. But the worst and saddest case at Cabrini-Green was the killing of Dantrell Davis, a seven-year-old boy who was walking home with his mother from school, and was shot by a stray bullet in the fall of 1992. As the city of Chicago began to rebound in the 1990s and the downtown was expanding once again, gentrification became the buzzword for the Near North. Unlike the many public housing projects on the south side of the city, home to most of the African American population, the Cabrini-Green Homes was located right next to the famous Gold Coast. Here was a neighborhood ripe for development. The city began to consider redeveloping the area with mixed-income housing. It produced a "Plan for Transformation" in 1999 that called for the demolition of 18,000 public housing units, including all open-gallery high-rise buildings. The Cabrini-Green project was part of the demolition plan. The tenants of Cabrini-Green fought the plan. They knew that their project was poorly maintained and dangerous. However, many families had lived there for years and to them it was home. Also they understood that the new development might not be required to house the current tenants of Cabrini-Green. The new project was to be mixed-income and less concentrated, and would therefore not be able to accommodate all the thousands of poor tenants who currently lived in Cabrini-Green. The tenants protested but eventually lost the fight: the last high-rise was demolished in 2011. The new development, which is attracting a variety of middle- and low-income residents, offers subsidized housing to a select group of tenants from the old Cabrini-Green. The condo owners and the public housing tenants live together in nervous unfamiliarity. The puzzle of housing the poorest of the poor has not yet been solved.

FURTHER INFORMATION: IMPORTANT PRINT, ELECTRONIC, AND MEDIA RESOURCES

Austen, Ben. May 2012. "The Last Tower: The Decline and Fall of Public Housing." *Harpers.* https://harpers.org/archive/2012/05/the-last-tower/. Accessed May 7, 2017.

Bowly, Devereax, Jr. 2012. *The Poorhouse: Subsidized Housing in Chicago.* Carbondale: Southern Illinois University Press.

Chung, Payton. 2003. "Short History of Cabrini Green." Westnorth.com. https://westnorth.com/2003/01/02/short-history-of-cabrini-green/. Accessed May 7, 2017.

Goetz, Edward G. Autumn 2012. "The Transformation of Public Housing Policy, 1985–2011." *Journal of American Planning Association* 78 (4): 452–63. https://www-tandfonline-com.proxy3.library.mcgill.ca/doi/full/10.1080/01944363.2012.737983. Accessed April 12, 2017.

Jackson, Kenneth. 1985. *Crabgrass Frontier.* New York and Oxford: Oxford University Press.

Miller, Brian J. September 2008. "The Struggle over Redevelopment at Cabrini-Green, 1989–2004." *Journal of Urban History* 34 (6): 944–60.

Ta-Nehisi Coates. June 2014. "The Case for Reparations." *Atlantic.* https://www.theatlantic.com/magazine/archive/2014/06/the-case-for-reparations/361631/ Accessed May 7, 2017.

Vale, Lawrence. February 2012. "Housing Chicago: Cabrini-Green to Parkside of Old Town." *Places Journal.* https://placesjournal.org/article/housing-chicago-cabrini-green-to-parkside-of-old-town/?gclid=Cj0KEQjwi7vIBRDpo9W8y7Ct6ZcBEiQA1CwV2PaYaWOOZE_VtpxxyPmbmMz-aliO7QvD-p7oOocopRcaAqPu8P8HAQ#footnote_10. Accessed April 11, 2017.

Cabrini-Green in Popular Culture

Cabrini-Green was part of popular culture in the late 20th century. The situation comedy called *Good Times*, which was produced by Norman Lear, was shown on television from 1974 to 1979. It portrayed a family that lived in the Cabrini-Green housing project. In addition, the horror film *Candyman*, from 1992, took place at the housing project.

Levittown

Nassau County, New York
1947

BACKGROUND

World War II had ended. A constellation of factors created a crisis in the American housing market. The moribund economy of the Great Depression and the subsequent allocation of manufacturing resources to the war effort resulted in a dearth of residential construction that persisted for over a decade. Fearing that the soldiers would not make it home, many young couples opted to marry during the war, and even to have children. The calamitous result was that there were few places to live for these young families when the soldiers finally returned home in 1945. Articles in the newspapers related stories about desperate families setting up homes in shipping crates, box cars, and chicken coops. Others doubled up with extended family or lived in temporary structures erected during the war, like Quonset huts. The housing crunch had reached critical proportions. In response, the federal government passed laws that insured mortgages through the Federal Housing Administration (FHA) and the Veterans' Administration. These laws permitted Americans to purchase homes with little or no money down. With the insurance of the federal government behind them, developers jumped at the chance to build houses as quickly as possible and to make the maximum profit with little risk. For the first time, developers could get an FHA "commitment" to insure the mortgage, and then become a temporary mortgagor. With "production advances" from the bank, the developer could then use these funds, with almost no risk, to continue to build gigantic projects with thousands of new homes. Undeveloped areas and small farms in counties surrounding large cities were prime targets for development. Another influence in suburban development was the Jeffersonian ideal of the single-family home. This traditional concept was supported by a political bias against multi-family housing as possibly subversive, even communistic. Joseph McCarthy, the red-baiting Republican senator from Wisconsin, held hearings in 1947–48 where he derided public housing and multi-family dwellings as a "breeding ground for communists" (Hayden 2003, 131). He teamed up with the National Association of Manufacturers and the developer of

Levittown, William Levitt, who testified against federal funding of housing, in addition to the abolishment of zoning and building codes, and the elimination of union labor in housing construction. However, the federal government was helpful to the private housing industry. Between 1946 and 1953, insured by the FHA and the Veterans' Administration, private builder-developers received loans from banks to construct 10 million new homes. This was a new phenomenon. In previous times, houses were most often built by small contractors or by the owners themselves. Even in the earlier housing boom of the 1920s, developers would purchase land; divide it into lots; build services like sewers, electric, and roads; and then sell the lots to owners or contractors who would build the houses. However, after World War II, huge builder-developer companies took over the housing industry with their speed of construction, their ability to handle government paperwork, and their lower prices. However, they often did not provide the services necessary for the development, like sewers and roads, leaving that cost up to the local governments.

The most influential builder-developer in the postwar years was Levitt and Sons, Inc. Abraham Levitt was a builder who launched his company in 1929, building upper-middle-class homes in the Long Island suburb of Rockville Center. Levitt and Sons continued to grow, building a subdivision in 1934 in Manhasset called "Strathmore." The company was hired to build several developments for wartime workers during World War II, which gave the developer experience in streamlining the construction, making for a quick turnaround. In addition, one of the sons, William, served in the Navy Seabees, the naval construction force, during the war. The family firm was well positioned to respond to the demand for housing once the war ended. It began to acquire 4,000 acres of land in the town of Hempstead, in Nassau County on Long Island. This land was previously used for potato farming. This was to become the first of the Levitt's legendary investments in middle-class suburban development, and the first to be named Levittown.

CHARACTERISTICS AND FUNCTIONALITY

The 7-square-mile tract of land was acquired by the Levitts in 1947. The Levitts named the development "Island Trees," although it was renamed Levittown in 1948. The patriarch, Abraham Levitt, was a former lawyer and horticulturalist. Although he lived in Manhattan in an apartment, the Jeffersonian concept of American families tending a garden in a small, suburban haven of greenery appealed to him. His son Alfred never finished college, but knew enough about drafting and architectural design to create the simple floor plans used in the Levittown houses. William, known as Bill, was the salesman and public relations man par excellence, who was responsible for the tremendously positive press coverage provided to the firm. The Levitts devised an innovative method of construction that was based on the concept of assembly lines. This method had never been utilized in residential construction. The Levitts laid out their new development with standard-sized 60- by 100-foot lots, along slightly curving streets. They used "vertical integration," a technique utilized by steel tycoon Andrew Carnegie during the Gilded Age. By vertically integrating, the company purchases and controls the sources of the necessary products for the industry, ensuring predictable costs and availability. With Carnegie, it was steel. With the Levitts, it was all the products necessary to build houses. They set up a subsidiary called the North Shore Supply Company. This company controlled the supply of the lumber, nails, and even the appliances that were provided to the houses. The Levitts purchased a lumber company in California that provided the wood. The construction of the houses was similarly set up like an assembly line in an automobile factory. Palettes of construction materials were delivered to the site and dropped off at 60-foot increments along the new roads. The materials were packaged according to need, with the items needed first located at the top. Workers did their work using power tools, like assembly-line workers, specializing in one thing only. They would perform their one task, even if it was painting a wall white, and then move on to the next house to paint an identical wall white. Unions were denied access to the building sites, which did result in some union picket lines. However, despite the tedious nature of the tasks assigned to the construction workers, they were paid handsomely, even better than union wages. The most complicated tasks were performed at a nearby assembly shop, with the completed sections delivered to the site. At its peak, the construction system invented by the Levitts produced one new house every 16 minutes.

The first group of houses in the development was completed and rented to an eager population. In October 1947, desperate families of veterans lined up for the chance to rent one of these new homes for $60 a month. The 1,800 houses in the first batch were initially rentals only, with an option to purchase after a year. The price of the houses after that year was a mere $6,990. The cost of the mortgage and taxes on these homes was actually less than the rent, so virtually everyone took advantage of the opportunity to buy. As the process of building continued, the houses were sold outright beginning in 1949. The first houses built by the Levitts were Cape Cod designs. These houses were small, at only 750 square feet. They were built "slab on grade," meaning that there was a concrete slab supporting the house, with no basement, making the construction of the house simpler. The house had only one floor, with an "expansion attic," which gave the homeowner the opportunity for "do it yourself" projects in the future if additional space was needed. There was a living room, kitchen, two bedrooms, and one bathroom in each house. No garage was included, although there was a driveway. The living room was 12 by 16 feet, with a fireplace. In 1949, a new version of the Levitt house was introduced called the Ranch. This house had a similar layout, but was slightly larger and had a carport. These houses sold for $9,500.

KEY STATISTICS

The original Levittown was built between 1947 and 1951 in the town of Hempstead in Nassau County, New York. It is almost seven square miles in area. It is not an incorporated town or village, but is called a "census designated place." When completed, it had more than 17,400 houses with a population of 82,000. Each house had a Bendix washer and a General Electric stove and some were even outfitted with a built-in television set. The Levittown Cape Cods were situated on a 60- by 100-foot lot, and the house measured 30 feet long by 25 feet deep. It had a high gable roof with windows on each end that could accommodate an additional room if finished. The houses were a simple rectangle and were extremely modest in design, although there were a few colonial details like shutters on the windows.

CULTURAL SIGNIFICANCE

William Levitt has become known as the "father of the modern American suburb," and Levittown has become the symbol of the postwar American suburb, with all its plusses and minuses. Levittown provided a needed housing option for many young families suffering from the unprecedented housing crisis after World War II. The houses were inexpensive. Although small, they provided a release valve for the families that were bunking with relatives or in various other inadequate conditions. Levittown was 40 miles outside of the city, but it gave its residents a home and a yard of their own. Many people loved it, and many friends were made among the hundreds of families that moved there. But it was not a panacea, and it unequivocally denied access to a certain group of people. The first contracts written by Levitt and Sons specified explicitly that the residents must be white, stating that the home could not "be used or occupied by any person other than members of the Caucasian race." The clause was taken out in 1948, due to a Supreme Court decision that found such clauses "unenforceable and contrary to public policy." However, Levittown continued to deny access to racial minorities, despite the law. The belief was that properties' values would fall if a minority moved in. The federal government's mortgage program that provided 5 percent down, 30-year mortgages in Levittown was a boon to the families who needed homes, as long as they were white.

The influence of Levittown on American life has been incalculable. Throughout the country, thousands of similar projects took advantage of the federal government's mortgage guarantees to build the suburban developments that litter the formerly undeveloped land that surrounds the cities. Five salient characteristics of the American suburbs that were built in the postwar years have been identified by Kenneth Jackson in his book *Crabgrass*

Frontier. First, they had a peripheral location, away from the city. Second, they had a low density, with single-family detached homes instead of townhouses or apartment buildings. Third, they displayed a similarity in design that made the whole project seem monotonous and repetitive. Fourth, due to the availability of government financing, mass production, and a booming economy, single-family homes were accessible to more working-class families for the first time. And fifth, Jackson states, was the economic and racial homogeneity of the new suburbs. African Americans were denied access to most of the postwar suburbs. By providing such attractive and inexpensive housing options for the white working class, the black working class remained in the urban areas, which exacerbated the pattern of "white flight," and severely hurt the economies of the cities. The homogeneity of the postwar suburbs also produced a conformity that has been criticized by a number of sociologists and writers as a cultural wasteland. However, despite its faults, the efficient production of so many inexpensive suburban dwellings that provided homes for so many Americans after the war was described by Kenneth Jackson as "a unique achievement in the world" (Jackson 1985, 245).

FURTHER INFORMATION: IMPORTANT PRINT, ELECTRONIC, AND MEDIA RESOURCES

Coates Ta-Nehisi. June 2014. "The Case for Reparations." *Atlantic*. https://www.theatlantic.com/magazine/archive/2014/06/the-case-for-reparations/361631/. Accessed May 7, 2017.

Hayden, Dolores. 2003. *Building Suburbia: Green Fields and Urban Growth, 1820–2000*. New York: Vintage Books.

Jackson, Kenneth T. 1985. *Crabgrass Frontier: The Suburbanization of the United States*. New York and Oxford: Oxford University Press.

Jones, Janelle. February 13, 2017. "The Racial Wealth Gap: How African-Americans Have Been Shortchanged Out of the Materials to Build Wealth." Economic Policy Institute. Working Economic Blog. https://www.epi.org/blog/the-racial-wealth-gap-how-african-americans-have-been-shortchanged-out-of-the-materials-to-build-wealth/. Accessed January 19, 2018.

Lambert, Bruce. 1997. "At 50, Levittown Contends with Its Legacy of Bias." *New York Times*. http://www.nytimes.com/1997/12/28/nyregion/at-50-levittown-contends-with-its-legacy-of-bias.html. Accessed February 22, 2017.

Marshall, Colin. 2015. "Levittown, the Prototypical American Suburb." *Guardian*. https://www.theguardian.com/cities/2015/apr/28/levittown-america-prototypical-suburb-history-cities. Accessed February 18, 2017.

Rothstein, Richard. 2017. *The Color of Law: A Forgotten History of How Our Government Segregated America.* New York: Liveright.

The Racial Wealth Gap and the Legacy of Housing Discrimination

Racial discrimination in federal housing policy during the 20th century has been one of the leading causes and a little-known dirty secret in the rise of racial inequality and what is now known as the "wealth gap." Today, African Americans' average incomes are approximately 60 percent that of whites' average incomes. Distressing as that is, the real crisis is the gap in wealth. African Americans' wealth averages 5 percent of the wealth of their white counterparts. Wealth is the measurement of total assets as opposed to income. Assets include the value of homes, cars, personal items, businesses, investments, and savings. So, although African Americans may have jobs with incomes comparable to whites, they have nowhere near the backup wealth that allows for retirement savings or college savings or the ability to provide an inheritance to children. Without the assets provided by wealth accumulation, families lack the buffer to help them through an economic downturn. This lamentable current situation was shaped by racially biased policies put in place by federal, state, and local governments, beginning in the 1930s that intensified in the years after World War II. This resulted in what amounted to government-sponsored racial segregation that had calamitous consequences.

These policies were institutionalized, varied, and pervasive. One of them was redlining. The policy known as "redlining" was initiated by the federal government in the 1930s when maps were created for every city in the country to identify locations where they would insure mortgage loans. Neighborhoods were identified with color coding, and areas that were outlined in red were black neighborhoods. The government considered those neighborhoods too risky to insure mortgages, thereby preventing residents in those neighborhoods from purchasing their homes. In addition, the official policy of the Federal Housing Administration (FHA) was to deny African Americans the opportunity to purchase homes in the newly created suburbs. The fear was that property values would go down, thereby putting the FHA-insured mortgages at risk. However, there was no statistical evidence for this reasoning. Suburban developments like Levittown in Long Island maintained these racially discriminatory policies for years. The manual created by the FHA, called the *Underwriting Manual*, which outlined rules for approving mortgage applications, specifically identified "inharmonious racial groups," thereby ensuring racial segregation. After World War II, with the endemic national housing shortage, black and white veterans alike were gainfully employed and in need of a place to live with their families. The FHA and the Veterans' Administration mortgages disallowed African Americans from qualifying for the mortgages, or for moving to houses in the suburbs. The white working-class families that were given this opportunity have benefited mightily from this perk. Most of them have gained wealth through the equity in their homes. In fact, two-thirds of all wealth for American families derives from their home equity. This wealth is used to pay for college, retirement, and old age, or as a buffer during hard times. Middle-class white families are also likely to enjoy a small inheritance from the value of their parents' home. However, African American families were often left in apartments or public housing in the inner cities, with no home equity and no wealth to pass along to their children. This persistent wealth gap has only worsened even as the segregationist government policies have been discarded. During the recent housing bubble, predatory lenders targeted minority families who were looking to buy into the American dream by purchasing a home, exposing them to high-interest, high-leverage loans. The foreclosure rate was higher for black families. When the bubble burst, the unemployment rate for African Americans was double that of whites. With the historic lack of wealth accumulation hindering their recovery from the crisis, minorities were hit the hardest during the recent Great Recession. Many Americans are not cognizant of this history of institutionalized racism, and they wonder why black families remain trapped in poverty. The regrettable history of these government policies provides one of the principal answers.

Seaside

Seaside, Florida
1981

BACKGROUND

The innovative real estate development system initiated by the William Levitt on Long Island in the late 1940s inspired hundreds of developments nationwide after World War II. Levitt condensed the construction method into a Ford-like assembly line system for large-scale suburban housing development. He rapidly and inexpensively produced houses for desperate families who were searching for housing during the postwar baby boom. Levitt's techniques of constructing hundreds of nearly identical houses on large tracts of former potato farms in the far reaches of Long Island were groundbreaking. But the completion of Levittown in 1947 was not the sole cause of the suburban sprawl that we encounter today. A constellation of crucial factors conspired to steer the nation into an explosion of suburban development in the decades following World War II. The severe housing crunch that faced the country was met head-on by several laws passed by Congress in the 1940s. The laws that insured mortgages through the Federal Housing Administration (FHA) and the Veterans' Administration gave working-class families a first-time opportunity to purchase a house with little or no money down. In addition, the FHA commitment to insure the mortgages gave developers the insurance to go ahead with the development of huge housing tracts. The data-driven methods of construction that had been developed during the war led to efficiencies that stimulated the construction of thousands of cookie-cutter houses at minimal cost. However, not everyone benefited from the favorable mortgage terms. The inclusion of racist language in the laws passed by Congress led to a legacy of discrimination that denied access to African Americans in these new suburban communities and also contributed to the disintegration of the economies in the nation's inner cities. In addition, zoning laws influenced the spread of suburban sprawl. Although introduced as a useful tool that segregated the smoky, malodorous, polluting factories from residential areas, the codification of the separation of all uses of land within a community was a major contributor to the appearance of the American suburbs. Zoning laws strictly segregated uses into residential, commercial, and industrial, thereby encouraging the spread of gigantic tracts of land dedicated solely to housing development. Adjacent smaller tracts were assigned to commercial development, connected by miles of new roadways. All this new construction required the use of the automobile. This resulted in the type of suburban sprawl that proliferated throughout the United States in the decades following World War II and continues today.

Before the introduction of the Levittown model of suburban development in the late 1940s, suburbs were developed in a very different manner. What came to be known as "streetcar suburbs" were built in the late 19th century and early 20th century in villages and towns within the range of the new form of transportation called the streetcar, or trolley. These trains allowed for short commutes from the new suburbs into the nearby city. Even after the invention of the automobile, streetcar suburbs were still being built through the 1930s. These towns featured a variety of houses, usually on small lots within walking distance to a main street where the commercial district was located. The development of the streetcar suburbs was very different from what was done in the late 20th century. Developers would purchase a tract of land and divide it up into lots. They would sell the lots to a small contractor, a carpenter, or an individual family, and the houses would then be built. This method resulted in more housing stock with more variety, and the community was more walkable.

By the 1970s, a group of American architects and urban planners examined the state of residential development in the United States and they hated what they saw. The low-density development gobbling up tracts of farmland farther and farther away from the urban centers, and totally car-dependent, seemed wasteful and unhealthy to this group of planners. Looking for inspiration from history, this group, who eventually took on the moniker "New Urbanists," studied several earlier precedents. The 19th-century movement that promoted so-called garden cities was one of their inspirations. This theory of urban planning, born in Britain, sought to break up the large, unwieldy cities into small satellite cities surrounding the city in concentric rings that were connected by transit. A number of new towns were built in the United States in the early 20th century based on these theories. Another influence was the American City Beautiful movement, which also dates from the turn of the 20th century. One of the leading proponents was John Nolen, a landscape architect who is credited with designing 27 new towns in the United States. Nolen believed in the Progressive ideals of civic virtue and public service. He embraced the concept of "environmentalism," which at that time meant that the good design of skilled professionals could improve human society. He believed in the importance of cities, but maintained that they could be improved by appropriate planning. The New Urbanists also found inspiration in an Austrian architect and planner named

Leon Krier, who has advocated for the use of traditional town planning as opposed to the typical modern use of segregated land-use zones. Another precedent of some of the ideas promoted by the New Urbanists was Jane Jacobs, the author of *The Death and Life of Great American Cities*, published in 1961. Jacobs argued against zoning, and in favor of the diverse urban street life that is engendered by a city that grows organically and welcomes a variety commercial and residential uses.

CHARACTERISTICS AND FUNCTIONALITY

Seaside is located on the Gulf Coast on Florida's panhandle. It is a new town built from scratch, and designed by the married team of New Urbanist architects Andres Duany and Elizabeth Plater-Zyberk. The land was owned by a Miami developer Robert Davis, who had inherited the land from his grandfather in 1979. Davis hired the Miami architectural firm Duany Plater-Zyberk and Company and proceeded to explore the concept of designing a new town. Traveling around the coast of Florida and researching old Florida beach communities, Davis encouraged his architectural team to find inspiration in the simple, 19th-century wood beach house and the town surrounding it. Duany and Plater-Zyberk had put together an analysis of the towns they had seen and came up with a scheme utilizing what they considered the most successful features. Soon they had a plan for the new town, which included a codification of the salient features that they had identified. The plan for the town was set, including a detailed building code, and in 1981, the new town of Seaside was launched.

The town is laid out in between the Gulf of Mexico to the south, woodland to the north, a nature preserve to the west, and an existing development to the east. A state highway bisects the southern third of the property. The town square is located in the center of the property among natural gorges in the dunes. A grid of streets is aligned with the community to the east called Seagrove. In the town center, a large property dominates the landscape as it abuts the state highway. The civic center is on a diagonal street that juts out from the town center to the northwest. At the end of the northwest diagonal are the Smolian Circle and the town hall. The northeast diagonal leads to Seaside Avenue, which boasts the largest properties and most prestigious addresses. The Neo-Classical pool pavilion is located at the apex of the northeast diagonal. The town has seven smaller streets running north–south. The lots are smaller and are made for middle-class housing.

The buildings in Seaside must conform to the detailed building codes written by the architects. These codes include rules for the massing, scale height, and footprint. Additional regulations cover the materials allowed to be used and the use of color, trim, lighting, fences, and even hardware. Houses were required to be made of wood, and had detached garages with alleys at the back of the houses. One of the interesting regulations in the town is the requirement for all houses to have front porches. The architects believed that porches encouraged friendly contact between neighbors. Although the team of Duany and Plater-Zyberk took pains to provide detailed codes and regulations for the appearance of the town of Seaside, they did not design any of the actual buildings. A number of prominent architects like Robert A. M. Stern, Leon Krier, and Steven Holl, as well as many others, designed the buildings within the town.

KEY STATISTICS

Seaside is an unincorporated town in Walton County, Florida. It comprises 80 acres on the Gulf of Mexico and has become a popular tourist destination. Its motto is "a simple, beautiful life." The science fiction film *The Truman Show* was filmed in Seaside in 1998.

CULTURAL SIGNIFICANCE

The New Urbanist movement in urban design has grown in popularity as well as in controversy. When Seaside was opened, it received a large dose of media coverage. Seaside is considered the first example of New Urbanist theories, but soon a group of like-minded architects and planners got together to draft a set of principles, which was later developed into the Charter for the Congress for the New Urbanism that was adopted in 1996. The charter includes the following principles: pedestrian-friendly streets and walkability; a grid of streets with a hierarchy of major and minor thoroughfares; mixed, not segregated, uses; a diverse range of housing size, type, and cost; emphasis on good quality architecture at human scale with a sense of place that nourishes the human spirit; a traditional neighborhood structure with a defined center and edge; the importance of the quality public realm and a range of uses and densities within a 10-minute walk; increased density; green transportation that encourages use of walking and biking; sustainability with minimal environmental impact; and finally, creating a high quality of life.

The charter of the New Urbanists is not only a collection of design concepts; it is also identified as a "normative theory," which indicates that it makes a judgment about right and wrong. The New Urbanists define the state of suburban sprawl in the United States as wrong and their precepts as right. They have been criticized from both sides of the political universe for their almost evangelical zeal and their absolute conviction that they have the answers to the problems of sprawl. Critics on the right think that planning should be left to the market forces and not strictly regulated as the New Urbanists insist. Besides, they contend, most Americans want to live in the suburbs with their large house with a beautiful kitchen, many bathrooms, and a three-car garage. They do not mind the driving and the traffic. Critics in the center and left have complained that this vision will always have a limited impact. How many new towns are going to be designed since the suburban genie has already been let out of the bottle decades ago? The towns that have been built, like Seaside and another Florida community built by the Disney Corporation called Celebration, have been derided as exercises in escapist nostalgia. The fact that Seaside was used as a prop for a film, *The Truman Show*, that portrayed a fake town that was secretly a reality show exemplifies its apparent appearance of inauthenticity. In addition, critics also worry about the fate of the urban poor. But New Urbanists would argue that their ideas can be translated into various locales, including as infill projects within inner cities. The vision of the New Urbanists as seen in the town of Seaside, Florida, is in the realm of the long list of utopian movements that have been strewn through American history. Certainly the New Urbanists have identified serious issues with urban planning, or the lack of it, that have taken over large swaths of the country. Their novel ideas of solving the issues of sprawl must be considered as we confront the problems of suburban sprawl more and more each day.

FURTHER INFORMATION: IMPORTANT PRINT, ELECTRONIC, AND MEDIA RESOURCES

Duany, Andres, Elizabeth Plater-Zyberk, and Jeff Speck. 2000. *Suburban Nation: The Rise of Sprawl and the Decline of the American Dream*. New York: North Point Press.

Ellis, Ciff. 2002. "The New Urbanism: Critiques and Rebuttals." *Journal of Urban Design* 7 (3): 261–91. http://www.tandfonline.com/doi/abs/10.1080/1357480022000039330. Accessed October 16, 2017.

Hayden, Dolores. 2003. *Building Suburbia: Green Fields and Urban Growth*. New York: Vintage Books.

Jackson, Kenneth. T. 1985. *Crabgrass Frontier: The Suburbanization of the United States*. New York and Oxford: Oxford University Press.

LaFrank, Kathleen. "Seaside, Florida: 'The New Town: The Old Ways.'" *Perspectives in Vernacular Architecture*. Vol. 6. Shaping Communities, 111–21. https://www.jstor.org/stable/3514366?seq=1#page_scan_tab_contents. Accessed October 11, 2017.

NewUrbanism.org. http://www.newurbanism.org/newurbanism.html. Accessed October 18, 2017.

Stephenson, Bruce. May 2002. "The Roots of the New Urbanism: John Nolen's Garden City Ethic." http://cnuflorida.org/resources/new-urbanism-florida-articles/the-roots-of-new-urbanism-john-nolens-garden-city-vision-for-florida/. Accessed October 18, 2017.

Upton, Dell. 2003. "New Urbanism." In *Encyclopedia of Community*, ed. Karen Christensen and David Levinson, 992–97. Thousand Oaks, CA:

SAGE. http://sk.sagepub.com/reference/community/n353.xml. Accessed October 16, 2017.

Warner, Sam Bass. 1962. *Streetcar Suburbs: The Process of Growth in Boston 1870–1900*. Cambridge, MA: Harvard University Press.

Examples of American New Urbanist Communities

Besides Seaside, there are a number of other New Urbanist communities in the United States. Some are new towns, and others are developments in older communities that utilize some or all of the New Urbanist principles. Here is a list of a few of the New Urbanist communities in the United States:

Celebration, Florida: Built in the 1990s and located in the Orlando area close to Walt Disney World, Celebration is a town that was actually built and managed by the Disney Development Corporation (DDC). The DDC was impressed with Seaside and sought to build a similar traditional community using New Urbanist principles. Disney commissioned a number of very prominent architects to design individual buildings in Celebration. They include Michael Graves, Robert A. M. Stern, Philip Johnson, and Robert Venturi and Denise Scott Brown.

L'On, Mount Pleasant, South Carolina: L'On is a New Urbanist community, northeast of Charleston. It was designed by the planning firms Dover, Kohl and Partners, and Duany Plater-Zyberk and Company. Founded in 1995, it is one of the early examples of New Urbanist town planning.

Kentlands, Gaithersburg, Maryland: Built on a historic farm estate, Kentlands was founded in 1988. The firm of Duany Plater-Zyberk was responsible for the urban planning. Kentlands and its sister community Lakelands comprise two of the largest New Urbanist ventures in the United States, with a combined population of over 8,000.

Military Architecture

Japanese American Relocation Camp

Pentagon

Japanese American Relocation Camp

Rohwer, Arkansas
1942

BACKGROUND

The surprise attack on Pearl Harbor that terrified the American public on December 7, 1941, set the stage for a dark period of racism in the United States. The Japanese, who were allies of the Germans in the Axis Powers, were already distrusted by many Americans, especially on the West Coast. In fact, there was a history of prejudice against Asians in the United States, dating back to the mid-19th century. Thousands of Chinese workers had immigrated to the country to build the transcontinental railroad. The states on the West Coast also saw an influx of Chinese immigrants during the California Gold Rush in 1849. San Francisco welcomed the Chinese workers, at least briefly, due to the acute labor shortage. However, once the Gold Rush was over, bias against the success of the hardworking Chinese began to surface. The state supreme court of California decided the case *People v. Hall* in 1854, which denied any Chinese person the right to testify against a white person. The fate of the Chinese worsened in 1869 with the completion of the western section of the transcontinental railroad. Thousands of unemployed workers surged into the cities of California looking for work, and the wages of the working class were depressed as a result. A movement began to flourish in California to ban the Chinese from entering the country. Nationally, however, the idea of excluding Chinese immigrants was not popular in the years after the Civil War. The eastern, southern, and midwestern states did not have many Asian immigrants, and therefore regarded the issue as a regional complaint. But in the 1870s, the representatives of the western states convinced Congress to pass a law denying entry for Chinese immigrants into the United States. It was vetoed by President Rutherford B. Hayes in 1878. The pressure from the western states proved unsustainable, however, and in 1882, President Chester Arthur signed the first Chinese Exclusion Act. This was intended as a temporary law, with a 10-year sunset provision. However, in 1892, the law was renewed. In 1902, President Theodore Roosevelt removed the sunset provision and made the law permanent.

Japanese immigrants came to the United States later than the Chinese. Most of them moved to Hawaii after, in 1884, the emperor allowed workers to leave the country to work on the sugar plantations. Soon they were relocating to the states of California, Oregon, and Washington. Before long, white Americans developed a deep distrust of the Japanese. The Congress had already passed a law that denied access for the Chinese to enter the country. Here was another foreign and exotic ethnic group that looked different and had a very distinct culture. In addition, white Americans were wary of the way that the Japanese revered their ancient culture. They did not assimilate as quickly as most of the other immigrant ethnic groups. This created even more suspicion among the white populace. Western representatives began to agitate for a Japanese Exclusion Act. Although the act never passed the Congress, President Theodore Roosevelt made a backroom deal with the Japanese government regarding a school segregation law. San Francisco passed a law that segregated Japanese students in the public schools. The Japanese citizenry protested mightily and got the attention of the Japanese government, which was not pleased with the discriminatory law. Roosevelt got the San Francisco school system to rescind its law. However, in return, the Japanese government promised to limit passports issued to Japanese laborers, thereby reducing Japanese immigration to the United States. This became known as the "Gentlemen's Agreement" of 1907–08. Although aimed specifically at one ethnic group, it was not very effective at discriminating against the Japanese. The loophole that allowed all family members of Japanese who were already here, and anyone who had already visited the country, to come back in left a gaping hole. Japanese kept coming into the United States, despite the racist law that attempted to deny access to them. Shockingly, in the United States, all Asian immigrants were prevented from becoming U.S. citizens by law until the passage of the Immigration and Nationality Act (also known as the McCarran-Walter Act) of 1952. On the West Coast, the white population continued to distrust the Japanese, and claimed that they were trying to "take over" California. Laws were passed that prevented immigrants from owning land. The enterprising Japanese, who were anxious to purchase property, would put the land in the name of their American-born children, thereby circumventing the law. During the 1920s, racial prejudice was intensifying throughout the country. Jim Crow laws were being passed in the South; the Ku Klux Klan was gaining in power, with a growing movement nationwide for laws that promoted white supremacy. The movement culminated in the passage of the 1924 Immigration Act, which was the most restrictive law ever passed in the country regarding immigration. The law established quotas from certain European countries, in an attempt to limit the number of "undesirable" immigrants like Italians and Jews. The bill also finally included the Asian Exclusion Act, which had been advocated for by the governments of the western states for years. At last, the racist propaganda promoted by white nationalists on the West Coast convinced much of the population in the rest of the country that Asians were dangerous because of their purported secretiveness and inscrutability and their strong cultural ties. The actions of the Japanese government during the 1930s did not help matters—it invaded China, occupied Manchuria, and withdrew from the League of Nations. Even though the nation was apprehensive about the actions of Hitler in Germany, Americans were also keeping an eye on Japan, which aligned with Germany as an Axis power in 1936. The sudden attack on Pearl Harbor created a panic and hysteria against the Japanese that soon resulted in the creation of the Japanese American relocation camps.

The anti-Japanese hysteria was fueled by West Coast newspapers and by members of the California government. These politicians included the state attorney general Earl Warren who would later become the leader of the liberal Warren Court of the U.S. Supreme Court. They claimed that the only way to protect the West Coast from Japanese invasion was to remove all people of Japanese heritage from the area. They spoke of a so-called Fifth column of espionage and spying. Years of racist commentary by the white-run media and governments had created an endemic distrust of the Japanese and suspicion of their allegiance to the United States. Following the advice of Earl Warren and John DeWitt, military commander for the Western Command, President Franklin Roosevelt declared the entire West Coast a military zone in Executive Order No. 9066 on February 16, 1942. This order gave the power to General DeWitt to remove all persons of Japanese ancestry from the Pacific Coast states. The attorney general of the United States, Francis Biddle, contended that the move was unconstitutional. Some of Roosevelt's advisors insisted that the Japanese were as patriotic as any Americans. But newspapers continued to claim that Japanese were a menace to the region, and could not be trusted to be loyal to the U.S. government when the country was at war with Japan.

The removal took place over the next six months. Families were given a week to sell their businesses and homes to white neighbors. Many were forced to sell at a great loss. They were not told where they were going or how long they would be gone. At first, they were bussed to assembly centers near their homes. These centers included fair grounds and racetracks where they were held in primitive conditions for several months while the government scouted for locations to set up the relocation camps. Ten sites were chosen. These sites were in Arizona, Utah, Colorado, Wyoming, California, Idaho, and Arkansas. All the sites were in areas that were desolate, in deserts or abandoned farmland far from population centers. They were, however, close to a railroad. After several months, all the internees were packed into railroad cars and taken to the camps with their paltry belongings in hand. One of the camps was located in Rohwer, Arkansas, in an area of former cotton fields that the federal government had purchased for the Farm Security Administration to be donated to poor subsistence farmers. By the end of the war, 117,000 Americans of Japanese origin were relocated to the internment camps. Two-thirds of those interned were U.S. citizens. Although Japanese immigrants, who were called "Issei," were not permitted to become citizens, their children who were born in the United States who were called "Nisei" were natural-born citizens. This incarceration of American citizens was later recognized by the American Civil Liberties Union as "the worst, single wholesale violation of the civil rights of Americans in our history."

CHARACTERISTICS AND FUNCTIONALITY

The relocation camp located in Rohwer, Arkansas, is typical of the 10 camps that the federal government erected in 1942. It was one of only two camps that were located in the South, as most of them were in western states. It accommodated over 10,000 people on a site of approximately 500 acres. The Missouri-Pacific Railroad passed by the site, carrying the interned Japanese families on the three-day train trip from locations around Los Angeles, California. The internees who went to Rohwer came from the Santa Anita racetrack in Arcadia, California, which was being used as an assembly center. The trains were jammed with families who had hastily packed up any belongings that they could, with suitcases and boxes stacked all around them. The camp at Rohwer was a city constructed for temporary use. The site was designed with a grid of streets, which were named "First Street" to "Eleventh Street" running north to south, and "A Street" to "K Street" running east to west. Most of the structures were barracks that were used for residences for the Japanese families, and the site was divided into residential blocks, with 12 barracks per block. The barracks were 20 feet deep by 120 feet long, and divided into six units, housing 250 people. Each family had a unit that usually consisted of one room. The hurriedly built structures were one-story wood-framed barracks with tar paper used as a siding. Inside, the wood structure was visible. Each family received a wood-burning stove and one cot for each person in the family. Bathrooms were not included in the residential units; toilets, bathing, and laundry facilities were located in separate facilities. Also, food was provided in communal mess halls. It looked like a military facility, and it functioned like one as well. As time went on, more structures were added to the camp. Schools were provided to the children, with teachers brought in from outside. The teachers lived at the camp as well. In the years that the Japanese families were interned at the camp, a social life developed. The families grew gardens; had chickens and hogs; and had clubs, church services, and dances. The Rohwer camp also contained a hospital building, a boiler house with a smokestack, recreations buildings, and a fire house. The other ubiquitous feature of all the camps was the barbed wire fencing, along with the watchtowers manned by armed military police. Rohwer had eight of these watchtowers.

A unique element of the Rohwer camp is the cemetery that was designed and built by the Japanese internees. Much of the camp was disassembled after the war but the cemetery monuments remained. There are 24 simple concrete headstones that identify the individuals who died while in the camp, and 2 major monuments that were completed in 1945. One is dedicated to the Japanese American soldiers who fought for the Americans during World War II. The monument is 15 feet tall and inscribed on it are the words "Dedicated to the men from Rohwer Center who gave their lives to America on foreign soil." This monument was designed and built by two internees Kaneo Fujioka and Kay Horisawa. The other large monument, also 15 feet tall, is dedicated to the internees who died while incarcerated at the camp. Its inscription states "May the people of Arkansas keep in beauty and reverence forever this ground where our bodies sleep." Another monument was added in 1982. It was designed by a former Rohwer internee Sam Yada, and is dedicated to the Japanese American 442nd Fighting Unit of the 100th Battalion, a unit that was the most highly decorated unit for its size in U.S. history.

KEY STATISTICS

The Rohwer camp was located at a rectangular site north of the center of the town of Rohwer and west of the Arkansas Highway 1. The Missouri-Pacific railroad tracks also lay to the west. It was 11 miles north of the town of McGehee and 110 miles southeast of the city of Little Rock, Arkansas. The entire camp was 5,000 feet long and 3,250 feet wide. It was initially opened on September 18, 1942, and closed on November 30, 1945. It housed over 10,000 internees during World War II.

CULTURAL SIGNIFICANCE

The incarceration of over 100,000 Japanese Americans without due process during World War II is now considered a shameful episode in American history. Though President Roosevelt was cautioned against it as unconstitutional by his Attorney General Francis Biddle, he listened to his more alarmist military advisors like General John DeWitt, who is quoted as saying "A Jap's a Jap. They are a dangerous element, whether loyal or not." The American public, fueled by anti-Japanese hysteria, accepted the rounding up of fellow Americans almost without question. There was no requirement that the army prove that the actions made the country safer. There was no outcry that fellow citizens of Italian or German descent (also descendants of Axis powers) be likewise incarcerated. The distrust of the Japanese ethnic group was so pervasive that it was almost accepted unconditionally. Although the American Civil Liberties Union protested the actions and a number of internees sued in federal court, the Supreme Court upheld the incarceration on the grounds of national security in the case *Korematsu v. The United States* in 1944. The Japanese families that were interned lost $500 million in assets that had been their homes and businesses. Many of the Japanese who were held in the camps had poorer health outcomes in their later years as compared to Japanese Americans who were not interned. Japanese family ties were damaged by the communal organization of the camps. In time, the federal government admitted its miscalculation. Congress passed a law in 1988, Public Law 100-383, that officially apologized for the episode and provided $20,000 in reparations to the 60,000 surviving internees.

FURTHER INFORMATION: IMPORTANT PRINT, ELECTRONIC, AND MEDIA RESOURCES

Aitken, Robert, and Marilyn Aitken. "Japanese American Internment." *Litigation* 37 (2, Winter 2011): 59–62, 70. JSTOR. http://www.jstor.org/stable/23075502. Accessed October 7, 2017.

"Japanese behind the Wire." Library of Congress. https://www.loc.gov/teachers/classroommaterials/presentationsandactivities/presentations/immigration/japanese4.html. Accessed October 10, 2017.

"Japanese Relocation during World War II." Educational Resources, National Archives. https://www.archives.gov/education/lessons/japanese-relocation. Accessed October 10, 2017.

Kitagaki, Paul, and T. A. Frail. January 2017. "The Injustice of Japanese-American Internment Camps Resonates Strongly to This Day." *Smithsonian Magazine*. https://www.smithsonianmag.com/history/injustice-japanese-americans-internment-camps-resonates-strongly-180961422/. Accessed October 10, 2017.

National Park Service. "Rohwer Relocation Center Memorial Cemetery." https://www.nps.gov/nhl/find/statelists/ar/RohwerRelocation.pdf. Accessed October 10, 2017.

George Takei, Speaking at the Dedication of the Japanese American Internment Museum, at the Site of the Internment Camp in Rohwer, Arkansas

George Takei, famous for his role as Hikaru Sulu in the original *Star Trek* television series, spent two years in the Rohwer Relocation Camp during World War II. Now in his 70s, he has become an activist for civil rights and lesbian, gay, bisexual, and transgender rights. This excerpt from his speech describes the men who volunteered to serve in the U.S. military after having been sent to the relocation camps.

They were young men who went from imprisonment here, in this internment camp, to fight for this country: a country that was imprisoning us and taking all our rights away, including the word "citizen." And now they wanted us to serve in the military. And they, indeed, did serve, with amazing, incredible heroism. They fought with unbelievable courage and, indeed, with incredible patriotism, and they sustained the highest combat casualty rate of any unit of its size. They fought in some of the most impossible battles.

. . . A few of those men who perished in that battle are on that list here in the cemetery. They fought for their country with unbelievable heroism, and their patriotism was beyond American patriotism. They fought to prove they were Americans. They had to prove they're Americans—and they didn't just fight for mom's apple pie, as almost all the others did. They fought to get "mom" out of imprisonment. They are true, exemplary American heroes.

Source: Takei, George. "George Takei's Rohwer Dedicatory Speech." April 13, 2013. Rohwer Japanese American Relocation Center. http://rohwer.astate.edu/george-takeis-speech/. Accessed October 10, 2017.

PhotoDisc, Inc.

The Pentagon

Arlington, Virginia
1943

BACKGROUND

Across the world, one building stands as a symbol for America's military might and its role as a superpower: the Pentagon. Constructed during World War II, the Pentagon is not only the physical headquarters for the U.S. Department of Defense, but also serves as the metaphor for American military power during World War II, the Cold War, and today's post–Cold War world. The very size of the building illustrated that the U.S. military would no longer be a small, continental defense force but rather be the type of force that would be active across the globe, protecting free people from the Fascists, then the Communists, and finally other threats like Islamic extremists. The building has served as the "nerve center" for U.S. military operations from World War II to the killing of Osama bin Laden.

In addition to its role as the center of America's military might, the Pentagon is also unique in that it is the world's largest office building. Constructed during World War II in less than 16 months, the building was both designed and built in a flurry, yet it remains totally functional for today's military needs. According to architectural historian Witold Rybczynski, "The Pentagon is not generally considered a significant work of architecture . . . but perhaps it should be . . . the Pentagon is the real thing: a globally recognized symbol" (Rybczynski 2007). The symbolic importance of the building has been illustrated as the site of awarding of medals to generals, the site of numerous anti-war protests during Vietnam, and the site of one of the attacks during the 9/11 terrorist strikes.

CHARACTERISTICS AND FUNCTIONALITY

The Pentagon was designed, in a Stripped Classical style, to serve as the office building for the greatly expanding U.S. military during World War II. Designed by George Bergstrom and David Witmer, the five-sided building contains five concentric pentagonal rings. The concentric pentagonal rings are designated from the center out as "A" through "E," with "F" and "G" in the basement. The offices in "E" ring are the only ones that have views of the outside, and are reserved for senior officials and generals.

The building has five floors above ground and two basement levels. It was constructed out of reinforced concrete with Indiana limestone covering the face of the building. Each of the main sides has its own entrance that has outward projections of colonnades, which form central porticos. The outer ring has walls that are 80 feet tall and 920 feet long. Each of the interior rings has the same height, but progressively shorter lengths. The building has more than 17 miles of corridors that connect the various offices through the building.

KEY STATISTICS

The key features of the Pentagon are both the shape of the building, which met the lay of the land, and its enormous size. Unlike other government buildings, the Pentagon is a five-sided building with over 6.50 million square feet of floor space. To put that into perspective, the Pentagon is as large as 114 American football fields, and when originally constructed was four times the size of the British War Office, the German War Ministry, and the Japanese General Staff buildings combined (Langmead 2009, 328). The massive size of the building was needed to house the commanders and staff of the U.S. military. Not only do the secretary of defense and the chiefs of staff of the military services have their offices in the outer ring, but also the Pentagon houses National Military Command Center, the primary communication center, or war room for the Joint Chiefs of Staff (the highest ranked generals in the military). The building also has over 23,000 military and civilian employees and contains over 20 restaurants, six zip codes, a chapel, and an athletic club. Although the Pentagon is huge, its layout allows for a person to walk between any two points in the building within approximately seven minutes. One of the most fascinating anecdotes in the building of the Pentagon is this: the Commonwealth of Virginia still had Jim Crow laws that required segregated bathrooms in the years that the Pentagon was being constructed. The Pentagon's architect was ordered to make sure he included separate facilities in order to accommodate these laws, and he complied. President Roosevelt had recently signed an executive order banning discrimination against government workers. When he visited the building while it was still under construction, he noticed a large number of bathrooms and questioned it. The bathrooms were already built, doubling the required number of bathrooms. They were never officially segregated, however. White workers did attempt to put signage on the doors but it was removed.

CULTURAL SIGNIFICANCE

The American military tradition originally advocated for a small professional army and navy that would be supplemented by a large influx of civilian soldiers only when necessary. However, with the changing nature of warfare in the industrial age, it was soon clear that original model might not work in the 20th century. In the late 1930s, the U.S. military began to expand to meet the threats of Nazi Germany and Imperial Japan. General George Marshall, U.S. Army Chief of Staff, realized the growing military needed a headquarters for the 24,000 members of the army staff. At first, he advocated using temporary buildings, but President Roosevelt wanted something more permanent. Brigadier General Brehon Somervell, the head of the Construction Division of the Quartermaster Corps, suggested constructing one building to house the entire War Department and ordered Major Hugh Casey, chief of design, and George Bergstrom, a well-known architect, to design a four-story, air-conditioned building to house 40,000 workers at the site of the old Washington-Hoover Airport in Virginia. They were given one weekend to make the plans. The initial plan called for a 5,100,000-square-foot building in a pentagon shape to fit within the five existing roads that bound the site. Because of the wartime rationing, the building was to be a maximum of four stories tall and use concrete rather than steel, which would result in saving 43,000 tons of steel for the war effort (Fine and Remington 1972, 431–39; Langmead 2009, 342).

Although Congress quickly appropriated the funding for the new building, there were still debates over its size, shape, and location. Congress and the president finally agreed on the site of the Arlington Farms, near Arlington Cemetery, as the best place for the new building. Although the new site did not have the constricting road system that the original building was designed to take into account, the architects decided against redesigning the pentagon shape so as not to delay the project.

Even before the site was determined, the army had selected the firm of John McShain, Inc., of Philadelphia (builders of the Washington National Airport in Arlington, the Jefferson Memorial in Washington, and the National Naval Medical Center in Bethesda, Maryland), along with Wise Contracting Company, Inc., and Doyle and Russell, both from Richmond, Virginia, to serve as the general contractors on the project. Because of the rushed nature of the project, the design work occurred simultaneously with construction. Although the drawings were completed in early October 1941, it was not until June 1942 that the final designs were completed. The urgency of the project was redoubled after the Japanese attack on Pearl Harbor in December 1941. As soon as individual sections of the building were completed, the military began using them. The army engineer placed in charge of the project was Colonel Leslie R. Groves, who would later direct the Manhattan Project, America's effort to develop the atomic bomb during World War II.

During World War II, the Pentagon served as the headquarters for all U.S. military activities; however, as the end of the war loomed, members of the government began planning on converting the Pentagon into a hospital or as a repository for the National Archives. As it turned out, that would never occur. As tensions with the Soviets rose after the Allied victory, it became apparent that for the first time in its history, the United States would not fully demobilize after the war, but would maintain a large peacetime standing army as a counter to the Soviets. The Pentagon would remain the central headquarters for that global military presence. Throughout the Cold War, U.S. military operations in Europe, Africa, Asia, and South America were planned and executed from the Pentagon. During the Vietnam War, the Pentagon was seen as a symbol of the war, and it became the site of numerous anti-war protests in 1967. It was even exorcised that year to remove the "demons of war." Norman Mailer, in his book *The Armies of the Night*, referred to the building as "the symbol, the embodiment . . . the true and high church of the military-industrial complex" (Mailer 1968, 113). In 1972, the Weather Underground detonated a bomb in a ladies' restroom to protest Nixon's bombing in Southeast Asia. In countless movies, television shows, and books, the Pentagon is seen as the command center for military operations. For example, the War Room scenes in Stanley Kubrick's iconic film *Dr. Strangelove* depict the president and the Joint Chiefs of Staff in a room with maps and displays to command military actions across the globe.

Sixty years after its ground breaking, on September 11, 2001, Al Qaeda terrorists crashed a jet aircraft into the Pentagon as part of their multi-pronged attack on the United States. Ironically, the portion of the Pentagon that was attacked had recently been remodeled as part of an effort to renovate the Pentagon and not all of the refurbished areas were yet opened for use. Consequently, only 70 civilians and 55 military personnel who were in the building were killed, rather than the thousands who would normally have been there. To demonstrate the nation's determination, the Defense Department immediately began "Operation Phoenix" to repair the building. The repairs were completed by September 11, 2002, on the first anniversary of the attack.

FURTHER INFORMATION: IMPORTANT PRINT, ELECTRONIC, AND MEDIA RESOURCES

Alexander, David. 2008. *The Building: A Biography of the Pentagon*. St. Paul, MN: MBI Publishing Company LLC and Zenith Press.

Fine, Lenore, and Jesse A. Remington. 1972. *The Corps of Engineers: Construction in the United States*. Washington, DC: Office of the Chief of Military History, U.S. Army.

Goldberg, Alfred. 1992. *The Pentagon: The First Fifty Years*. Washington, DC: Historical Office, Office of the Secretary of Defense.

Langmead, Donald. 2009. *Icons of American Architecture from the Alamo to the World Trade Center*. Westport, CT: Greenwood Press.

LeBrun, Nancy. 2002. *Inside the Pentagon*. Washington, DC: National Geographic.

Mailer, Norman. 1968. *The Armies of the Night*. New York: New American Library.

Rybczynski, Witold. June 10, 2007. "The Office." *New York Times Sunday Book Review*.

Vogel, Steve. 2007. *The Pentagon: A History: The Untold Story of the Wartime Race to Build the Pentagon—And to Restore It Sixty Years Later*. New York: Random House.

9/11 Attacks

On September 11, 2001, members of Al Qaeda, an Islamic terrorist group, hijacked four airliners and flew two of them into the World Trade Center twin towers in New York City and one into the Pentagon. The other plane crashed in Pennsylvania after the passengers fought with the hijackers. The attacks of 9/11 represented not only the largest terrorist attack in U.S. history, but also the largest loss of civilian life by an enemy attack. The attacks shocked the nation as millions gathered around their TVs to watch the rescue efforts in New York and Washington. Rather than frighten the United States, the attacks galvanized Americans resolve to fight the threat of Al Qaeda and their supporters and protectors in Afghanistan, the Taliban. By October 2001, President George W. Bush had ordered American military to remove the Taliban from Afghanistan, and later to remove Saddam Hussein from Iraq. The attacks on 9/11 started America's long war with Islamic terrorism that has seen American forces deployed all around the world.

As for the Pentagon, the crash of the aircraft caused the death of all 59 civilians and the 5 terrorists aboard the airliner, as well as 70 civilians and 55 military personnel in the Pentagon, and a partial collapse of that side of the building. There were many heroes that day at the Pentagon who helped rescue people in the rubble, including Secretary of Defense Donald Rumsfeld who ran from his office on the other side of the building to the site of the impact to help. The contractors working on the building set a goal of having the damage repaired in one year, which they accomplished. A memorial garden and park were opened in 2008 near the site.

Memorial Architecture

Lincoln Memorial

Vietnam Veterans Memorial

Lincoln Memorial

Washington, D.C.
1922

BACKGROUND

One of the most famous and beloved monuments in the nation's capital, Washington, D.C., is the Lincoln Memorial. It may seem surprising, though, that it was completed well into the 20th century on land that did not exist during Lincoln's lifetime. Attempts had been made to build a monument to the beloved assassinated president, and in 1867, a commission was set up to plan a monument. The commission went so far as to choose an architect, Clarke Mills, to design the structure. The completed design was in the style of the times. It represented a paean to the Union victory with a 70-foot-high structure, embellished with colossal statues of horses, freed slaves, Union generals, and abolitionists, and a statue of Lincoln on top. The grandiose, ostentatious style, typical of the age, would not have worn well today. The intent of the monument was to aggrandize the North's victory over the South. The design did not attract enough funding to follow through on the project, so it was dropped. The concept of building a memorial to Abraham Lincoln remained on the minds of the city planners in Washington, D.C., although the endeavor was not accomplished for decades.

Planners had struggled with planning the layout of the nation's capital for years. The original plan for Washington, D.C., was completed in 1791 by Pierre Charles L'Enfant. This plan included the inclusion of a National Mall and was based on rational, classical planning, with straight axes connecting the White House and the Capitol Building. Part of the design was completed, but styles changed, and the idea of classical symmetry was eschewed. In the 1850s, the influential landscape designer Andrew Jackson Downing designed a completely different plan for the National Mall. Downing, who had influenced the design of Central Park, proposed a naturalistic landscape with curving paths and thick, informal plantings in the manner of picturesque design. Construction on the mall continued as per Downing's plan during the rest of the 19th century, despite his untimely death in 1852. Tastes changed again, and after the Columbian Exhibition in Chicago in 1893, the new City Beautiful Movement held sway. The City

Beautiful Movement's precepts again turned to classical symmetry, based on the Beaux-Arts design, which was popular at the time. A new plan was devised in 1902 by the McMillan Commission that followed the principles of the City Beautiful Movement. These principles called for broad avenues, wide vistas, and more grass. The winding paths and the thick shrubbery were removed, and the narrow expanse of grass, flanked by rows of trees and broad, straight paths and the rectangular reflecting pool extended the vistas all the way from the Capitol to the site of the new Lincoln Memorial. The National Mall as it appears today is based on the City Beautiful concepts proposed by the McMillan Plan. The new Potomac Park, built on landfill next to the Potomac River, was proposed by the McMillan Commission as a location for a memorial to Abraham Lincoln. This was the location that was eventually chosen.

However, the choice of the new Potomac Park was not without controversy. One senator, Shelby M. Cullom of Illinois, served as the champion of the Lincoln Memorial project. He proposed bills to set up a new commission unsuccessfully five times, with his first attempt in 1901. Finally, on his sixth try, the bill passed in 1910. The former president of the United States, William Howard Taft, was selected as the president of the Lincoln Memorial Commission. By 1913, the Commission had selected the architect, Henry Bacon and the location, Potomac Park. The commission followed the direction of the 1902 McMillan Commission to place the Lincoln Memorial at the end of the mall in the Potomac Park's newly reclaimed land. Some opponents complained that former swamp land was an inappropriate location for the memorial. They suggested that the memorial be placed across the Potomac in Arlington, Virginia. But the notion of placing the monument to Lincoln in a Confederate state, the home state of the Confederate president Robert E. Lee, was an anathema to many. Critics also decried the distance between the Capitol and the memorial. A number of prominent architects proposed alternates to the location, closer to the Capitol. The design of the structure was criticized as well. The proposal of the Greek Temple was condemned by some as too grand as a representation of the humble president from Illinois. They suggested that a log cabin be built instead. In general, though, the entire concept of the memorial was radically different from the one proposed soon after Lincoln's death. The politics had changed. The Radical Republicans who ruled in the years after the Civil War were no longer in power. Although the memory of the Civil War remained fresh for many Americans, the meaning of the monument that glorified the victorious president was reconciled. The memorial would not represent the bloody military triumph of the North against the South. It would represent the saving of the Union and the anguish the president faced as he wrestled with these issues. This interpretation of the memorial to Lincoln omitted reference to the abolition of slavery. Charles McKim, renowned architect of the firm McKim, Mead and White, and influential member of the Lincoln Memorial Commission, argued that the monument should portray the president as a man who transcended the ugliness of the war and its connotations. The commission fought off the various criticisms and stuck to its proposal. The location was to be in Potomac Park as an extension of the National Mall, and the architect was to be Henry Bacon.

CHARACTERISTICS AND FUNCTIONALITY

The Lincoln Memorial was completed in 1922. The architect, Henry Bacon, was a successful Beaux-Arts architect from New York City. He worked for the iconic Beaux-Arts firm of McKim, Mead and White before starting his own firm in 1897. Bacon worked with the Beaux-Arts sculptor Daniel Chester French, who was responsible for the statue of Abraham Lincoln inside the building. The ceremony to mark the groundbreaking for the memorial was held on February 12, Lincoln's birthday, in the year 1914. An allocation of $300,000 was made to begin the work. The design of the structure is based on the Parthenon in Athens, a 5th-century Greek temple that is considered a masterpiece of classical architecture. Henry Bacon had traveled in Greece and was inspired by the design and democratic ideals of the Ancient Greeks. Bacon altered two major features as opposed to the original Parthenon, in his final design, however. He changed the roof line, which in the Greek version is a gable roof, into a flat-roofed attic that is set back and rises above the entablature. In addition, he reoriented the front of the building, turning it 90 degrees, so that the long side of the temple is at the front instead of the side.

The Lincoln Memorial is called a peripteral Greek temple, which indicates that it has columns on all four sides of the building. The exterior is constructed with Colorado-Yule marble. The foundation is made of concrete, and encompassed by a rectangular 14-foot-high retaining wall. A peristyle, or portico, surrounds the building with 36 fluted Doric columns. The 36 columns represent the number of states in the Union at the time of Lincoln's death. In addition to the 36 columns, another 2 fluted Doric columns flank the entrance. All the columns, as well as the exterior walls, incline inward slightly. This idiosyncratic feature was inserted intentionally so that the building would not appear asymmetrical from afar. Above the columns is a frieze that contains the names of the 36 states in the Union and the years that they entered the Union. The names are separated by medallions of wreaths. Above the frieze, the cornice contains a carved scroll with lion heads and palmetto cresting. The attic frieze contains inscriptions of the country's 48 states, which comprised the nation at the time of the completion of the monument. The entrance to the memorial, which is on the east side of the building, is approached by a series of monumental stairs, rising from the end of the reflecting pool. There are several groups of steps, separated by landings.

Near the entrance to the building are two low walls, called buttresses, on either side of the steps. On the top of the buttresses are 11-foot-high carved tripods, or three-legged vessels, made of Tennessee marble.

The interior of the memorial shrine is constructed of Indiana limestone. The structure is divided into three rooms, and each room is divided by a row of four Ionic columns. On the walls of the rooms at the north and south side are inscriptions of two of Lincoln's most famous speeches: the Gettysburg Address and the Second Inaugural Address. Above the inscriptions are murals, representing Freedom, Liberty, Immortality, Justice, and the Law on one side, and Unity, Fraternity, and Charity on the other side, both painted by Jules Guerin. The ceilings are covered in marble soaked in beeswax, which improved the translucency of the marble, letting more light into the space. In the center of the structure is the seated figure of Lincoln himself, designed by Daniel Chester French and executed by the Piccirilli brothers, from the New York City marble shop of the same name. The monumental statue was carved in New York and transported in pieces to Washington, D.C., where the Piccirilli brothers assembled it. Originally planned to be 10 feet tall, it was greatly enlarged when the designers realized that it would appear too insignificant within the grand space. Its final size is 19 feet tall and 19 feet wide. Since the figure is seated, the standing figure of Lincoln would be 28 feet tall. The Lincoln statue is made of Georgia white marble and sits on an oblong pedestal made of Tennessee white marble. Above Lincoln's head, between two pilasters, is an epitaph, written by New York City newspaper columnist Royal Cortissoz. It states: "In this temple, as in the hearts of the people for whom he saved the Union, the memory of Abraham Lincoln is enshrined forever." Cortissoz regarded this succinct statement his proudest achievement. The sculptor Daniel Chester French studied many portrayals of Lincoln for his inspiration to design the sculpture, including photographs, eyewitness descriptions, and the actual castings of his hands made in 1960. Lincoln is portrayed in contemplation, with his left hand clenched in steadfast resolve and the right hand open in peaceful forgiveness. His face displays a thoughtful expression, pondering the serious choices confronting him. The Lincoln Memorial was completed in eight years, on time, and opened in 1922.

KEY STATISTICS

The Lincoln Memorial is located at the foot of 23rd Street, N.W. in Washington, D.C. It sits at the west end of the National Mall in Potomac Park on the east bank of the Potomac River. Constitution Avenue borders it to the north, Independence Avenue to the south, and the reflecting pool of the Mall to the east. The structure measures 189 feet wide by 118 feet deep. It

is 99 feet tall. The columns in the peristyle are 44 feet tall, with a diameter at the base of 7.5 feet. The foundation ranges in depth from 44 to 65 feet from grade to bedrock. The site comprises 109 acres. The final cost of the memorial was the following: $2,957,000 for the building itself and $88,400 for the statue of Lincoln. Total cost for the project was $3,045,400. The dedication ceremony for the memorial was held on Memorial Day, May 30, 1922.

CULTURAL SIGNIFICANCE

The significance of the Lincoln Memorial has grown since its initial dedication. The politics of the post–Civil War era led to a postponement of the construction of the memorial for over 40 years. The agreement to build the shrine came when the Republicans and Democrats resolved to portray the memorial as a remembrance of the saving of the Union. The issue of slavery and the emancipation of the slaves by Lincoln were virtually ignored. In fact, the dedication event itself was segregated, as much of Washington, D.C., was during the Jim Crow era. The monument remains a highly affecting memorial, however. Its placement at the end of the National Mall facing the reflecting pool gives it gravitas. The seated, solitary figure of Abraham Lincoln reflects the integrity and humanity of the man as he struggled with the consummate issues of the day. However, despite its discounting of the issue of slavery, the memorial has become a site for civil rights protests over the years. In 1939, after being refused by the Daughters of the American Revolution (DAR) to sing a planned-for spring concert at the DAR-owned Constitution Hall in Washington, renowned African American contralto Marian Anderson sang an Easter concert on the steps of the Lincoln Memorial in front of a crowd of 75,000 fans. Anderson, who had sung with the New York Philharmonic and at Carnegie Hall, was soon supported by a variety of civil rights groups, as well the First Lady Eleanor Roosevelt, who resigned her membership with the DAR. Mrs. Roosevelt worked with the head of the Walter White of the National Association for the Advancement of Colored People and the U.S. secretary of the interior Harold Ickes to arrange an alternative venue for Anderson. They selected the steps of the Lincoln Memorial as their location, and the anniversary of Lincoln's death, Easter Sunday, as their date. Anderson performed a number of songs, including some gospel songs and "America," also known as "My Country, 'Tis of Thee." Marian Anderson later performed at Constitution Hall. She performed at the inaugurations of both Dwight D. Eisenhower and John F. Kennedy. She also performed at the more famous event that took place in front of the Lincoln Memorial—the March on Washington for Jobs and Freedom, where Martin Luther King Jr. gave his iconic "I Have a Dream Speech."

FURTHER INFORMATION: IMPORTANT PRINT, ELECTRONIC, AND MEDIA RESOURCES

Allen, Erin. April 9, 2014. "The Sound of Freedom: Marian Anderson at the Lincoln Memorial." Library of Congress Blog. https://blogs.loc.gov/loc/2014/04/the-sound-of-freedom-marian-anderson-at-the-lincoln-memorial/. Accessed September 27, 2017.

Gillette, Howard, Jr. 2004. "The Lincoln Memorial and American Life by Christopher A. Thomas" (Review). *Indiana University of Magazine of History* 100 (4): 397–99. https://scholarworks.iu.edu/journals/index.php/imh/article/view/12096/17899. Accessed September 27, 2017.

Kakutani, Michiko. August 27, 2013. "The Lasting Power of Dr. King's Speech." *New York Times*. http://www.nytimes.com/2013/08/28/us/the-lasting-power-of-dr-kings-dream-speech.html. Accessed January 24, 2018.

"Lincoln Memorial Building Statistics." https://www.nps.gov/linc/learn/historyculture/lincoln-memorial-building-statistics.htm. Accessed September 27, 2017.

"Martin Luther King, Jr. and the Global Freedom Struggle—March on Washington for Jobs and Freedom." Stanford University—Martin Luther King, Jr. Research and Education Institute. http://kingencyclopedia.stanford.edu/encyclopedia/encyclopedia/enc_march_on_washington_for_jobs_and_freedom/index.html. Accessed September 27, 2017.

Moeller, G. Martin, Jr. 2012. *AIA Guide to the Architecture of Washington, D.C.* Baltimore, MD: Johns Hopkins University Press.

National Park Service. 1981. "Lincoln Memorial." https://npgallery.nps.gov/pdfhost/docs/NRHP/Text/66000030.pdf. Accessed September 27, 2017.

National Park Service. August 16, 2017. "Lincoln Memorial History and Culture." https://www.nps.gov/linc/learn/historyculture/index.htm. Accessed September 27, 2017.

Martin Luther King Jr.'s "I Have a Dream" Speech

Martin Luther King Jr. delivered his most celebrated speech on the steps of the Lincoln Memorial in front of 250,000 civil rights demonstrators on August 28, 1963. The so-called March on Washington for Jobs and Freedom was organized to put pressure on President John F. Kennedy to initiate strong civil rights legislation in Congress. President Kennedy supported the march, hoping that a peaceful, well-attended march would influence public opinion toward support of the passage of a civil rights bill. Kennedy watched the speech on television in the White House. King gave his speech at the end of a long program that included musical performances by gospel singer Mahalia Jackson and contralto Marian Anderson, who had performed at the Lincoln Memorial once before, in 1939. Legendary folk singers Bob Dylan, Peter, Paul and Mary, and Joan Baez also performed. Martin Luther King Jr. was known for his inspiring oratorical gifts. But no one was prepared for the soaring rhetoric delivered by Dr. King that day. He began the speech with a beautifully written but woeful description of the intolerable conditions endured by black Americans in 1963. With references to the Constitution, the Gettysburg Address, and the 100th anniversary of the Emancipation Proclamation, King decried the promises that went unfulfilled for African Americans, who were still subjected to segregation and endemic prejudice. Halfway through the speech, Mahalia Jackson, sitting close to King on the dais, exhorted King to talk about the dream. Jackson was referring to a number of previous speeches that King had made where he used hopeful imagery about having a dream that a taste of freedom would one day be enjoyed by African Americans. King promptly set aside his prepared remarks, vaulting from elegant prose to inspirational poetry. He began a peroration, the inspiring conclusion of a speech, with the phrase "I have a dream," which he used repeatedly in a rhetorical device called anaphora. With a voice rising to an emotional pitch, King captivated the huge crowd, who responded with "Amens" and other encouraging words. The "I Have a Dream" speech made by Dr. Martin Luther King that hot, steamy August day over 50 years ago in Washington, D.C., has become the inspiration for American children who recite the speech in school, as well as for aspiring protesters around the world. The Civil Rights Act was passed in 1964, with the Voting Rights Act following in 1965. The March on Washington, and in particular the glorious speech made by King that day on the steps of the Lincoln Memorial, served as a turning point in the history of American civil rights.

Brandon Bourdages/Dreamstime.com

Vietnam Veterans Memorial

Washington, D.C.
1982

BACKGROUND

The American experience in Vietnam was one of the most traumatic in American history. For the first time in the nation's history, the military had lost a war, and it was broadcast over television to American homes. With over 50,000 dead, countless wounded, and the nation torn apart politically from the war, Vietnam became a deep wound that touched at people's public and private lives. Returning veterans from the war did not receive the heroes' welcome that their fathers had received coming home from World War II. After the war, many tried to forget or put the war behind them, but some realized that, for the wound to heal, America needed to confront the Vietnam experience.

Constructed in the early 1980s, the Vietnam Veterans Memorial in Washington, D.C., was an attempt by the U.S. government to memorialize the dead from the Vietnam Conflict, and to begin the healing of the war that divided a nation in the 1960s and '70s. In stark contrast to the other monuments in Washington, the black granite wall listing the names of the Americans dead in the conflict does not celebrate the accomplishments of the nation; rather it pays respect to those who lost their lives in the conflict. At first, the memorial was controversial; however, since then Americans have accepted it as a fitting way to remember those who died in that unfortunate conflict in Southeast Asia.

CHARACTERISTICS AND FUNCTIONALITY

Unlike many of the other memorials and monuments in Washington, the Vietnam Veterans Memorial is a simple structure made of two 246-foot-long walls made of gabbro, a coarse-grained igneous rock, that rise from the corners to an apex. The shiny, black walls start at a height of 8 inches and move to approximately 10 feet at the apex. The shape of the wall was designed to illustrate a "wound that is closed and healing" (www.VirtualWall.org).

Carved on the wall are the names of the Americans who died in the war. Uniquely, the names are placed in order of how they died in the war, providing the visitor with a day-by-day story of the human cost of the war. The names are catalogued in books and on line, so that visitors can find loved ones on the wall. It has become a practice for visitors to take rubbings of the names using pencils, crayons, and many others on paper as a way to bring home the name. Veterans and others also leave mementos and other items at the wall to honor the dead. These items are collected by the National Park Service and catalogued for preservation.

In addition to the wall, a bronze statue titled The Three Servicemen and the Vietnam Women's Memorial, a memorial dedicated to the women of the United States who served in the Vietnam War, have been added to the two-acre park. These were not part of the original design.

KEY STATISTICS

The Vietnam Veterans Memorial sits on two acres near the Lincoln Memorial on the National Mall, on the site of a former navy building that was demolished after World War II. The selection of the memorial's site on the National Mall indicated its importance to the nation since this is the site of many of the most important buildings in Washington. The Vietnam Veterans Memorial Fund, Inc. (VVMF), raised close to $9,000,000 through private contributions by more than 275,000 individuals, groups, and corporations to fund the construction of the wall. No federal funds were spent on the construction.

The memorial has two 246-foot-long walls that rise to a 10-foot apex where they meet. The height of both walls gradually decreases to eight inches. There are 58,286 names listed on the Vietnam Veterans Memorial that were either "Killed in Action" (KIA) or who were "Missing in Action" (MIA). The names are grouped by year and are in approximate order of when they died in the conflict. Kiosks at either end of the wall provide finding aids for the wall.

CULTURAL SIGNIFICANCE

During the late 1970s, the nation was still coming to grips with the debacle of the Vietnam War and the political and social upheaval of the 1960s. Many people advocated just forgetting the war and moving on; however, many who served or who lost loved ones in the war did not want to just forget it. Also, popular culture began to explore the Vietnam experience. Movies like *The Deer Hunter* and *Apocalypse Now* and books like *A Rumor of War* and *Dispatches* brought attention to the war and its effects. After seeing *The Deer Hunter*, Jan Scruggs, a veteran of the war, began to think of ways to commemorate the war. At a meeting of the Vietnam Veterans of America, Scruggs and Bob Doubek, another veteran, formed the VVMF on May 28, 1979. After some resistance, the VVMF had raised over $8 million in two years.

After obtaining the funding and the location near the Lincoln Memorial, the VVMF held a design competition in 1981 with 1,421 designs submitted and a cash prize of $50,000. The blind jury awarded the prize to Maya Lin, an Asian American undergraduate student in architecture at Yale. As a 21-year-old student of Asian descent, Lin is convinced that her design would never have been selected without the aid of a jury who had no knowledge of the designer responsible for the work. In fact, after being awarded the prize, her design was unpopular with political conservatives. They saw it as not typical of war memorials, believing that it did not honor the soldiers who died. Many important supporters of the program, including Ross Perot, James Watt, and James Webb, withdrew their support. However, after Lin testified before Congress, and other architects lent their support, the plan was executed and the memorial was dedicated on November 13, 1982.

Since its construction, the nation and veterans have warmed to the memorial and its memorialization of the war and its effects. In 2007, the American Institute of Architects named the Memorial number 10 on its list of America's favorite architecture. Over 3,000,000 visitors a year visit the site. The memorial was also listed as a National Historic Landmark the same year it was constructed.

FURTHER INFORMATION: IMPORTANT PRINT, ELECTRONIC, AND MEDIA RESOURCES

Fithian, David Brooks. 1994. *A Dark and Shining Stone: Symbol Contests and the Vietnam Veterans Memorial*. New Haven, CT: Yale University Press.

Lopes, Sal. 1987. *The Wall: Images and Offerings from the Vietnam Veterans Memorial*. New York: Collins.

Scruggs, Jan C., and Joel L. Swerdlow. 1985. *To Heal a Nation: The Vietnam Veterans Memorial*. New York: Harper & Row.

Tritle, Lawrence A. 2012. "Monument to Defeat: The Vietnam Veterans Memorial in American Culture and Society." In *Cultures of Commemoration*, ed. Polly Low, Graham Oliver, and P. J. Rhodes, 159–79. London: British Academy.

Mobile Walls

One of the most interesting aspects of the Vietnam Veterans Memorial is the creation of smaller, exact replica, mobile walls that travel the nation. One of the main purposes of the Vietnam Veterans Memorial was to help members of the general public who were touched

by the war to heal. Unfortunately, many of them could not travel to Washington, D.C., to see the wall, and their loved ones' name, and that is why the mobile walls project came into effect.

Soon after the dedication of the memorial, John Devitt founded Vietnam Combat Veterans, Ltd., and constructed a half-size replica of the Vietnam Veterans Memorial, named "The Moving Wall." Starting in 1984, this mobile monument began traveling the nation stopping in towns and cities of all sizes as a way to bring the memorial to the people. The mobile wall was so popular that several other traveling walls were constructed to meet the demands. Other groups have also designed and constructed mobile walls, and two permanent replicas were constructed near the Wildwoods Convention Center, New Jersey, and in Winfield, Kansas. Finally, online versions of the wall have been created in cyberspace as other ways to disseminate the message of the wall.

BIOGRAPHICAL APPENDIX

Anderson, Marian: An African American contralto who performed between 1925 and 1965 and was celebrated for her beautiful voice. She is also known for her work in civil rights. After being denied by the Daughters of the American Revolution to perform at Constitution Hall in Washington, D.C., in 1939, President and Mrs. Franklin Roosevelt arranged to have her sing in front of the Lincoln Memorial to a crowd of over 75,000.

Bacon, Henry: An American architect in the Beaux-Arts style, Henry Bacon is most known for his design of the Lincoln Memorial in Washington, D.C., completed in 1922.

Bergstrom, George: An American architect who is best known for designing the Pentagon in Arlington, Virginia, completed in 1943.

Bunshaft, Gordon: An architect who was a partner in the firm Skidmore, Owings and Merrill, and specialized in the Modernist style. His most famous work is Lever House, in New York City.

Burnham, Daniel: An architect and partner in the firm of Burnham and Root in Chicago, Burnham was known for his work on the 1893 World's Columbian Exposition in Chicago as well as several early skyscrapers like the Flatiron Building in New York City. He was also a city planner, and worked on plans for the master plan for Washington, D.C.

Cassatt, Alexander: The president of the Pennsylvania Railroad, Cassatt was responsible for the construction of the tunnels and terminal at Pennsylvania Station in New York. His sister was the American Impressionist painter Mary Cassatt.

Childs, David M.: A partner in the architectural firm Skidmore, Owings and Merrill, Childs is the principal designer for the new One World Trade Center, completed in 2014.

Disney, Walt: A pioneer in the animation industry, Disney founded Disney Studios and began producing innovative animated films in the 1930s. In the 1950s, Disney opened the amusement park Disneyland in Anaheim, California. He later opened Disneyworld in Orlando, Florida.

Duany, Andres: An American architect and urban planner of Cuban descent, Duany is a proponent of the movement called "New Urbanism" that attempts to counteract the deleterious effects of suburban sprawl.

Dundy, Skip: One of the developers of the groundbreaking amusement park in Coney Island called Luna Park, which was opened in 1903.

Eisenhower, Dwight D.: After serving as a general in the U.S. Army, Eisenhower was elected the 34th president of the United States in 1953, serving for two terms. He was a proponent of building the Interstate Highway System, which was approved by Congress in 1956.

Firestone, Harvey: Founder of the Firestone Tire and Rubber Company, Firestone was one of the leading industrialists of the early 20th century.

Ford, Henry: Founder of the Ford Motor Company, Henry Ford was also the first to utilize the assembly line technique in automobile manufacturing. His innovation made the automobile inexpensive enough for most middle-class Americans to buy, which transformed American culture.

Gandhi, Mahatma: Leader of the independence movement in India during the early 20th century. He was also a proponent of nonviolent civil disobedience, a protest method that inspired Martin Luther King Jr. in the United States during the American civil rights movement.

Gehry, Frank: An American contemporary architect of Canadian descent who is known for his idiosyncratic style. His most famous buildings include the Walt Disney Concert Hall in Los Angeles, California, and the Guggenheim Museum in Bilbao, Spain.

Graham, Billy: An evangelical preacher who attained celebrity status, Graham was also an advisor to many American presidents.

Graham, Bruce: A Colombian-born American architect who designed in the International Style, Graham worked with Fazlur Khan for the architectural firm Skidmore, Owings and Merrill. With Khan, Graham was responsible for the design of the Willis Tower (Sears Tower) and the Hancock Tower, both in Chicago.

Graham, John: A prominent British-born American architect, Graham formed a firm with his son John Graham Jr. The Grahams were responsible for designing a number of early shopping malls in the 1950s, including Northgate Shopping Center in Seattle.

Grauman, Sid: An early promoter of the film industry, Grauman built some of Hollywood's most famous movie palaces, including Grauman's Chinese Theatre.

Graves, Michael: An American architect and industrial designer of the late 20th century, Graves was known for his Postmodernist style. He designed the Portland Public Service Building, and a number of household items that were sold at Target.

Gropius, Walter: The founder of the Bauhaus School and one of the pioneers of the Modernist movement in architecture.

Groves, Colonel Leslie R.: An officer in the Army Corps of Engineers, Groves oversaw the construction of the Pentagon, and directed the Manhattan Project, a secret project that developed the atomic bomb during World War II.

Gruen, Victor: An Austrian American architect who became famous for his designs of enclosed shopping malls. Late in his life, he moved back to Austria and denounced the shopping mall, calling them "bastard developments."

Hoover, Herbert: The 31st president of the United States, Hoover, a Republican, served two terms but was defeated in a landslide by Democrat Franklin D. Roosevelt in 1932 after the onset of the Great Depression.

Hughes, Howard: A hugely successful investor and businessman in the 20th century, Hughes was also a pilot, film producer, and founder of Hughes Aircraft Company in 1932. Late in life, he became an eccentric recluse.

Hyde, Henry Baldwin: Founder of the Equitable Life Assurance Company in 1959, Baldwin grew the company into the largest in the world by the turn of the 20th century.

Jacobs, Jane: An activist and author in the mid-20th century, Jacobs wrote *The Death and Life of Great American Cities*, one of the most influential books regarding the importance of street life and diversity in cities.

Johnson, Philip: One of the most prominent American architects of the 20th century, Johnson was the preeminent Modernist in his early years, turning to Post-Modernism in his later work. He designed the interior of the Seagram Building, a Modernist masterpiece in New York City.

Kahn, Albert: The so-called Architect of Detroit, Kahn designed many industrial buildings in Michigan in the early 20th century, including the Ford River Rouge Complex in Dearborn.

Kaufmann, Edgar, Sr.: A successful entrepreneur in the early 20th century, Kaufmann owned Kaufmann's Department Store in Pittsburgh, Pennsylvania. He commissioned Frank Lloyd Wright to design his country house in the hills of western Pennsylvania, which became Wright's masterpiece, Fallingwater.

Khan, Fazlur Rahman: A Bangladeshi American engineer and architect, Khan was credited with inventing new engineering solutions for skyscraper design, including the bundled tube structural system, used on the Sears Tower (now known as the Willis Tower).

King, Martin Luther, Jr.: The hero of the American civil rights movement, King was instrumental in combating racial inequality using nonviolent civil disobedience. He won the Nobel Peace Prize in 1964 and was assassinated by James Earl Ray on April 4, 1968, setting off riots across the country.

Koolhaas, Rem: An influential Dutch architect and theorist, Koolhaas has been awarded a number of American commissions, including the Seattle Central Library. He has also written books on urbanism and design, including *Delirious New York* (1978) and *S,M,L,XL* (1995.)

Kroc, Ray: Kroc invested in the fast-food chain McDonald's in 1954, and franchised it, making it the fast-food juggernaut that it is today. He was not, however, the founder of the chain.

LaGuardia, Fiorello: Known as "the Little Flower," LaGuardia was the 99th mayor of New York City, serving from 1934 to 1945. He has been credited with being one of America's greatest mayors, cleaning up corruption and restoring faith in city politics.

Lamb, William: The principal architect of the iconic Art Deco skyscraper the Empire State Building, Lamb was a partner in the firm Shreve, Lamb and Harmon.

Lapidus, Morris: A Russian-born American architect, Lapidus worked in retail design before having a chance to design buildings. He used his theatrical design skills to great effect in his Miami hotels, which include the Fontainebleau Hotel and the Eden Roc. His style has become known as "Miami Modern" or "MiMo."

Le Corbusier: One of the pioneers of the Modern Movement in architecture and design, Le Corbusier, a Swiss-French architect, had great influence on the design of American public housing in the mid-20th century. These projects often used his "towers in the park" concept, which was introduced in his master plan for the "Radiant City," originally published in 1924. This type of planning has since been discredited by many urban planners as isolating and unsafe.

Levitt, William: A real estate developer in New York, Levitt originated the assembly line type system of construction in his pioneering suburban development Levittown on Long Island in the late 1940s, which influenced the growth of the suburbs nationwide.

Lewis, Jerry Lee: One of rock and roll's early stars, Lewis is known for his energetic style of singing and playing the piano. He was one of a series of early rock and roll stars who were discovered at the Sun Record Studio in Memphis.

Libeskind, Daniel: A Polish American architect, Libeskind is best known for his design of the master plan for the replacement of the original World Trade Center, which was destroyed on September 11, 2001.

Lin, Maya: Maya Lin was discovered as a 21-year-old Yale design student when she won the competition for the design of the proposed Vietnam Veterans Memorial. Her design for the "Wall" has been lauded as a groundbreaking design. She has gone on to design memorials, architecture, landscape architecture, and sculpture.

Lindbergh, Charles: The handsome American aviator Charles Lindbergh became world famous after he completed the first solo transatlantic flight from New York to Paris in 1927. His fame grew with the media coverage of the kidnapping and murder of his young son. Lindbergh was later criticized for his noninterventionist "America First" stance before the United States declared war on Germany and Japan in 1941. He subsequently professed support for the war publicly.

Marshall, General George: A celebrated general during World War II, Marshall went on to serve as secretary of state and secretary of defense under President Truman. He is best known for his contribution to the creation of the Marshall Plan, which helped Europe rebuild after the war.

McCarthy, Joseph: A Republican senator from Wisconsin, Joseph McCarthy is best known for accusations that Communists had infiltrated the American government. His smear tactics against many prominent politicians and entertainment figures destroyed many careers. His power was diminished after the Army-McCarthy hearings and he was censured by the Senate in 1954.

McKim, Charles Follen: An American architect who practiced in the Beaux-Arts style at the end of the 19th and beginning of the 20th century, McKim was a partner in the celebrated firm McKim, Mead and White.

Moretti, Luigi: An Italian architect of the Modern Movement, Moretti's most famous building in the United States is the Watergate Complex in Washington, D.C.

Moses, Robert: Known as "the master builder," Robert Moses wielded virtually unbridled power for over half a century in New York in his multiple unelected titles. He was responsible for much of the infrastructure in the New York City region built in the early to mid-20th century. His focus on the automobile to the detriment of mass transit has been highly criticized, as has his disregard for vibrant urban neighborhoods that he destroyed in order to build highways. Although his reputation has been somewhat resurrected recently, he remains a polarizing figure.

Novack, Ben: Ben Novack was the eccentric but visionary developer of the Fontainebleau Hotel in Miami Beach, Florida, the first hotel built in the Miami Modern style in the 1950s.

Perkins, Carl: One of the many stars discovered in the 1950s at the Sun Studio in Memphis, Perkins was known for his rockabilly style. His songs have influenced many later rock and roll artists, including the Beatles, Elvis Presley, and Johnny Cash.

Phillips, Sam: Founder of Sun Records in Memphis, Tennessee, Sam Phillips is credited with discovering some of the most celebrated early rock and roll artists, including Elvis Presley, Carl Perkins, Jerry Lee Lewis, and Johnny Cash.

Plater-Zyberk, Elizabeth: An American architect and urban planner, Plater-Zyberk has been influential in the New Urbanism movement. She works with her husband Andres Duany in the firm DPZ Partners, based in Miami, Florida.

Presley, Elvis: Known as the "king of rock and roll," Elvis Presley was a cultural icon of the 20th century. His career began in Memphis after he was discovered by Sam Phillips at Sun Studio in 1954. He soon became a sensation, with his unique style of singing and performing. Presley made a number of successful films in the 1950s and 1960s.

Raskob, John Jacob: John Jacob Raskob was a businessman and investor in the 1920s and 1930s, best known for building the Empire State Building in 1931.

Rockefeller, David: The youngest of the six children of John D. Rockefeller Jr. and brother of Nelson, David Rockefeller was a banker. He served as the chairman and CEO of the Chase Manhattan Bank, now known as JP Morgan Chase. He was also instrumental in the construction of the World Trade Center in lower Manhattan in the 1960s, in the hopes that the new complex would revitalize the flagging neighborhood that was located near the location of his bank.

Rockefeller, Nelson: Nelson Rockefeller, grandson of millionaire industrialist John D. Rockefeller, was a liberal Republican politician who served as governor of New York State during the years 1959–1973 and as vice president of the United States from 1974 to 1977 under President Gerald Ford.

Roosevelt, Franklin D.: Franklin Delano Roosevelt was the 32nd president of the United States, a Democrat, serving from 1933 to 1945. He died in office after being elected for a record four terms. He shepherded the country through the Great Depression, passing many new laws with his agenda that he called the New Deal. He also led the nation through World War II. He is considered one of the greatest American presidents.

Scruggs, Jan: Jan Scruggs is an army veteran who founded the Vietnam Veterans Memorial Fund, which was responsible for the construction of the Vietnam Veterans Memorial in Washington, D.C. Scruggs raised $8 million from private sources for the project, and successfully steered the project through many hurdles related to controversy regarding its location and design.

Siegel, Benjamin "Bugsy": A handsome and charismatic Jewish gangster in the 1930s and 1940s, Siegel was known for his involvement in the development of the Las Vegas strip, building the Flamingo Hotel in 1946. He was murdered at his girlfriend's home in Beverly Hills in 1947.

Smith, Alfred E.: Alfred E. Smith was a popular politician who was elected governor of New York State four times and ran for president in 1928 as a Democrat. Smith lost the election to the Republican Herbert Hoover. As a Roman Catholic of Irish descent, Smith was criticized by many voters who claimed that he would take his guidance from the Pope. After losing the election in 1928, Smith became president of Empire State, Inc., the entity responsible for the construction of the Empire State Building in New York City.

Somervell, Brigadier General Brehon: A decorated officer in the army during World War II, Somervell was instrumental in completing the construction of the Pentagon in Washington, D.C.

Strauss, Joseph B.: An American structural engineer, Joseph Strauss was celebrated for his pioneering work in the design of bascule bridges, also known as drawbridges. His greatest achievement, however, was the construction of the Golden Gate Bridge in San Francisco, which is a suspension bridge. The Golden Gate Bridge was the longest suspension bridge in the world from its opening in 1937 until it was surpassed by the Verrazano-Narrows Bridge in New York in 1964.

Thompson, Frederic: With Skip Dundy, Frederic Thompson was one of the developers of the innovative amusement park in Coney Island called Luna Park, opened in 1903.

van der Rohe, Ludwig Mies: One of the founders of the Modernist Movement in architecture, Mies van der Rohe was a German who emigrated to the United States during World War II. His spare designs were illuminated by his motto "less is more." His American work includes the International Style icon, the Seagram Building in New York City.

Wagner, Robert F., Jr.: A four-term Democratic mayor of New York City, Robert F. Wagner Jr. was responsible for the creation of the New York City Landmarks Preservation Commission after the outcry that ensued following the demolition of the Beaux-Arts masterpiece Pennsylvania Station in 1963.

Warren, Earl: Earl Warren was a politician and jurist who served as governor of California and subsequently chief justice of the Supreme Court from 1953 to 1969. The Warren Court was known for its liberal decisions in many landmark cases.

Wilkerson, William R.: Founder of the *Hollywood Reporter* and owner of the nightclub Ciro's in Hollywood in the 1930s and 1940s, Wilkerson was also the original developer of the Flamingo Hotel on the Las Vegas Strip, until being forced out by the mobster Bugsy Siegel.

Witmer, David: A chief architect for the War Department, David Witmer was one of the architects of the Pentagon, built in 1943.

Wright, Elizur: A mathematician, Elizur Wright is considered the father of life insurance and life insurance regulation. His ideas reformed the life insurance business in the mid-19th century. He was also known as an ardent abolitionist.

Wright, Frank Lloyd: One of America's greatest architects, Frank Lloyd Wright had a long and successful career. His early work was in the Prairie Style, inspired by his Midwest background. Wright's design for the country house built for department store magnate Edgar Kaufmann, Fallingwater, is considered his masterpiece.

Yamasaki, Minoru: Minoru Yamasaki was an American architect whose most famous work was the World Trade Center in New York City, completed in 1973.

GLOSSARY OF TERMS

Acroteria: An architectural ornament placed on a pedestal. It is most commonly located at the ends or the apex of a pediment.

Apex: Highest point of a structure.

Arcade: In architecture, an arcade is a series of arches. It can be a covered walkway supported by arches, or a row of arches along a wall.

Arch-gravity dams: A dam design that uses a curved dam and its geographical location to hold back the pressure of the water.

Bascule bridge: A bascule bridge is a movable bridge, also called a drawbridge. It can be single or double, with a "leaf" that lifts up, allowing boat traffic to pass.

Bundled tube structure: In structural engineering, a tube is a structural system where, to resist wind, seismic, and impact loads, a building is designed to act like a hollow cylinder, cantilevered perpendicular to the ground. In a bundled tube structure, instead of one tube, a building consists of several tubes tied together to resist lateral forces. The Sears Tower (Willis Tower) is an example of a bundled tube structure.

CAD: CAD, or computer-aided design, is the use of computers to draw, analyze, create, and calculate in architectural and engineering design.

Cantilever: A long projecting beam or girder fixed at only one end.

Central business district: Also called a "CDB," in city planning, the central business district is the main commercial and business center of a city or a town.

Chippendale: A furniture style from the mid-1700s in England based on the designs of Thomas Chippendale.

Coffers: Recessed panels, often used in ceilings, soffits, or vaults. They are usually squares, rectangles, or octagon-shaped.

Colonnade: A long sequence of columns located on a classical building.

Concrete: A building material using loose aggregate held together with cement to form a strong masonry material.

Corbel: In architecture, a corbel is a type of bracket. It is a structural piece of stone, wood, or metal, jutting from a wall to carry a weight.

Crenellation: A crenellation is a rampart built around the top of a castle with regular gaps for firing arrows or guns.

Curtain wall: A curtain wall is a nonbearing wall, often of windows or metal panels. The wall is attached to the frame of the building but does not carry any load in the structure.

Deconstructivism: A movement of Postmodern architecture, which gives the impression of the fragmentation of the constructed building. It is characterized by an absence of harmony, continuity, or symmetry. Frank Gehry has been identified as a deconstructivist, although he does not self-identify as one.

Doric order: One of the three orders of ancient Greek architecture. The Doric order has simple circular capitals at the top of columns.

Egg-and-dart: In architecture, a design shape used in moldings. It consists of an egg-shaped object alternating with an element shaped like an arrow, anchor, or dart.

Eminent domain: The right of a government or its agent to take private property for public use, with payment of compensation.

Entablature: A horizontal, continuous lintel on a classical building supported by columns or a wall.

Exoskeleton: An external skeleton that protects the body. In architecture, the exoskeleton is an external support that is part of the building's structure.

Gabbro: A large, dark, igneous rock, similar to basalt.

Greek frieze: In Greek and Roman architecture, a frieze is the middle of the three main divisions of an entablature, which is the section resting of the capital, above the columns.

Hydroelectricity: Electricity produced using water-powered techniques.

I-beam: A steel beam with an I or H cross-section, used in modern construction.

Keystone: A keystone is a wedge-shaped stone at the apex of a masonry arch.

KIA: Killed in Action.

Limited-access highway: A highway with access only at specific intervals, usually through the use of on and off ramps; also called a controlled-access highway or freeway.

Lunette: A lunette is a half-moon shaped space, often where the upper part of a wall intersects with a vault. When a lunette is used as a window it is commonly called a half-moon window.

Manhattan schist: A metamorphic rock found in Manhattan. It is the bedrock that is used to support the tall buildings found in New York City.

MIA: Missing in Action.

Military-industrial complex: The term for the growing political power of the military and the businesses that supplied it during the Cold War. President Eisenhower warned of the power of the group in his farewell address when he stated "we must guard against the acquisition of unwarranted influence, whether sought or unsought, by the military-industrial complex."

Modern architecture: A 20th-century architectural style that runs counter to classical architectural styles by trying to incorporate changes to society and technology into architecture. Best known for its use of "form follows function" pursuit of design. Architects who utilized this design style were known as "Modernists."

Mullions: Vertical bars between the panes of glass in a window, or a door.

National Command Authority: The term used for the president and secretary of defense who command military actions for the United States.

National Military Command Center: The communication center or war room in the Pentagon where U.S. military actions across the globe are controlled.

New Deal: A series of programs, instituted by President Franklin Roosevelt, intended to alleviate the suffering caused by the Great Depression. These programs include Social Security, although there were many others that were in effect between 1933 and 1938.

Nomenclature: The system of naming things. In architecture, it is the specialized vocabulary used to describe architectural elements.

NORAD: The North American Air Defense Command. A joint U.S.-Canadian command responsible for protecting the United States and Canada from aerial attack.

Nuclear weapons: Weapons that rely on nuclear reaction to cause massive amounts of destruction.

Peristyle: A peristyle is a continuous porch formed by a row of columns surrounding the perimeter of building or a courtyard, commonly found in a Greek temple.

Pilaster: An upright architectural member that is rectangular in plan that usually projects a third of its width or less from the wall. It resembles a column, but, unlike a column, it is attached to the wall.

Glossary of Terms

Pilings: A form of construction of a foundation of a building. It involves drilling a borehole into the ground, and then placing concrete and reinforcing iron or steel into the hole.

Portico: In classical architecture, a porch leading to an entrance.

Post-tensioning: Post-tensioning is a method of strengthening reinforced concrete by applying tension to the reinforcing rods after the concrete has set.

Pylon: A vertical sign, usually freestanding.

Quonset huts: A Quonset hut is a lightweight prefabricated structure of corrugated galvanized steel having a semicircular cross-section, used during World War II as temporary shelter.

Radome: A dome or other structure protecting radar equipment and made from material transparent to radio waves.

Redlining: The practice of refusing a loan or insurance to someone because they live in an area deemed to be a poor financial risk. This practice was often used by banks to prevent African Americans from investing in white neighborhoods.

Soffit: The underside of a part or member of a building.

Spillways: A structure associated with a dam that is used to control the flow of water.

Streetcar suburbs: A streetcar suburb is a residential community whose growth and development was influenced by the use of streetcar lines as a primary means of transportation.

Stripped classical style: An architectural style that was popular in federal buildings in the 1930s through 1950s. The style takes the basic traditions of the classical style, but removes most of the ornamentation.

Tar paper: A heavy paper impregnated with tar and used as a waterproofing material in building. Often used a roofing, it can also be used to as inexpensive waterproof siding.

Thin-shell concrete: In architecture, a thin-shell concrete structure is a structure composed of a relatively thin shell of concrete, usually with no interior columns.

Transom: In architecture, a transom is a transverse horizontal structural beam or bar, or a crosspiece separating a door from a window above it. Also refers to the window above a door within the horizontal structural beam.

Tri-partite: Divided into three sections.

Truss: A framework, typically consisting of rafters, posts, and struts, supporting a roof, bridge, or other structure.

Vertical integration: Vertical integration occurs when a company expands its business operations into different steps on the same production path, such as when a manufacturer owns its supplier and/or distributor. Henry Ford attempted vertical integration in his River Rouge plant.

Weatherboard: The use of long, thin boards to cover exterior walls; sometimes called clapboard.

BIBLIOGRAPHY

Aitken, Robert, and Marilyn Aitken. Winter 2011. "Japanese American Internment." *Litigation* 37 (2): 59–62, 70. JSTOR. http://www.jstor.org/stable/23075502. Accessed October 7, 2017.

Al, Stefan. 2017. *The Strip: Las Vegas and the Architecture of the American Dream*. Cambridge, MA: The MIT Press.

Alexander, David. 2008. *The Building: A Biography of the Pentagon*. St. Paul, MN: MBI Publishing Company LLC and Zenith Press.

Allen, Erin. April 9, 2014. "The Sound of Freedom: Marian Anderson at the Lincoln Memorial." Library of Congress Blog. https://blogs.loc.gov/loc/2014/04/the-sound-of-freedom-marian-anderson-at-the-lincoln-memorial/. Accessed September 27, 2017.

Allen, Frederick Lewis. 1952. *The Big Change: America Transforms Itself 1900–1950*. New York: Harper and Row.

American Experience. PBS.org. October 15, 2000. "Attica Prison Riot." http://www.pbs.org/video/2112801229/. Accessed July 31, 2017.

American Experience. PBS.org. February 28, 2011. "Triangle Fire." http://www.pbs.org/wgbh/americanexperience/films/triangle/. Accessed January 20, 2017.

American Experience. PBS.org. January 29, 2013. "Henry Ford." http://www.pbs.org/video/american-experience-henry-ford-film/. Accessed September 22, 2017.

American Rails. 2016. "Pennsylvania Station, An Architectural Wonder." http://www.american-rails.com/pennsylvania-station.html. Accessed July 10, 2017.

Austen, Ben. May 2012. "The Last Tower: The Decline and Fall of Public Housing." *Harpers*. https://harpers.org/archive/2012/05/the-last-tower/. Accessed May 7, 2017.

Bagli, Charles V. May 4, 2013. "102 Floor, 10 Million Bricks and Tangled History." *New York Times*. http://www.nytimes.com/2013/05/05/business/

empire-state-building-has-a-tangled-history.html. Accessed March 24, 2017.

Becker, Lynn. 2004. "Sleekness in Seattle: Rem Koolhaas, Joshua Ramus, OMA and the Seattle Public Library." *Repeat*. http://lynnbecker.com/repeat/seattle/seattlepl.htm. Accessed May 25, 2017.

Berger, Joseph. March 22, 2011. "Triangle Fire: The Building Survives." *New York Times*. http://www.nyc.gov/html/lpc/downloads/pdf/reports/brown.pdf. Accessed January 19, 2017.

Betsky, Aaron. November 7, 1991. "Architecture: Mann's Chinese Theatre: Illusion at Its Best." *Los Angeles Times*. http://articles.latimes.com/1991-11-07/news/we-1473_1_mann-s-chinese-theater. Accessed March 3, 2017.

Betsky, Aaron. August 13, 2012. "One World Trade Center's Decent into 'Meh.'" *Architect Magazine*. http://www.architectmagazine.com/design/one-world-trade-centers-descent-into-meh_o. Accessed June 10, 2017.

Bloomberg Business Week. October 6, 2003. "Frank Gehry's High-tech Secret." https://www.bloomberg.com/news/articles/2003-10-05/frank-gehrys-high-tech-secret. Accessed February 27, 2017.

Boorstin, Daniel J. 1973. *The Americans: The Democratic Experience*. New York: Vintage Books.

Bowly, Devereax, Jr. 2012. *The Poorhouse: Subsidized Housing in Chicago*. Carbondale: Southern Illinois University Press.

Brake, Alan G. September 12, 2015. "Postmodern Architecture: The Portland Municipal Services Building, Oregon, by Michael Graves." *Dezeen*. https://www.dezeen.com/2015/09/12/postmodernism-architecture-portland-municipal-services-building-michael-graves/. Accessed March 10, 2017.

Brangham, William. July 21, 2015. "How a Coney Island Sideshow Advanced Medicine for Premature Babies." PBS Newshour. http://www.pbs.org/newshour/updates/coney-island-sideshow-advanced-medicine-premature-babies/. Accessed February 5, 2017.

CBS Miami. 2012. "Narcy Novack Sentenced to Life in Family Killings Case." http://miami.cbslocal.com/2012/12/17/sentencing-day-in-narcy-novack-family-killings-case/. Accessed February 18, 2017.

Charles River Editors. 2017. *The Sears Tower: History of Chicago's Most Iconic Landmark*. Middletown, DE: Charles River Editors.

Charleton, James H. 1984. "Los Angeles Memorial Coliseum." National Park Service. https://npgallery.nps.gov/pdfhost/docs/NHLS/Text/84003866.pdf. Accessed October 14, 2017.

Cheek, Lawrence. March 26, 2007. "On Architecture: How the New Central Library Really Stacks Up." *Seattle PI.* http://www.seattlepi.com/ae/article/On-Architecture-How-the-new-Central-Library-1232303.php. Accessed May 25, 2017.

Chung, Payton. 2003. "Short History of Cabrini Green." Westnorth.com. https://westnorth.com/2003/01/02/short-history-of-cabrini-green/. Accessed May 7, 2017.

City of Miami Planning Department. 2009. "Morris Lapidus/Mid 20th Century Historic District Designation Report." http://mimoonthebeach.com/pdfs/Morris%20Lapidus_Mid%2020th%20Century_FINAL_low%20res.pdf#page=3. Accessed February 9, 2017.

Classic Las Vegas. 2007. "The Fabulous Flamingo Hotel History—The Wilkerson-Siegel Years—The History of the Las Vegas Strip." https://web.archive.org/web/20160111084052/; http://classiclasvegas.squarespace.com/a-brief-history-of-the-strip/2007/9/23/the-fabulous-flamingo-hotel-history-the-wilkerson-siegel-yea.html. Accessed November 1, 2017.

Duany, Andres, Elizabeth Plater-Zyberk, and Jeff Speck. 2000. *Suburban Nation: The Rise of Sprawl and the Decline of the American Dream.* New York: North Point Press.

Dunlap, David W. June 12, 2012. "1 World Trade Center Is a Growing Presence, and a Changed One." *New York Times.* https://cityroom.blogs.nytimes.com/2012/06/12/1-world-trade-center-is-a-growing-presence-and-a-changed-one/. Accessed June 11, 2017.

Dunlop, David. December 7, 2016. "Symbol of Jet Age Is Bound for a New Era." *New York Times*, p. A23.

Dupre, Judith. 2016. *One World Trade Center: Biography of a Building.* New York, Boston, and London. Little, Brown and Company.

Educational Resources, National Archives. 2017. "Japanese Relocation during World War II." https://www.archives.gov/education/lessons/japanese-relocation. Accessed October 10, 2017.

Ellis, Ciff. 2002. "The New Urbanism: Critiques and Rebuttals." *Journal of Urban Design*, 261–91. http://www.tandfonline.com/doi/abs/10.1080/1357480022000039330. Accessed October 16, 2017.

Ellis, Luke, Bruce M. Nash, and Max Raphael. 2005. *Hoover Dam.* New York: A & E Home Video.

Empire State Realty Trust. Empire State Building Fact Sheet. 2015. http://www.esbnyc.com/sites/default/files/esb_fact_sheet_4_9_14_4.pdf. Accessed March 27, 2017.

Esri, Natasha Geiling. November 25, 2014. "The Death and Rebirth of the American Mall." *Smithsonian Magazine*. http://www.smithsonianmag.com/arts-culture/death-and-rebirth-american-mall-180953444/. Accessed February 18, 2017.

Fallingwater. 2017. "Fallingwater Facts." http://www.fallingwater.org/38/. Accessed July 2, 2017.

Fiederer, Luke. 2016. "AD Classics: TWA Flight Center/Eero Saarinen." *ArchDaily*. http://www.archdaily.com/788012/ad-classics-twa-flight-center-eero-saarinen. Accessed January 30, 2017.

Fine, Lenore, and Jesse A. Remington. 1972. *The Corps of Engineers: Construction in the United States*. Washington, DC: Office of the Chief of Military History, U.S. Army.

Fithian, David Brooks. 1994. *A Dark and Shining Stone: Symbol Contests and the Vietnam Veterans Memorial*.1

Fox, Justin. January 26, 2004. "The Great Paving." *Fortune* 149 (2): 86–90. http://archive.fortune.com/magazines/fortune/fortune_archive/2004/01/26/358835/index.htm. Accessed November 29, 2017.

Frank Lloyd Wright Foundation. 2012. "The Life of Frank Lloyd Wright." http://franklloydwright.org/frank-lloyd-wright/. Accessed July 2, 2017.

Fried, Benjamin. July 1, 2004. "Mixing with the Kool Crowd." Project for Public Spaces. https://www.pps.org/reference/mixing-with-the-kool-crowd/. Accessed May 25, 2017.

Friedman, Alice T. 2000. "The Luxury of Lapidus: Glamour, Class, and Architecture in Miami Beach." *Harvard Design Magazine*11: 39–47. http://www.nyc-architecture.com/ARCH/ARCH-Lapidus.htm. Accessed February 9, 2017.

Gelernter, Mark. 1999. *A History of American Architecture: Buildings in Their Cultural and Technological Context*. Hanover and London: University Press of New England.

Gillette, Howard, Jr. 2004. "The Lincoln Memorial and American Life by Christopher A. Thomas" (Review). *Indiana University of Magazine of History* 100 (4): 397–99. https://scholarworks.iu.edu/journals/index.php/imh/article/view/12096/17899. Accessed September 27, 2017.

Gilpin, Kenneth N. July 16, 1998. "Richard McDonald, 89, Fast-Food Revolutionary." *New York Times*. http://www.nytimes.com/1998/07/16/business/richard-mcdonald-89-fast-food-revolutionary.html. Accessed August 13, 2017.

Gladwell, Malcolm. March 15, 2004. "The Terrazzo Jungle." *New Yorker*. http://www.newyorker.com/magazine/2004/03/15/the-terrazzo-jungle. Accessed February 18, 2017.

Glantz, James, and Eric Lipton. 2003. *City in the Sky: The Rise and Fall of the World Trade Center*. New York: Times Books, Henry Holt and Company.

Glatt, John. 2013. *The Prince of Paradise: The True Story of a Hotel Heir, His Seductive Wife, and a Ruthless Murder*. New York: St. Martin's Press.

Goetz, Edward G. Autumn 2012. "The Transformation of Public Housing Policy, 1985–2011." *Journal of American Planning Association* 78 (4): 452–63. https://www-tandfonline-com.proxy3.library.mcgill.ca/doi/full/10.1080/01944363.2012.737983. Accessed April 12, 2017.

Goldberg, Alfred. 1992. *The Pentagon: The First Fifty Years*. Washington, DC: Historical Office, Office of the Secretary of Defense.

Goldberger, Paul. 1979. *The City Observed: New York—A Guide to the Architecture of Manhattan*. New York: Vintage Books.

Goldberger, Paul. October 10, 1982. "Architecture of a Different Color." *New York Times*. http://www.nytimes.com/1982/10/10/magazine/architecture-of-a-different-color.html?pagewanted=all. Accessed March 12, 2017.

Goldberger, Paul. September 24, 2001. "The Skyline: Building Plans." *New Yorker*. http://www.newyorker.com/magazine/2001/09/24/building-plans. Accessed June 4, 2017.

Goldberger, Paul. September 29, 2003. "Good Vibrations." *New Yorker*. Conde Nast Publications. http://go.galegroup.com.proxy.library.csi.cuny.edu/ps/i.do?&id=GALE|A106518159&v=2.1&u=cuny_statenisle&it=r&p=AONE&sw=w. Accessed February 26, 2017.

Goldberger, Paul. May 24, 2004. "High-Tech Bibliophilia." *New Yorker*. http://www.newyorker.com/magazine/2004/05/24/high-tech-bibliophilia. Accessed May 25, 2017.

Goldberger, Paul. September 12, 2011. "Shaping the Void: How Successful Is the New World Trade Center?" *New Yorker*. http://www.newyorker.com/magazine/2011/09/12/shaping-the-void. Accessed June 10, 2017.

Gray, Christopher. September 24, 1995. "Streetscapes/Public Housing; In the Beginning, New York Created First Houses." *New York Times*. http://www.nytimes.com/1995/09/24/realestate/streetscapes-public-housing-in-the-beginning-new-york-created-first-houses.html. Accessed December 28, 2016.

"Greensboro Lunch Counter Sit-In." December 9, 1998. https://www.loc.gov/exhibits/odyssey/educate/lunch.html. Accessed August 17, 2017.

Grimes, William. March 10, 2010. "Bruce Graham, Chicago Architect Who Designed Sears Tower, Dies at 84." *New York Times*. http://www.

nytimes.com/2010/03/10/arts/design/10graham.html. Accessed April 14, 2017.

Hajdu, David. December 3, 2015. "Sam Phillips: The Man Who Invented Rock and Roll by Peter Guralnick." *New York Times*. https://www.nytimes.com/2015/12/06/books/review/sam-phillips-the-man-who-invented-rock-n-roll-by-peter-guralnick.html. Accessed October 6, 2017.

Harris, Gale. March 25, 2003. "Brown Building (Originally Asch Building) Designation Report." *Landmarks Preservation Commission*. Designation List 346. LP-2128. http://www.nyc.gov/html/lpc/downloads/pdf/reports/brown.pdf. Accessed January 17, 2017.

Hayden, Dolores. 2003. *Building Suburbia: Green Fields and Urban Growth, 1820–2000*. New York: Vintage Books.

Hess, Alan. March 1986. "The Origins of McDonald's Golden Arches." *Journal of the Society of Architectural Historians* 45 (1): 60–67. http://www.jstor.org.proxy.library.csi.cuny.edu/stable/990129?seq=1#page_scan_tab_contents. Accessed August 1, 2017.

Hess, Alan. August 14, 2013. "The Oldest McDonald's as Architecture." Alan Hess on Architecture. http://alanhess.blogspot.com/2013/08/the-oldest-mcdonalds-as-architecture.html. Accessed August 1, 2017.

Hilke, Jens. "History and Cultural Impact of the Interstate Highway System." University of Vermont. http://www.uvm.edu/landscape/learn/impact_of_interstate_system.html. Accessed November 13, 2017.

Hiltzik, Michael A. 2010. *Colossus: Hoover Dam and the Making of the American Century*. New York: Free Press.

Historic American Buildings Survey (HABS) No. NY-6371, Trans World Airlines Flight Center, John F. Kennedy International Airport, Jamaica Bay, Queens (subdivision), Queens, New York. http://lcweb2.loc.gov/master/pnp/habshaer/ny/ny2000/ny2019/data/ny2019data.pdf. Accessed January 27, 2017.

History and Facts—Willis Tower. http://www.willistower.com/history-and-facts. Accessed April 10, 2017.

Hott, Lawrence, and Tom Lewis. September 27, 1997. "Divided Highways: The Interstates and the Transformation of American Life." https://www.youtube.com/watch?v=PLr-8QPbiAY. Accessed November 29, 2017.

Huxtable, Ada Louise. October 30, 1963. "Farewell to Penn Station." *New York Times*. https://nycarchitectureandurbanism.files.wordpress.com/2015/03/huxtable-farewell-to-penn-station-1963.pdf. Accessed July 10, 2017.

Huxtable, Ada Louise. May 29, 1966. "Who's Afraid of Big, Bad Buildings?" *New York Times*. https://timesmachine.nytimes.com/timesmachine/1966/05/29/140000432.html?pageNumber=92. Accessed May 12, 2017.

Hyde, Charles K. 1966. "Assembly-Line Architecture: Albert Kahn and the Evolution of the U.S. Auto Factory." *Journal of the Society for Industrial Archeology* 22 (2): 5–24. http://www.jstor.org/stable/pdf/40968351.pdf?refreqid=excelsior%3Aec43689eb2bb59d2f93b24fcddc6fd91. Accessed September 10, 2017.

Immerso, Michael. 2002. *Coney Island: The People's Playground*. New Brunswick, NJ, and London: Rutgers University Press.

International Civil Rights Center & Museum. 2010. "The Greensboro Chronology." https://www.sitinmovement.org/history/greensboro-chronology.asp. Accessed August 17, 2017.

Jackson, Kenneth T. 1985. *Crabgrass Frontier: The Suburbanization of the United States*. New York and Oxford: Oxford University Press.

Jacobs, Jane. 1961. *The Death and Life of Great American Cities*. New York: Vintage Books.

Jones, Rennie. October 23, 2013. "AD Classics. Walt Disney Concert Hall/Frank Gehry." *ArchDaily*. http://www.archdaily.com/441358/ad-classics-walt-disney-concert-hall-frank-gehry. Accessed February 27, 2017.

Kamin, Blair. October 18, 2014. "One World Trade Center 'A Bold but Flawed Giant.'" *Chicago Tribune*. http://www.chicagotribune.com/news/columnists/ct-one-world-trade-center-review-kamin-met-1019-20141017-column.html. Accessed June 10, 2017.

Kasson, John F. 1978. *Amusing the Million: Coney Island at the Turn of the Century*. New York: Hill and Wang.

Kheel Center, Cornell University. 2015. "The 1911 Triangle Factory Fire." http://www.ilr.cornell.edu/story/fire.html. Accessed April 13, 2018.

Kimmelman, Michael. May 28, 2014. "Finding Space for the Living at a Memorial." *New York Times*. https://www.nytimes.com/2014/05/29/arts/design/finding-space-for-the-living-at-a-memorial.html. Accessed June 11, 2017.

Kimmelman, Michael. November 29, 2014. "A Soaring Emblem of New York, and Its Upside-Down Priorities." *New York Times*. https://www.nytimes.com/2014/11/30/nyregion/is-one-world-trade-center-rises-in-lower-manhattan-a-design-success.html?_r=0. Accessed June 10, 2017.

King, Elizabeth. "The Rise and Fall of the American Shopping Mall." *Broadly, Vice Media*. https://broadly.vice.com/en_us/article/the-rise-and-fall-of-the-american-shopping-mall. Accessed February 18, 2017.

Kitagaki, Paul, and T. A. Frail. January 2017. "The Injustice of Japanese-American Internment Camps Resonates Strongly to This Day." *Smithsonian Magazine.* https://www.smithsonianmag.com/history/injustice-japanese-americans-internment-camps-resonates-strongly-180961422/. Accessed October 10, 2017.

Koolhaas, Rem. 2000. Laureate Biography. The Pritzker Architecture Prize. http://www.pritzkerprize.com/2000/bio. Accessed May 29, 2017.

LaFrank, Kathleen. "Seaside, Florida: The New Town: The Old Ways." *Perspectives in Vernacular Architecture. Vol. 6. Shaping Communities*, 111–21. https://www.jstor.org/stable/3514366?seq=1#page_scan_tab_contents. Accessed October 11, 2017.

Lambert, Bruce. 1997. "At 50, Levittown Contends with Its Legacy of Bias." *New York Times.* http://www.nytimes.com/1997/12/28/nyregion/at-50-levittown-contends-with-its-legacy-of-bias.html. Accessed February 22, 2017.

Lambert, Phyllis. 2013. *Building Seagram.* New Haven, CT, and London: Yale University Press.

Lambert, Tim. "A History of Los Angeles." http://www.localhistories.org/losangeles.html. Accessed October 12, 2017.

Lamster, Mark. April 3, 2013. "A Personal Stamp on the Skyline." *New York Times.* http://www.nytimes.com/2013/04/07/arts/design/building-seagram-phyllis-lamberts-new-architecture-book.html. Accessed March 12, 2017.

Landmarks Preservation Commission. November 9, 1982. "Lever House." Designation List 161. LP-1277. http://s-media.nyc.gov/agencies/lpc/lp/1277.pdf. Accessed March 13, 2017.

Landmarks Preservation Commission. October 3, 1989. "Seagram Building, Including the Plaza." Designation List 221. LP-1664. http://s-media.nyc.gov/agencies/lpc/lp/1664.pdf. Accessed March 13, 2017.

Landmarks Preservation Commission. July 19, 1994. "Trans World Airline Flight Center at New York International Airport." Designation List 259. LP-1916. http://s-media.nyc.gov/agencies/lpc/lp/1915.pdf. Accessed January 27, 2017.

Landmarks Preservation Commission Nomination. November 12, 1974. "First Houses." LP-0876. http://www.neighborhoodpreservationcenter.org/db/bb_files/74-FIRST-HOUSES.pdf. Accessed January 13, 2017.

Langmead, Donald. 2009. *Icons of American Architecture from the Alamo to the World Trade Center.* Westport, CT: Greenwood Press.

Las Vegas Online Entertainment Guide. 2005. "History of Las Vegas." http://www.lvol.com/lvoleg/hist/lvhist.html. Accessed November 1, 2017.

LeBrun, Nancy. 2002. *Inside the Pentagon*. Washington, DC: National Geographic, Library of Congress.

Library of Congress. 2004. "Japanese behind the Wire." https://www.loc.gov/teachers/classroommaterials/presentationsandactivities/presentations/immigration/japanese4.html. Accessed October 10, 2017.

Lind, Carla. 1996. *Frank Lloyd Wright's Fallingwater*. Portland, OR: Archetype Press.

Lindsay, Drew. October 1, 2005. "The Watergate: The Building That Changed Washington." *Washingtonian*. https://www.washingtonian.com/2005/10/01/the-watergate-the-building-that-changed-washington/. Accessed July 21, 2017.

Lopes, Sal. 1987. *The Wall: Images and Offerings from the Vietnam Veterans Memorial*. New York: Collins.

Los Angeles Coliseum Commission. 2014. "Coliseum History—LA Coliseum." http://www.lacoliseum.com/index.php/coliseum-history/. Accessed October 11, 2017.

Los Angeles Conservancy. 2016. "Chinese Theatre." https://www.laconservancy.org/locations/tcl-chinese-theatre-0. Accessed March 3, 2017.

Los Angeles Conservancy. 2017. "Los Angeles Memorial Coliseum—Los Angeles." https://www.laconservancy.org/issues/los-angeles-memorial-coliseum. Accessed October 11, 2017.

Louchheim, A. B. April 27, 1952. "Building in the New Style." *New York Times*. http://www.nytimes.com/1952/04/27/archives/newest-building-in-the-new-style.html. Accessed March 14, 2017.

Love, Kenneth. 2006. "Saving Fallingwater." Documentary. Kenneth A. Love International.

Mallhistory.com. 2013. "Northgate Mall." http://www.mallhistory.com/malls/northgate-mall-seattle-wa. Accessed February 18, 2017.

Manieri, Ray. Fall 1979/Winter 1980. "Downtown Greensboro Historic District." Old Greensboro Preservation Society. For National Park Service. http://www.hpo.ncdcr.gov/nr/GF0042.pdf. Accessed August 19, 2017.

Marshall, Colin. 2015. "Levittown, the Prototypical American Suburb." *Guardian*. https://www.theguardian.com/cities/2015/apr/28/levittown-america-prototypical-suburb-history-cities. Accessed February 18, 2017.

May, Lary, ed. 1988. *Recasting America: Culture and Politics in the Age of the Cold War*. Chicago, IL: University of Chicago Press.

McGuigan, Cathleen. August 18, 2003. "A Mighty Monument to Music: Frank Gehry's Swooping, Soaring Walt Disney Concert Hall Is the Architect's Masterwork—And the Mirror of This Own Restless Energies." *Newsweek*.

http://onesearch.cuny.edu/primo_library/libweb/action/display.do?frbrVersion=2&tabs=detailsTab&ct=display&fn=search&doc=TN_gale_ofa108321611&indx=6&recIds=TN_gale_ofa108321611&recIdxs=5&elementId=5&renderMode=poppedOut&displayMode=full&frbrVersion=2&vl(62436675UI0)=any&query=any%2Ccontains%2Cwalt+disney+concert+hall&dscnt=0&search_scope=everything&scp.scps=scope%3A%28CUNY_BEPRESS%29%2Cscope%3A%28SI%29%2Cscope%3A%28AL%29%2Cprimo_central_multiple_fe&onCampus=true&vid=si&queryTemp=walt+disney+concert+hall&institution=SI&tab=default_tab&vl(freeText0)=walt%20disney%20concert%20hall&group=GUEST&dstmp=1488138072814. Accessed February 26, 2017.

McNerthney, Casey. February 17, 2013. "Northgate—Nation's First Suburban 'Mall'—Announced 65 Years Ago This Week." Seattlepi.com. http://www.seattlepi.com/local/seattle-history/article/Northgate-nations-first-suburban-mall-4286441.php. Accessed February 18, 2017.

Meares, Hadley. July 21, 2016. "The People's Playground." Curbed LA. https://la.curbed.com/2016/7/21/12215982/los-angeles-olympics-coliseum-history. Accessed October 11, 2017.

Menand, Louis. November 16, 2015. "The Elvic Oracle—Did Anyone Invent Rock and Roll?" *New Yorker*. https://www.newyorker.com/magazine/2015/11/16/the-elvic-oracle. Accessed October 3, 2017.

Miller, Brian J. September 2008. "The Struggle over Redevelopment at Cabrini-Green, 1989–2004." *Journal of Urban History* 34 (6): 944–60.

Miller, Donald L. 1996. *City of the Century: The Epic of Chicago and the Making of America*. New York: Simon & Schuster.

Moeller, G. Martin, Jr. 2012. *AIA Guide to the Architecture of Washington, D.C.* Baltimore, MD: Johns Hopkins University Press.

Morgan, Neville (Producer) and Guralnick, Peter (Writer). 2000. "Sam Phillips—The Man Who Invented Rock and Roll." Documentary. A&E Television Networks. https://www.youtube.com/watch?v=tYcadYXsTyM. Accessed October 3, 2017.

Morgan, Ted. July 13, 1986. "Intrigue and Tyranny in Motor City." *New York Times*. http://www.nytimes.com/1986/07/13/books/intrigue-and-tyranny-in-motor-city.html?pagewanted=all&mcubz=0. Accessed September 22, 2017.

Muschamp, Herbert. April 18, 1999. "Best Building; Opposites Attract." *New York Times Magazine*. http://www.nytimes.com/1999/04/18/magazine/best-building-opposites-attract.html. Accessed March 17, 2017.

Muschamp, Herbert. October 23, 2003. "Architecture Review; A Moon Palace for the Hollywood Dream." *New York Times*. http://www.nytimes.

com/2003/10/23/arts/architecture-review-a-moon-palace-for-the-hollywood-dream.html. Accessed February 22, 2017.

Muschamp, Herbert. May 16, 2004. "Architecture: The Library That Puts on Fishnets and Hits the Disco." *New York Times*. http://www.nytimes.com/2004/05/16/arts/architecture-the-library-that-puts-on-fishnets-and-hits-the-disco.html?_r=0. Accessed May 25, 2017.

Napoli. Lisa. November 1, 2016. "The Story of How McDonald's First Got Its Start." Smithsonian. Com. http://www.smithsonianmag.com/history/story-how-mcdonalds-first-got-its-start-180960931/. Accessed August 1, 2017.

National Park Service. 1977. "Ford River Rouge Complex." https://npgallery.nps.gov/pdfhost/docs/NHLS/Text/78001516.pdf. Accessed September 24, 2017.

National Park Service. 1977. National Register of Historic Places Inventory—Nomination Form. "Equitable Building." http://npgallery.nps.gov/nrhp/GetAsset?assetID=67601cac-4e94-4aad-91a0-d743b12d4336. Accessed December 4, 2016.

National Park Service. September 7, 1979. "Hoover Dam." National Register of Historic Places Inventory-Nomination Form. https://npgallery.nps.gov/pdfhost/docs/NHLS/Text/81000382.pdf. Accessed December 18, 2017.

National Park Service. 1981. "Lincoln Memorial." https://npgallery.nps.gov/pdfhost/docs/NRHP/Text/66000030.pdf. Accessed September 27, 2017.

National Park Service. 1989. "Triangle Shirtwaist Factory." National Register of Historic Places Designation Report. https://focus.nps.gov/pdfhost/docs/NHLS/Text/91002050.pdf. Accessed January 23, 2017.

National Park Service. 1991. "Rohwer Relocation Center Memorial Cemetery." https://www.nps.gov/nhl/find/statelists/ar/RohwerRelocation.pdf. Accessed October 10, 2017.

National Park Service. 1998. "Aviation in American History." Guidelines for Evaluating and Documenting Historic Aviation Properties, National Register of Historic Places Bulletin. https://www.nps.gov/nr/publications/bulletins/aviation/nrb_aviation_II.htm. Accessed January 30, 2017.

National Park Service. 2002. "Sun Record Company/ Memphis Recording Service." https://www.nps.gov/nhl/find/statelists/tn/SunRecord.pdf. Accessed October 6, 2017.

National Park Service. 2005. "Watergate, Washington, DC." http://www.watergate50.com/preservation/2005_hNRHPregAp.pdf. Accessed July 25, 2017.

National Park Service. 2008. "Fontainebleau Hotel." https://npgallery.nps.gov/NRHP/GetAsset/ba895a1a-3110-4396-b7cb-f4dec3dee3f7?branding=NRHP. Accessed February 9, 2017.

National Park Service. October 25, 2011. "Portland Public Service Building." National Register of Historic Places Registration Form. https://www.portlandoregon.gov/omf/article/509212. Accessed March 12, 2017.

National Park Service. July 31, 2017. "Lincoln Memorial Building Statistics." https://www.nps.gov/linc/learn/historyculture/lincoln-memorial-building-statistics.htm. Accessed September 27, 2017.

National Park Service. August 16, 2017. "Lincoln Memorial History and Culture." https://www.nps.gov/linc/learn/historyculture/index.htm. Accessed September 27, 2017.

NewUrbanism.org. http://www.newurbanism.org/newurbanism.html. Accessed October 18, 2017.

The Official Report of the New York State Special Commission on Attica. 1972. New York: Bantam Books. Digitized by New York State Library, 222 Madison Avenue, Albany, NY 12230. 2011. http://www.nysl.nysed.gov/mssc/attica/atticareport.pdf. Accessed July 31, 2017.

Ouroussoff, Nicolai. September 2012. "Why Is Rem Koolhaas the World's Most Controversial Architect?" *Smithsonian Magazine*. http://www.smithsonianmag.com/arts-culture/why-is-rem-koolhaas-the-worlds-most-controversial-architect-18254921/. Accessed May 25, 2017.

Paradis, Thomas W. 2011. *The Illustrated Encyclopedia of American Landmarks*. Leicester: Lorenz Books.

PBS Independent Lens. 2003. Rebecca Cerese and Dr. Steven Channing. "February One: The Story of the Greensboro Four." http://www.pbs.org/independentlens/februaryone/. Accessed August 20, 2017.

Pierpont, Claudia Roth. November 18, 2002. "The Silver Spire—How Two Men's Dreams Changed the Skyline of New York." *New Yorker*. https://www.newyorker.com/magazine/2002/11/18/the-silver-spire. Accessed March 27, 2017.

Pilat, Oliver, and Jo Ranson. 1941. *Sodom by the Sea: An Affectionate History of Coney Island*. Garden City, NY: Doubleday, Doran & Company, Inc.

Pitts, Carolyn. January 26, 1976. "Fallingwater: National Register of Historic Places Inventory—Nomination Form." National Park Service. http://www.dot7.state.pa.us/CRGIS_Attachments/SiteResource/H000868_01J.pdf. Accessed July 2, 2017.

Plotsky, Eric J. 1999. "The Fall and Rise of Pennsylvania Station: Changing Attitudes toward Historic Preservation in New York City." Massachusetts Institute of Technology Masters in City Planning Thesis.

Plunz, Richard. 1990. *A History of Housing in New York City*. New York: Columbia University Press.

Port Authority of New York and New Jersey. 2017. "History of the Twin Towers—World Trade Center." https://www.panynj.gov/wtcprogress/history-twin-towers.html. Accessed June 4, 2017.

Port Authority of New York and New Jersey. 2017. "One World Trade Center." http://www.panynj.gov/wtcprogress/index.html. Accessed June 10, 2107.

Preservation Greensboro. 2016. "F. W. Woolworth Co. Building/ International Civil Rights Center & Museum." PocketSights. https://pocketsights.com/tours/place/F-W-Woolworth-Co-Building-International-Civil-Rights-Center-Museum-132-South-Elm-Street-4645. Accessed August 19. 2017.

Robins, Anthony W. May 19, 1981. "Empire State Building." Designation List 143. LP-2000. Landmarks Preservation Commission. http://s-media.nyc.gov/agencies/lpc/lp/2000.pdf. Accessed March 24, 2017.

Robinson, David. 1968. *Hollywood in the Twenties*. New York: Paperback Library.

Rose, Mark H., and Raymond A. Mohl. 2012. *Interstate: Highway Politics and Policy since 1939*. Knoxville: University of Tennessee Press.

Roth, Leland M. 1979. *A Concise History of American Architecture*. Boulder, CO: Westview Press.

Roth, Leland M., and Amanda C. Roth Clark. 2016. *American Architecture: A History*. Boulder, CO: Westview Press.

Rothstein, Mervyn. January 19, 2001. "Morris Lapidus, an Architect Who Built Flamboyance into Hotels, Is Dead at 98." *New York Times*. http://www.nytimes.com/2001/01/19/arts/morris-lapidus-an-architect-who-built-flamboyance-into-hotels-is-dead-at-98.html. Accessed February 18, 2017.

Rybczynski, Witold. June 10, 2007. "The Office." *New York Times Sunday Book Review*.

San Francisco Planning Commission. Resolution 14754. December 17, 1998. "The Golden Gate Bridge." Draft Landmarks Board Case Report.

Schlosser, Eric. 2012. *Fast Food Nation*. New York: Mariner Books.

Scruggs, Jan C., and Joel L. Swerdlow. 1985. *To Heal a Nation: The Vietnam Veterans Memorial*. New York: Harper & Row.

Seattle Public Library. 2004. "History of the Central Library." http://www.spl.org/locations/central-library/cen-about-the-central-library/cen-history. Accessed May 25, 2017.

Seeing Stars—The Movie Palaces. 2005. "Grauman's Chinese Theatre." http://www.seeing-stars.com/theatres/chinesetheatre.shtml. Accessed March 3, 2017.

Shiel, Mark. 2012. *Hollywood Cinema and the Real Los Angeles*. London: Reaktion Books.

Shiff, Blair. May 27, 2017. "The History of the Golden Gate Bridge as It Turns 80." ABC News. http://abcnews.go.com/Lifestyle/history-san-franciscos-landmark-golden-gate-bridge-turns/story?id=47657315. Accessed October 31, 2017.

Sigmund, Pete. June 2, 2006. "The Golden Gate: 'The Bridge That Couldn't Be Built.'" ConstructionEquipmentGuide.com. https://www.construction equipmentguide.com/redirect/7045?story=7045&headline=The%20 Golden%20Gate:%20%EBThe%20Bridge%20That%20Could-n%EDt%20Be%20Built%ED. Accessed October 19, 2017.

The Skyscraper Center. 2015. "Willis Tower." https://skyscrapercenter.com/building/willis-tower/169. Accessed April 10, 2017.

Slade, Kathleen E. 2012. "Attica State Correctional Facility: The Causes of the Riot of 1971." *The Exposition* 1(1): Article 3. http://digitalcommons.buffalostate.edu/cgi/viewcontent.cgi?article=1000&context=exposition. Accessed July 1, 2017.

Smith, Lindsey. January 2, 2015. "Happy 80th Birthday to America's First Experiment in Public Housing." http://bedfordandbowery.com/2015/01/happy-80th-birthday-to-americas-first-experiment-in-public-housing/. Accessed December 28. 2016.

Smithsonian Air and Space Museum. 2007. "Air Travel in a Changing America/America by Air." 2007. https://airandspace.si.edu/exhibitions/america-by-air/online/jetage/jetage04.cfm. Accessed January 30, 2017.

Stanford University—Martin Luther King, Jr. Research and Education Institute. 2007. "Martin Luther King, Jr. and the Global Freedom Struggle—March on Washington for Jobs and Freedom." https://kinginstitute.stanford.edu/encyclopedia/march-washington-jobs-and-freedom. Accessed September 27, 2017.

Stanton, Jeffrey. 1998. "Coney Island—Luna Park." http://www.westland.net/coneyisland/articles/lunapark.htm. Accessed January 23, 2017.

Stein, Leon. 1962, 1990. *The Triangle Fire*. Ithaca, NY, and London: Cornell University Press.

Steinhauer, Jennifer. July 18, 1997. "Woolworth Gives Up on the Five-and-Dime." *New York Times*. http://www.nytimes.com/1997/07/18/business/woolworth-gives-up-on-the-five-and-dime.html?mcubz=0. Accessed August 17, 2017.

Stephenson, Bruce. May 2002. "The Roots of the New Urbanism: John Nolen's Garden City Ethic." http://cnuflorida.org/resources/new-urbanism-florida-articles/the-roots-of-new-urbanism-john-nolens-garden-city-vision-for-florida/. Accessed October 18, 2017.

Stevens, Joseph E. 1988. *Hoover Dam: An American Adventure*. Norman: University of Oklahoma Press.

Stromberg, Joseph. May 11, 2016. "Highways Gutted American Cities. So Why Did They Build Them?" *Vox*. https://www.vox.com/2015/5/14/8605917/highways-interstate-cities-history. Accessed November 13, 2017.

Sullivan, David A. 2015. "Coney Island History: The Story of Thompson & Dundy's Luna Park." Heart of Coney Island. http://www.heartofconeyisland.com/luna-park-coney-island.html. Accessed January 23, 2017.

Ta-Nehisi Coates. June 2014. "The Case for Reparations." *Atlantic*. https://www.theatlantic.com/magazine/archive/2014/06/the-case-for-reparations/361631/. Accessed May 7, 2017.

TCL Chinese Theatres. 2004. "History—TCL Chinese Theatres." http://www.tclchinesetheatres.com/tcl-chinese-theater-history/. Accessed March 1, 2017.

Thompson, Heather Ann. May 25, 2014. "Empire State Disgrace: The Dark, Secret History of the Attica Prison Tragedy." *Salon*. http://www.salon.com/2014/05/25/empire_state_disgrace_the_dark_secret_history_of_the_attica_prison_tragedy/. Accessed July 27, 2017.

Thompson, Heather Ann. 2016. *Blood in the Water: The Attica Uprising of 1971 and Its Legacy*. New York: Pantheon Books.

Tritle, Lawrence A. 2013. "Monument to Defeat: The Vietnam Veterans Memorial in American Culture and Society." In *Cultures of Commemoration*, ed. Polly Low, Graham Oliver, and P. J. Rhodes, 159–79. *Proceedings of the British Academy*. London: British Academy.

Tyson, Peter. April 30, 2002. "Twin Towers of Innovation." *Nova Online*. http://www.pbs.org/wgbh/nova/tech/twin-towers-of-innovation.html. Accessed May 21, 2017.

Upton, Dell. 1998. *Architecture in the United States*. Oxford: Oxford University Press.

Upton, Dell. 2003. "New Urbanism." In *Encyclopedia of Community*, ed. Karen Christensen and David Levinson, 992–97. Thousand Oaks, CA: SAGE. http://sk.sagepub.com/reference/community/n353.xml. Accessed October 16, 2017.

U.S. Department of Transportation, Federal Highway Administration. 2004. "Two Bay Area Bridges—The Golden Gate and San Francisco-Oakland Bay Bridge." https://www.fhwa.dot.gov/infrastructure/2bridges.cfm. Accessed October 31, 2017.

U.S. Department of Transportation, Federal Highway Administration. 2017. "The Dwight D. Eisenhower System of Interstate and Defense Highways Part VII—Miscellaneous Interstate Facts." https://www.fhwa.dot.gov/highwayhistory/data/page07.cfm. Accessed November 29, 2017.

Vale, Lawrence. February 2012. "Housing Chicago: Cabrini-Green to Parkside of Old Town." *Places Journal*. https://placesjournal.org/article/housing-chicago-cabrini-green-to-parkside-of-old-town/?gclid=Cj0KEQjwi7vIBRDpo9W8y7Ct6ZcBEiQA1CwV2PaYaWOOZE_VtpxxyPmbmMz-aliO7QvD-p7oOocopRcaAqPu8P8HAQ#footnote_10. Accessed April 11, 2017.

A View on Cities. 2008. "Sears Tower." http://www.aviewoncities.com/buildings/chicago/searstower.htm. Accessed April 14, 2017.

Vogel, Steve. 2007. *The Pentagon: A History: The Untold Story of the Wartime Race to Build the Pentagon—And to Restore It Sixty Years Later*. New York: Random House.

Wald, Matthew L. September 2, 2001. "Rescuing a World-Famous but Fragile House." *New York Times*. http://www.nytimes.com/2001/09/02/us/rescuing-a-world-famous-but-fragile-house.html. Accessed July 2, 2017.

Warner, Sam Bass. 1962. *Streetcar Suburbs: The Process of Growth in Boston 1870–1900*. Cambridge, MA: Harvard University Press.

Watergate (documentary series). 1994. BBC and Discovery. Directed by Mick Gold, produced by Paul Mitchell and Norma Percy. https://www.youtube.com/watch?v=fRCih5rUiVQ. Accessed July 24, 2017.

Weingroff, Richard F. Summer 1996. "Federal-Aid Highway Act of 1956: Creating the Interstate System." U.S. Department of Transportation, Federal Highway Administration. Vol. 60. No. 1. https://www.fhwa.dot.gov/publications/publicroads/96summer/p96su10.cfm. Accessed November 13, 2017.

Western Construction News. 1931. "Hoover Dam Specifications." *Western Construction News* 6 (1).2

White, Norval, and Elliot Willensky. 1978. *AIA Guide to New York City*. New York: Collier Books.

Wilma, David. August 2, 2001. "Northgate Shopping Mall (Seattle) Opens on April 21, 1950." Historylink.org. http://www.historylink.org/File/3186. Accessed November 6, 2016.

Wiseman, Carter. 2000. *Twentieth-Century American Architecture: The Buildings and Their Makers*. New York and London: W. W. Norton.

Wright, Gwendolyn. 2008. *USA: Modern Architectures in History*. London: Reaktion Books.

WTTW. "Ten Buildings That Changed America. #8—Portland Municipal Services Building." http://interactive.wttw.com/tenbuildings/portland-municipal-services-buildin. Accessed March 12, 2017.

INDEX

Ackerman, Frederick L., 217
African Americans: *Birth of a Nation*, portrayal in, 98; Black Panther Party, 19; discrimination against, 43, 160, 239, 243; Ford Motor Company, 93; Great Migration, 18; Jim Crow laws, 105–8; Los Angeles, 9; Martin Luther King, Jr., 274; popular music, 133–37; public housing, 219, 231–32; racial wealth gap, 240; Tenderloin District, 7
Age of Enlightenment, 17
Airline industry, 5, 55, 158, 173–79
Allen, Frederick Lewis, 97
American Institute of Architects (AIA), 115, 226, 279
Amusement parks: Disneyland, 20, 77; Luna Park, 73–78, 161
Anderson, Marian, 272
Anti-Semitism: Henry Ford, 93; immigration quotas, 252; restricted policies in hotels, 160
Apartment buildings: Cabrini-Green Homes, 229–33; Dakota Apartments, 22; First Houses, 215–20; racial wealth gap, 241; Watergate Complex, 181–85
Arad, Michael, 208–9
Arizona: Hoover Dam, 25–28
Arlington, Virginia, 259–63

Army Corps of Engineers: Hoover Dam, 25
Art Deco style: Empire State Building, 111–15, 189; First Houses, 218; Golden Gate Bridge, 34–35; Hoover Dam, 26; Miami Beach buildings, 157–58; Woolworth's store, 107
Asch Building (also known as the Brown Building), 63–70
Asian Exclusion Act, 252
Assembly lines: automobile manufacturing, 39, 91–94; commercial food preparation, 150; home construction, 237, 243
AT&T Building, 50
Attica State Prison, 17–23; design, 18, 20–21; lawsuits, 21; prison riot, 21
Auburn system, 17–18
Autobahn, 41
Automobiles: Ford River Rouge Complex, 89–95; Interstate Highway System, 39–45; McDonald's, 149; Northgate Shopping Center, 127–31

Bacon, Henry, 268–69
Baseball: Los Angeles Memorial Coliseum, 14

311

Bassett, Edward M.: 1916 Zoning Resolution, 87
Baths of Caracalla, 4
Battle of the Overpass, 94
Bauhaus, 165
Beardsley, William J., 20
Beaux-Arts style: Carrere and Hastings, 114; Cass Gilbert, 109, 111; City Beautiful movement, 268; Lincoln Memorial, 269; Los Angeles Memorial Coliseum, 12; Pennsylvania Station, 3–4; Woolworth Building, 109, 111
Bel Geddes, Norman, 40
Bergstrom, George, 259
Berkowitz, David, 22
Black Canyon, 26, 120
Black Panther Party, 19
Blanck, Max: Asch Building, 64–65, 68, 70
Boulder City, Nevada, 26, 120
Bowen, William: Los Angeles Memorial Coliseum, 10, 14
Boynton, Captain Paul: Sea Lion Park, 75
Bridges: bascule, 32–33; Golden Gate Bridge, 31–36; Verrazano Narrows Bridge, 35
Brooklyn: Luna Park, 73–78
Brown v. Board of Education, 107
Buffalo, New York: Attica State Prison, 18; Pan American Exposition, 74–75
Building codes: Levittown, New York, 236; New York City, 66, 68, 210; Seaside, Florida, 245
Bundled tube structures, 189–90
Bureau of Public Roads, 39
Bureau of Reclamation, 25, 27
Burnham, Daniel, 12, 82–83

Cabrini-Green Homes, 229–33
California: Black Panther Party, 19; Golden Gate Bridge, 31–36; Gold Rush, 119, 251; Googie Style, 123; Grauman's Chinese Theatre, 97–102; Hoover Dam, 25, 27; Interstate Highway System, 45; Japanese American relocation camps, 250–57; Los Angeles Memorial Coliseum, 7–15; McDonald's, Downey, California, 148–53; Walt Disney Concert Hall, 200–205
Campaign finance laws, 185
Cape Cod houses, 237–38
Carnegie, Andrew, 55–56, 237, 272
Cassatt, Alexander, 3, 5, 7
Celebration, Florida, 247–48. *See also* Disney Corporation; New Urbanism
Centennial Fair, Philadelphia, 73
Central Library, 55–60
Central Park, 73, 267
Chandler, Harry, 10
Chapman, Mark David, 22
Cheesman Dam, 27
Chicago, Illinois: Cabrini-Green Homes, 229–33; Chicago Housing Authority, 231–32; "The Ledge," 191; Mies van der Rohe, 165–66; Pritzker Architecture Prize, 60; Sears Tower, 187–91, 196, 212; Skidmore, Owings and Merrill, 142; skyscrapers, 82–83; "White City" (World's Columbian Exposition), 3, 12, 74, 267
Childs, David M., 208–9
Chinese Exclusion Act, 251
Chrysler Building, 27, 85, 111–14
City Beautiful movement, 12, 244, 267–68

City planning, 12, 87, 142, 201
Civic architecture, 3–60; Attica Correctional Facility, 17; Central Library, 55; Golden Gate Bridge, 31; Hoover Dam, 25; Interstate Highway System, 39; Los Angeles Memorial Coliseum, 9; Pennsylvania Station, 3; Portland Public Service Building, 47
Civil rights movement, 21, 106, 133; African Americans, 102–8, 273–74; Japanese, 251–57; prison reform, 21–22; women's rights, 65
Civil War, 81–82, 98, 251, 268, 272
Classicism: Asch Building, 67; Empire State Building, 114; Lincoln Memorial, 267–69; Pennsylvania Station, 4; Pentagon, 259; Portland Public Service Building, 47–50; Seagram Building, 167–68; Woolworth's Store, 107
Cold War, 41, 259, 262
Colorado River flooding, 25–26
Commercial architecture, 63–212; Asch Building (now known as Brown Building), 63; Empire State Building, 111; Equitable Building, 81; Flamingo Hotel, 119; Fontainebleau Hotel, 157; Ford River Rouge Complex, 89; Grauman's Chinese Theatre, 97; Lever House, 141; Luna Park, 73; McDonald's, 149; Northgate Shopping Center, 127; One World Trade Center, 207; Seagram Building, 165; Sears Tower (currently known as the Willis Tower), 187; Sun Record Studio, 133; TWA Flight Center, 173; Walt Disney Concert Hall, 201; Watergate Complex, 181; Woolworth's Store, 105; World Trade Center Twin Towers, 193
Community Development Association (Los Angeles Memorial Coliseum), 11
Computer-aided design (CAD), 184, 203–4
Coney Island, 74–78, 161. *See also* Couney, Dr. Martin; Incubator exhibit, Coney Island; Luna Park, Coney Island; Steeplechase Park
Congregate system in prisons, 17
Consumers: consumerism, 129; consumer products, 51, 73, 141; consumer society, 77
Corinthian columns (Pennsylvania Station), 4
Couney, Dr. Martin, 78. *See also* Incubator exhibit, Coney Island
Court of Honor: Los Angeles Coliseum, 13; Luna Park, 76
Cross-Country Motor Transport Corps, 40

"Darkness and Dawn," Omaha Trans-Mississippi Exposition, 74
Davis, Brody, Bond, 210
Dearborn, Michigan, 89–95
The Death and Life of Great American Cities (Jane Jacobs), 85, 245
Delirious New York (Rem Koolhas), 56
Department stores, 63, 113, 128, 131
Discrimination: housing policy, 240, 243; racial discrimination, 260; religious discrimination, 19
Disney Corporation, 247; Disney, Lillian, 202; Disney, Walt, 76–77; Disneyland, 20, 77

Domestic architecture, 215–48; Cabrini-Green Homes, 229; Fallingwater, 223; First Houses, 215; Levittown, 235; Seaside, 243
Doric columns, 4, 269
Downing, Andrew Jackson, 267
Duany, Andres, 245–48. *See also* Plater-Zyberk, Elizabeth; Seaside, Florida
Dundy, Elmer ("Skip"), 74–77

Eden Roc Hotel: discrimination against African Americans, 160; *Fontainebleau Corporation v. 4525, Inc.* court case, 158–59
Edison, Thomas, 76, 89–90, 98
Eisenhower, Dwight D., 39, 41–42, 272
Ellis, Charles, 34
Eminent domain, 43, 194, 216, 230
Empire State Building, 36, 111–17
Equitable Building, 81–87
Equitable Life Assurance Society, 81–83
Exposition Park, California, 10–11, 13

Fairs: Centennial Fair, Philadelphia, 73; Exposition Park, 10–11, 13; New York World's Fair, 1939, Futurama, 40; Omaha Trans-Mississippi Exposition, 74; Panama-Pacific International Exposition, 31; Pan American Exposition, 74; Paris Exposition Internationale des Arts Decoratifs et Industriels Modernes, 111; "White City" (World's Columbian Exposition), 3, 12, 73–74, 267
Fallingwater, 223–27; renovations of, 227

Fast food, 149, 153–54
Federal Aid Road Highway Act (1916), 39; Federal Aid Highway Act (1921), 40; Federal Aid Highway Act (1956), also known as the Interstate Highway Act, 41, 173
Federal Housing Administration (FHA), 43, 231, 235, 240, 243; discriminatory policies, 43, 240; redlining, 231
Ferguson, Colin, 22
First Houses, 215–20
Flagler, Henry Morrison, 157
Flamingo Hotel, 119–24
Flint, Frank P., 10
Fontainebleau Hotel, 157–62; in popular culture, 162
Football, 10–11, 14, 260
Ford, Henry, 39, 89–95
Ford River Rouge Complex, 89–95
Foreclosure rate, 241
Forecourt of the Stars, 100
French, Daniel Chester, 269–70
Furniture: Gehry, Frank, 201; Saarinen, Eero, 175; Wright, Frank Lloyd, 225

Garden cities, 244. *See also* City Beautiful movement; New Urbanism
Garland, William May, 10–11, 14–15
Gehry, Frank, 201, 203, 205
General Motors, 40, 93–94, 112
Giannini, A. P., 33
Gibson Girl, 63
Gilbert, Cass, 84, 109, 111
Gilded Age, 63, 237
Goldberger, Paul: Lever House, 144; Portland Public Service Building, 51; Seagram Building, 169; Seattle Central Library,

58; Walt Disney Concert Hall, 203; World Trade Center Twin Towers, 196
Golden Gate Bridge, 31–36; suicides, 36
Gold Rush (California), 9, 31–32, 119, 251
Gompers, Samuel, 64
Good Roads Movement, 39
Googie Style, 123, 151–52
Graham, Billy, 14
Graham, Bruce, 188–89
Graham, Ernest R., 82–83
Grand Central Terminal, 106, 166, 177
Grauman's Chinese Theatre, 97–102; Grauman, Sidney Patrick, 99
Graves, Michael, 47–52
Great Depression: Attica Correctional Facility, 18; Empire State Building, 116; Fallingwater, 223; Golden Gate Bridge, 35; Hoover Dam, 25; housing industry, effect on, 127, 235; Los Angeles Memorial Coliseum, 13; Luna Park, 77; McDonald brothers, 149; Miami Beach, 157; national road system, 40; public housing, 215, 229; Seattle, 55; skyscraper construction, effect on, 189, 193
Great Migration, 18, 231
Greenfield Village, 93
Greensboro, South Carolina, 105–8; "Greensboro Four," 105–8
Gruen, Victor, 129
Guggenheim Museum (Bilbao), 202–3, 205

Harris, Isaac, 64, 70
Hempstead, New York, 236, 238
Highway Trust Fund, 41, 43–44

Historic preservation, 6
Hitler, Adolf, 13
Hollywood, California, 10, 15, 121–22, 149, 179; Grauman's Chinese Theatre, 97–102
Hoover, Herbert, 28, 112
Hoover, J. Edgar, 182
Hoover Dam (Boulder Dam), 25–28, 120
Hotels: Flamingo Hotel, 119–24; Fontainebleau Hotel, 157–62; Watergate Hotel, 183–85
Housing: housing policy, 232, 240; mixed income, 232. *See also* Discrimination
Housing bubble, 241
Housing developments: Levittown, 235–40, 243–44; Seaside, 243–48
Hughes, Howard, 175, 179
Humana Building, 50
Huxtable, Ada Louise, 6, 161, 197
Hyde, Henry Baldwin, 82

Immigration, 97, 251–52; Immigration Act of 1924, 252; Immigration and Nationality Act (McCarran-Walter Act), 252
Incarceration: of Japanese during World War II, 254–56; rates of, 21; systems of, 18
Incubator exhibit, Coney Island, 78
Industrial Revolution, 73
International Ladies' Garment Workers' Union, 64, 69
International Orange (Golden Gate Bridge), 35
International style, 47–48, 56, 85, 111, 116; Fallingwater, 226; Fontainebleau Hotel, 159; Lever House, 143–44; Seagram Building, 166–68; TWA Flight Center, 175–77

Interstate Highway System, 5, 39–45, 158, 173
Islam, 19, 259, "War on Terror," 198–99, 263
Island Trees, New York, 236

Jackson, George, 19
Jackson, Kenneth (*Crabgrass Frontier*), 238–39
Jacobs, Charles, 4
Jacobs, Deborah, 57
Jacobs, Jane: *The Death and Life of Great American Cities,* 85, 245
Japanese American internment, 251–57; cemetery at Rohwer internment camp, 255
Japanese American relocation camp, 251–57
Jim Crow laws: discriminatory laws in 1920s, 252; Lincoln Memorial dedication, 272; Pentagon, construction of, 260; popular music, discrimination in, 133; Woolworth's Store, 105, 107
John A. Roebling's Sons Company, 34
John F. Kennedy International Airport (JFK), 174–75
Johnson, Philip, 48, 50, 167, 169, 248

Kahn, Albert, 90–91
Kaskey, Raymond (Portlandia), 49
Kaufmann, Edgar, Sr., 224
Kennedy, John F., 272–73
Kentlands, Gaithersburg, Maryland, 248
Khan, Fazlur Rahman, 188–89
King, Martin Luther, Jr.: "I Have a Dream" speech, 272–74; riots after the assassination of, 232; Woolworth's store, 106
Koolhas, Rem, 56, 58–60
Kroc, Ray, 151–54

LaGuardia, Mayor Fiorello, 174, 217
Lake Mead, 26, 120
Lambert, Phyllis, 167, 169
Landmarks Preservation Commission, 6
Lapidus, Morris, 158–62
Las Vegas, Nevada: Flamingo Hotel, 119–21, 123–24, 161; Hoover Dam, 26–27
Le Corbusier, 167; Modernism, 47–48, 111, 165, 226; "tower in the park," 230–31
Ledge attraction, Willis Tower, 190–91
L'Enfant, Pierre Charles, 267
Lever Brothers, 141–42, 144, 166
Lever House, 85, 141–46, 166–67
Levitt, Abraham, 236
Levitt, William, 236, 238, 243
Levitt and Sons, Inc., 236, 238
Levittown, 235–40, 243–44
Libeskind, Daniel, 205, 208
Libraries for All, 56, 59
Life insurance, Equitable Life Assurance Society, 81–84
Limited-access highways, Interstate Highway System, 41
Lin, Maya, 279
Lincoln Highway, 40
Lincoln Memorial, 267–70
Lindbergh, Charles, 174
L'On, Mount Pleasant, South Carolina, 248
Long Island, 150; Levittown, 236, 240, 243
Los Angeles, California: Academy Awards, 101; Grauman's Chinese Theatre, 100–101; Hoover Dam, 25, 27; Japanese, relocation of, 254; Los Angeles Highway, 121; Los Angeles Memorial Coliseum, 9–15; McDonald's, 149, 151; Million Dollar Theatre,

99; rail connection to Las Vegas, 119; San Francisco, comparison to, 31; Walt Disney Concert Hall, 201–5; William R. Wilkerson, 121
Los Angeles Memorial Coliseum, 9–14
Luckman, Charles, 142, 166–67
Luna Park, Coney Island, 73–78, 161

Malls, 43, 188; "dead malls," 131; Northgate Shopping Center, 127–31
Manhattan Project, 142, 261
Manifest destiny, 39, 82
Marin County, California, 32, 35
Mass production: Levittown, 239
McAneny, George, 1916 Zoning Resolution, 87
McCarthy, Joseph, 235
McCormick Campus Center at the Illinois Institute of Technology, Rem Koolhaas, 56
McDonald's, 149–54; McDonald brothers, 149–54
McKane, John Y., 74–75
McKim, Charles Follen, 3–4, 268
McKim, Mead and White, 143, 269
McMillan Commission, 268
Memorial architecture, 267–80; Lincoln Memorial, 267; Vietnam Veterans Memorial, 277
Memphis, Tennessee, 133–38
Meston, Stanley Clark, 150–51
Mexican War, Treaty of Guadalupe Hidalgo, 31
Meyer and Holler, 99
Miami Beach: Art Deco hotels, 157; Fontainebleau Hotel, 157–62
Miami Modern (MiMo), 159

Middle class: automobiles for, 39, 89; housing, 215, 232, 236; Michael Graves, 47; popular music, 133–34; racial wealth gap, 241; Seaside, 245; shopping malls, 130; vacation travel, 160; zoning, effects of, 86
Middletown: A Study in Modern American Culture, 89
Military architecture, 251–63; Japanese American relocation camp, 251; The Pentagon, 259
Million Dollar Quartet, 138
Mobile walls, 279–80
Model-T Ford, 39, 90–93
Moderne style, 12, 34–35, 158
Modernist design, 48, 141, 165–66, 184, 226
Moisseiff, Leon D., Golden Gate Bridge, 34
Moretti, Luigi, 181–82, 184
Morgan, J. P., 65
Mormons, 119
Morrow, Irving, Golden Gate Bridge, 34
Moses, Robert, 85, 217
Movie palaces, 99–101
Movies, 98, 102
Municipal Housing Authority Act, 216
Muslims, in Attica Correctional Facility, 19
Mutual Life Insurance Company, 82

Nassau County, New York, Levittown, 235–36, 238
National Historic Landmarks: Hoover Dam, 27; Vietnam Veterans Memorial, 279; Woolworth Building, 109
National Historic Preservation Act, 6

National Labor Relations Act, 68
National Mall, 267–70, 272, 278
New Deal, 68, 216; New Deal Federal Artists Program, 218
New Urbanism, 246–48
New York: Asch Building, 63–70; Attica Correctional Facility, 18–19, 22; Empire State Building, 111–17; Equitable Building, 81–87; First Houses, 215–20; Lever House, 141–46; One World Trade Center, 207–12, 263; Pennsylvania Station, 3–7; Seagram Building, 165–70; TWA Flight Center, 173–79; Woolworth Building, 109; World Trade Center Twin Towers, 193–99
New York City Housing Authority (NYCHA), 216–17, 219
New York City Landmarks Preservation Commission, 6, 175, 177
New York Public Library, 58, 114
New York Times, 6, 69, 74, 144, 161, 168, 196–97; Pentagon Papers, 182
New York World's Fair, 1939, Futurama, 40
Nixon, Richard, 21, 182–83, 185
Normative theory, 246. *See also* New Urbanism
Northgate Shopping Center, 127–31
Novak, Ben, 158–60

Office buildings: Asch Building (also known as the Brown Building), 63–70; Empire State Building, 36, 111–17; Equitable Building, 81–87; Lever House, 85, 141–46, 166–67; One World Trade Center, 190, 197, 207–12; Seagram Building, 85, 144, 165–70; Sears Tower, 187–91, 196, 212; Watergate Complex, 181–85; World Trade Center Twin Towers, 188, 193–99, 207, 209, 211, 263
Office of Metropolitan Architecture (OMA), 56
Olmsted, Frederick Law, 73
Olympic Games, 11, 13
One World Trade Center, 190, 197, 207–12
Organic architecture, 224, 226
O'Shaughnessy, Michael, 32
Oswald, Russell, 19

Pace Associates, 230
Panama Canal, 27, 31
Pan American Exposition, Buffalo, New York, 74
Parkinson & Parkinson, 11–12
Penitentiaries, 17, 19
Pennsylvania Railroad, 3–5, 7
Pennsylvania Station, 3–7
Pennsylvania Turnpike, 40
Penology, 17, 22
Pentagon, 259–63
Pentagon Papers, 182
Peristyle, Los Angeles Memorial Coliseum, 12–13; Lincoln Memorial, 269, 272
Pershing Map, 40
Phillips, Sam, 134–38
Planned Unit Developments (PUDs), 181, 184. *See also* Watergate Complex
Plater-Zyberk, Elizabeth, 245–48. *See also* Duany, Andres; Seaside, Florida
Popular culture: Cabrini-Green Homes, 233; Fontainebleau Hotel, 162; rock and roll, 137
Portland, Oregon, 47–48, 50

Portland Public Service Building (Portland Building), 47–52
Post-Modernism, 48, 50–51
Preservation movement, 6
Presley, Elvis, 135–36, 138
Prison-industrial complex, 22
Prisons: Attica, 17–23; Auburn, 17–18; Clinton, 18; San Quentin, 19; Sing Sing, 18, 20, 75
Pritzker Architecture Prize, 56, 60
Prix de Rome (Rome Prize), 47
Progressive Era, 64, 73
Prohibition, 98, 120, 166, 229
Protests: civil rights, 98, 272; preservation, 6, 194; Vietnam War, 19, 182, 259, 262
Public housing: Chicago, 229–33; New York City, 215–20; racial wealth gap, effect of, 241; Senator Joseph McCarthy hearings, 235; St. Louis, 194
Public transportation, 43–44, 127, 215
Public Works Administration (PWA), 216
Puerto Ricans, 18

Quakers, 17
Queens, New York, 173–79
Quonset huts, 235

Racial segregation: in Las Vegas, 124; racial wealth gap, 240; redlining, 86; zoning laws, 85
Railroads, 5, 39, 187
Ramus, Joshua, Central Library, 56–57
Raskob, John Jacob, 112–13, 116
Rat Pack, 160. *See also* Fontainebleau Hotel
Rea, Samuel, 4
Redlining, 86, 231, 240
Regulations: Asch Building, 68; aviation, 174, 177; building codes, 245–46; Flamingo Hotel, 121; insurance, 81; Jim Crow laws, 105; zoning, 83–87, 143
Republican Party, 21
"Road Gang" lobbying syndicate, 41
Rock and roll, 135–37
Rockefeller, David, 193
Rockefeller, Nelson, 19, 21
Rockefeller drug laws, 21
Roosevelt, Eleanor, 217, 220, 272
Roosevelt, Franklin Delano: Golden Gate Bridge, 35; Hoover Dam, 26, 28; Interstate Highway System, 40; Japanese relocation, 253, 255; Los Angeles Memorial Coliseum, 14; New Deal legislation, 68, 216–17; Pentagon, 260–61; postwar reaction to, 141; Wagner Act, 94

Saarinen, Eero, 175–78
San Francisco, California, 9, 25, 40, 45, 251–52; Golden Gate Bridge, 31–36
San Quentin Prison, 19
Sausalito, California, 32, 35
Sea Lion Park, 75, 77
Seagram Building, 85, 144, 165–70
Sears, Roebuck and Company, 131; catalog, 73; Sears Tower, 187–91, 196, 212
Sears Tower (Willis Tower), 187–91
Seaside, Florida, 243–48; New Urbanism, 246–48
Seattle, Washington, 55–60
Seattle Central Library, 55–60
Segregation, 85–86, 124, 133, 240, 252, 274
Shreve, Lamb and Harmon, 114; Lamb, William, 114, 116
Siegel, Benjamin "Bugsy," 122–24

Silent Majority, 21
Six Companies, Inc., 25
Skidmore, Owings and Merrill (SOM), 142, 146, 188, 193, 208
Skyscrapers: Empire State Building, 111–17; Equitable Building, 81–87; One World Trade Center, 207–12; Sears Tower (Willis Tower), 187–91; tallest skyscrapers in the world, 212; World Trade Center Twin Towers, 193–99
Smith, Alfred E., 112
Snohetta, 210
Snyder, Meredith P., 10
"Sodom by the Sea," 74
Southern Pacific Railroad, 32
Southern strategy, 21
Steeplechase Park, 75
Strauss, Joseph B., 32–35
Suburbanization, 44, 85; streetcar suburbs, 244; suburban sprawl, 89, 243–44, 246–47
Sullivan, Joseph "Mad Dog," 23
Sullivan-Hoey Act, 68
Sun Record Studio, 133–38
Super Bowl, 14
Supreme Court, United States: *Brown v. Board of Education*, 107; executive privilege, 183; housing discrimination, 238; *Korematsu v. the United States*, 256; Warren, Earl, 253; zoning restrictions, 85
Sutter's Mill, 31
Sutton, Willie, 23

Takei, George, 257
Taliesin, 223
Technology: aviation industry, 174; construction techniques, 87, 145, 189; electrocution, 76; incubators, 78; Industrial Revolution, 73, 141; train, 3
Tenements, 63, 77; First Houses, 215–19
Terrorist attacks, 9/11, 198–99, 210, 259, 263
Thompson, Frederic (Luna Park), 74–77
Thompson, Heather Ann, 21
Tilyou, George C. (Steeplechase Park), 75
Tocqueville, Alexis de, 18
Topsy the Elephant, electrocution of, 76
Transcontinental railroad, 9, 251
Treaty of Guadalupe Hidalgo, 9, 31
Triangle Waist Company, 64, 67, 70
Truman Show, The, 246. See also Seaside, Florida
Tunnels, 3–5, 7, 20, 26, 194
Turner, Frederick Jackson, 39, 121
TWA Flight Center, 173–79

Underwriting Manual (FHA), 240
Unions, labor, 94, 217, 237
University of Southern California (USC), 10, 201

Van der Rohe, Mies, 47–48, 56, 111, 144, 159; Seagram Building, 165–70
Verrazano Narrows Bridge, 35
Vertical integration, 91–92, 99, 237
Veterans Administration (VA), 235–36, 240, 243
Vietnam Veterans Memorial, 277–80
Vietnam War, 19, 182, 262, 278

Wagner, Robert, 68
Walkability, 129, 244. See also New Urbanism
Walt Disney Concert Hall, 200–205

Walt Disney World, 248
War on drugs, 18
War on terror, 198–99
Warren, Earl, 253
Washington, DC: Lincoln Memorial, 267–70; National Mall, 267–70, 272, 278; Vietnam Veterans Memorial, 277–80; Watergate Complex, 181–85
Watergate Complex, 181–85; Watergate Hotel, 185; Watergate scandal, 182–85
Wealth gap, with African Americans, 240
White City, Chicago World's Columbian Exposition, 12, 74
White flight, 43, 130, 239
Wilkerson, William, 121–23
Willis Tower, 187–91
Wilson, Woodrow, 39, 97
Witmer, David, 259
Woolworth Building, New York, 109, 111
Woolworth's Store, Greensboro, South Carolina, 105–9
Working class: FHA regulations, 243; Levittown, 239; Luna Park, 73, 77; Model-T Ford, 90, 93; racial wealth gap, 240–41; "Roaring Twenties," 97
Works Progress Administration, 40, 217
World's Columbian Exposition, 3, 12, 73–74, 267

World Series, 14
World Trade Center Memorial, 208–9
World Trade Center Twin Towers, 188, 193–99, 207, 209, 211, 263
World War II: aviation industry, 174; Great Migration, 18, 231; Interstate Highway System, 41; Japanese internment, 255–57; Las Vegas, 120; Levitt and Sons, 236, 238; Los Angeles Memorial Coliseum, 13; Manhattan Project, 142, 261; Pennsylvania Station, 5; Pentagon, 259, 261; postwar economic boom, 122, 141, 150, 158, 160, 173; postwar growth of suburbs, 127, 188, 235, 243–44; public housing projects, 47, 230; use of Miami hotels during war, 158; Vietnam War, comparison to, 277
Wounded Warrior Home Project, 52
Wright, Elizur, 81
Wright, Frank Lloyd, 142, 144, 167, 223; Fallingwater, 223–27

Yamasaki, Minoru, 194
Yerba Buena (San Francisco), 31

Zoning laws: Equitable Building, 83, 85–86; Lever House, 143; Seagram Building, 169; Seaside, 243

ABOUT THE AUTHORS

Elizabeth B. Greene is an interior designer at the College of Staten Island. She received a bachelor's degree in art history from McGill University in Montreal, where her specialization was modern art and architecture. She attended the Columbia University Historic Preservation Program at the Columbia Graduate School of Architecture, Planning and Preservation. Greene is author of *Buildings and Landmarks of 19th-Century America: American Society Revealed* and of "Homes in the Gilded Era, 1881–1900" in *The Greenwood Encyclopedia of Homes through American History*.

Edward Salo, PhD, is assistant professor of history at Arkansas State University, Jonesboro, Arkansas. He was involved in historic preservation consulting for 15 years before coming to Arkansas State University.